meeting strangers, making friends

meeting strangers, making friends

MORE SURPRISING TRAVEL ADVENTURES FROM THE MINNESOTA STORYTELLER

TOM MATTSON

DUDLEY COURT PRESS
SONOITA, AZ

Published in the United States of America by Dudley Court Press
PO Box 102 Sonoita, AZ 85637
www.DudleyCourtPress.com

FRONT COVER PHOTO CREDIT: Tom Mattson.
Cover photo shows a scene from Shirakawa Village in Japan, at the end of a long ride into the mountains. Meet
the individuals pictured in Tom's stories about Bhutan and Cuba and on his website, www.TomsGlobe.com
BACK COVER AUTHOR PHOTO: Thomas Leonard Studio, www.ThomasLeonardStudio.com.
COVER AND INTERIOR DESIGN: Dunn+Associates, www.Dunn-Design.com

Publisher's Cataloging-in-Publication Data
Mattson, Tom, 1945- author.
Title: Meeting strangers, making friends : more surprising travel adventures
from the Minnesota storyteller / Tom Mattson.
Description: Sonoita, AZ Dudley Court Press, [2021]
Identifiers: ISBN: 978-1-940013-86-2 (paper) | 978-1-940013-87-9 (ebook) | LCCN: 2020925603
Subjects: LCSH: Mattson, Tom, 1945- —Travel. | Travelers' writings, American.
Americans—Foreign countries—Anecdotes. | Voyages and travels—Anecdotes.
Adventure and adventurers—Anecdotes. | American essays—21st century. | LCGFT: Travel writing.
BISAC: TRAVEL / Essays & Travelogues. | TRAVEL / Special Interest / Literary.
LITERARY COLLECTIONS / Essays.
LCC: G465 .M38 2021 | DDC: 910.4/1—dc23

Connect with Tom at www.TomsGlobe.com

Look for other books in this series at your favorite bookseller
or at www.DudleyCourtPress.com

I dedicate this book

to the many around the world

and at home who have opened proverbial doors

as I've sought to experience a life of wonder.

Each of these people, I'm sure,

opens doors for many others as well.

ACKNOWLEDGMENTS

In creating two adventure books of friends I've made and locales I've succumbed to, I've drawn on wisdom and advice from many abroad and at home. I acknowledged and celebrated a number of these people at the beginning of my first book, *The Other Worlds: Offbeat Adventures of a Curious Traveler.* I give them many thanks now, too.

For every person you read about in these stories, there are many others who also make enjoyable travels possible: those who give directions and offer suggestions; corner store clerks; hotel, café, and transportation personnel; park and plaza caretakers; volunteers in houses of worship; farmers and fishermen; librarians; curators and staff in the world's 55,000 museums; and inquisitive passersby.

My publisher, Gail Woodard of Dudley Court Press, has led the publishing process for *The Other Worlds* and this book. Her leadership, advice, and inside knowledge have been invaluable and an inspiration to me. And what a learning experience!

Gail has a great team and connections with some of the finest professionals in this country and beyond. Dudley Court Press Marketing Coordinator Carrie Le Chevallier, Project Coordinator Lora Arnold, and Copy Editor Pam Nordberg are superb! Book Designer Kathi Dunn of Dunn+Associates deserves widespread accolades for her cover and interior designs. Take a look at my first book and also appreciate her work on this book from cover to cover.

Editor Caroline Lambert has worked her magic with the 140,000 words in my two books. My final draft manuscript, born out of more than a dozen drafts, benefits immensely from Caroline's subsequent editing.

Larry Chance typed every word of this book and then dealt with my thousands upon thousands of handwritten revisions. Larry has also weighed in with valuable observations. Larry's late wife, Irene, was also key to the early stages of this book.

Barb Tucker of Andrew's Cameras has designed captivating promotional displays for my books and is a fountain of creative ideas.

Lori Thompson and Corey Mills of W.A. Fisher Co. are top talents in Minnesota. Lori, a graphic artist, created every map—black and white for the book, spectacular color for the website. She and I fine-tuned every last detail. Corey set up and maintains my website, TomsGlobe.com, and prepares my newsletter. Lori and Corey educate me each step of the way.

A great big thank you to all!

INTRODUCTION

Join me, please, on adventures to the far corners of our world. I promise we'll also discover intriguing, nearly hidden spots ever so close to home.

Once our journey begins, we find that we like meeting strangers. In fact, we soon love it.

Any one of the eight billion people on our planet, I venture to say, would love to meet Kunzang Choden. Let you and I do that—at her home out of a past century in Bhutan's lofty Himalaya Mountains. Hers is the 20th generation of her family to live on that land. And oh does she have stories to tell! Could one be about an abominable snowman or snowwoman?

In Peru's Andes Mountains, we meet another stranger. Mario Tribeño Mar, we learn, is a descendant of the Incas. Since we can barely communicate with Mario at first, how long might our friendship last? A half hour? Or much longer?

Our string of happenstances continues in other far corners. Phi Lay Ob drives a three-wheeled tuk-tuk in Battambang, Cambodia. After this once stranger becomes a friend, we hear a story of heartbreak and hope. Perhaps we believe it's a message that should be heard the world over.

As we approach the rim of a volcano—two and a half miles above sea level—we discover a small but thriving community. Among the residents are Maria and her family, the Pilatasigs. What are the chances that a traveler to Ecuador would meet Maria? One in a million? Let's discover the answer in the opening pages of *Meeting Strangers, Making Friends*.

Should we tell the generations younger than ours that they'll have to travel the world to discover the wonders of diversity? As close as Albuquerque, New Mexico, we'll find one epicenter of diversity. Then, come on my motorcycle with me for a hop, skip, and jump to Acoma Pueblo for the grandest feast of the year. Once atop the awesome mesa above the desert floor, let's hope to chat with Acoma tribal members. It might be possible to follow them into their family home and discover what goes on behind closed doors. Perhaps the essence of a feast day has not ebbed for the last 920 years in this "Sky City."

Close to home, we might urge young family members to become better friends with elderly relatives and neighbors. An account or two spun out later in this book introduces you to my 103-year-old cousin —who, over a full century, cared about, engaged, and even regaled the many who met her.

You may wonder if the characters in this book agree that their stories should be told. "Make my story travel!" each one urged once they learned I'd like to tell their stories. And so their stories have traveled— to the pages you are about to read. And possibly into the hearts of friends to whom you mention or gift this book.

• • •

Growing up a block from an iron mine on Minnesota's Mesabi Iron Range, I never envisioned I'd have a single adventure like those I now write about. I recount how I was introduced to curiosity and wonder at a young age, though, at the outset of my first book, *The Other Worlds: Offbeat Adventures of a Curious Traveler.* Building upon *The Other Worlds,* I'll enjoy having you with me for a few more years' worth of new offbeat adventures (of a still curious traveler).

For "extra chapters," photo-stories, links to videos, unique maps, and color photos from around our planet, visit www.TomsGlobe.com.

Jack Canfield, co-creator of the *Chicken Soup for the Soul* series, told me upon reading *The Other Worlds*, "You're seeing parts of the world that no one ever sees . . . meeting people from all walks of life, becoming good friends with them [and] writing about it in a way that is so captivating." The stories inspire him, he said, to experience what it is like to travel without planning the day or consulting a guidebook.

I hope this book does the same for you. So turn this page now, and we'll be off and running!

SOUTH
AMERICA

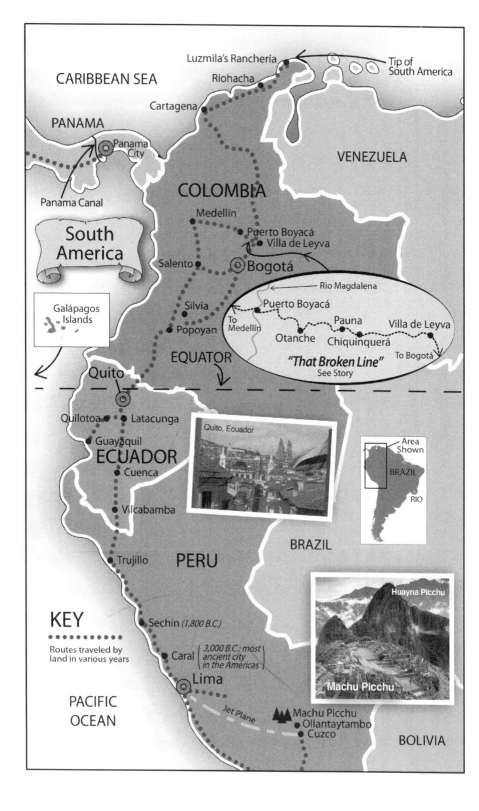

CARIBBEAN SEA

PANAMA

Panama City

Panama Canal

South America

Galápagos Islands

Luzmila's Ranchería

Tip of South America

Riohacha

Cartagena

VENEZUELA

COLOMBIA

Medellín

Puerto Boyacá

Villa de Leyva

Salento

Bogotá

Silvia

Popoyan

EQUATOR

Rio Magdalena

Puerto Boyacá

To Medellín

Otanche

Pauna

Villa de Leyva

Chiquinquerá

To Bogotá

"That Broken Line"
See Story

Quito

Quilotoa

Latacunga

Guayaquil

ECUADOR

Cuenca

Quito, Ecuador

Area Shown

BRAZIL

RIO

Vilcabamba

Trujillo

BRAZIL

PERU

KEY

Routes traveled by land in various years

Sechín *(1,800 B.C.)*

Caral

3,000 B.C.: most ancient city in the Americas

Lima

PACIFIC OCEAN

Jet Plane

Huayna Picchu

Machu Picchu

Machu Picchu

Ollantaytambo

Cuzco

BOLIVIA

ECUADOR

Those Who Have Missions, at 12,870 feet
FEBRUARY 13-15, 2015

Three strangers are on three different missions a number of years ago, in bright afternoon sunshine. A traveler snaps photos as fast as his brimming heart can focus, searching for precious views. A young woman sitting with two others on the rim of a volcanic crater tries to sell brightly painted *artesanía* to support her family. A guy in a Minnesota iron mining town, whose passport expired years earlier, wonders if he still has the family's Finnish *sisu*[1] to embark on journeys to strange places, without knowing a soul.

Have these missions come to successful conclusions in the ensuing years?

The photographer did snap one treasurable photo—three women vendors in the attire of the Kichwa people of Quilotoa above a crater lake—12,870 feet high in the Andes Mountains. The Finnish-American guy in the mining town without a passport was me, and with *sisu*, I made it to Cuenca, Ecuador, healthy and fit three days ago. If you were there, you too would surely visit the Museum of Aboriginal Cultures with its stone axes, chisels, arrowheads, and other treasures of 5,000 to 10,000 years ago, right up to the present—and counting. The trail through the museum ends in a gift shop. My eyes are drawn to an exquisite postcard on the rack—a photo of three young women selling artesanía on the rim of a volcano. Flipping the card over, I read, "Vendors of Tigua Crafts in Quilotoa."

---

[1] A Finnish word describing a reserve of power that enables extraordinary actions to overcome mentally or physically challenging situations—something closely related to "guts" in English.

"Since I'm going to Quilotoa in two days," I tell myself, "I'll buy this card as a memento."

"Hold your horses!" an inner voice tells me. "You know how photographers operate. The three women probably never saw this photo, let alone the postcard. Buy three more, and find these women!"

So I purchase four postcards at 25 cents each. I just won't mail mine home—at $2.50 a stamp.

"Wait!" I hear. That inner voice is sometimes a bother. "Buy three more cards and give each woman two. A grandmother would surely love one."

The postcard that caught the author's attention in Ecuador's Museum of Aboriginal Cultures. His mission suddenly became: "Purchase six and search for the women!"

Mission started. Not so fast! I soon conclude. Not knowing how potent the instant coffee on my breakfast table is, I overdose on caffeine. My heartbeat speeds up, but I can't feel a pulse for an hour. In a couple of past episodes, my nonexistent pulse was back to normal within 15 minutes. ("Don't worry," doctors concluded.) Still, I log on a hotel computer to check what condition my condition is in. ("Probably fine," according to the internet.) To be wise, though, I snuff out my plan to journey from 8,000-foot-high Cuenca to Quilotoa, altitude 12,870 feet. Instead, I'll enjoy pleasant places at lower heights (and lower heart rates).

But for the next 24 hours, Quilotoa—and the postcards—nag at me. Finally, I nearly blurt out loud, "Quilotoa it will be, come hell or erupting volcano!" Some 10 hours on four buses and over a day and a half later, Quilotoa it is. My head is lighter still, but at least I feel my pulse pound. I study some of Quilotoa's 300 residents, mixed with milling tourists on one of the biggest travel days of the year. It is Carnival (or Mardi Gras) in South America! I pick out a target for my question: "Do you know the women in this postcard?"

"Sí," the man answers.

"Where are they, por favor?"

"Maria is selling her husband's handicrafts in the community center a minute this way." (The vendors no longer sit on the rim of the crater, 1,300 feet above the surface of the bottomless lake. That old spot is now taken up by a restaurant.)

As my newfound guide leads me for the 60 seconds it takes to reach the art center, a young man named Wilmer runs up behind us. He's gotten word (word must travel fast in thin air) that I have a photo of his mother Maria, his aunt Delfina, and his cousin Sandra. Handing him a postcard, I suggest he walk ahead of me so he will be the one who hands it to his mother.

Before I can catch my breath, six identical postcards are being passed around a throng surrounding Maria (a throng must gather faster in thin air, without any word being uttered). Their smiles reveal that they all love the picture. After I take an unposed photo of the throng, which includes three of Maria's four sons, I have the option of bidding them adiós. I am, after all, on my way to the carnival in Chugchilán, down the road some broken pieces.

"Yes, I'll go right now," I tell myself. "Or not?"

That pesky inner voice pipes up, "No! There are things you must learn! Like, has Maria ever seen this postcard? And is she fulfilling her mission of supporting her family by selling artesanía?"

I approach Maria's son Wilmer with the first question. "No, she has not seen this postcard before," he tells me. "In fact, my mother didn't know it existed. She'd never even been shown the image on the photographer's camera. And she doesn't remember the photo being taken!"

"Would the photo be about three years old?" I ask Wilmer, since for some reason that's the number floating in my mind.

"No. My cousin Sandra is a teenager in the picture. Now she's married. She and her husband own a hotel in Baños, very popular for hot springs, river rafting, and mountain climbing. The photo is 12 or maybe 15 years old!"

When the photo was taken, Maria and her husband Jose had four young boys—together known as the Pilatasig family. In short order, I meet not only Wilmer, but also the eldest, Nelson, and the youngest, Klever, now a 17-year-old student. The fourth son, Patricio, has not yet returned from school.

I venture to guess that this same exquisite card will still be sold a dozen years from now. I decide that on my next trip to Ecuador I will: (1) Find the card distributor; (2) demand 100 copies at a steeply discounted price (or, "I'm a fading lawyer, but I'll make a federal case out of this for infringement of my three clients' privacy"); and (3) deliver the 100 cards to the women to sell or give free with each purchased handicraft—ever-the-salesman Klever can think of the right tie-in. (Yes, you might quibble with my tactics as I drift out of the picture.)

I now snap more photos and a video of the crowd around Maria, with commentary by Wilmer. The father, Jose Pilatasig, is at home, painting. All four sons—Nelson, Wilmer, Patricio, and Klever—are becoming painters too. This answers my second question: the family business seems to be booming.

I am curious about what creates the dazzling colors of the art. Wilmer leads me to the brothers' workshop. He hands me small jars of paint that produce the magic—"the same as those used by auto body repair shops," he says. I acquire a painting his father created on a sheepskin canvas. It portrays the Quilotoa crater, the lake, distant snow-covered volcanoes, the setting sun, townspeople going about their business, and all manner of animals going about theirs.

Wilmer not only paints but guides travelers on the family's two horses from the crater lake up the steep trail to the rim. He's traveled down and up hundreds of times, since he once rented out kayaks at a hostel on the lakeshore.

A wood-burning stove heats their workshop. I love such antique-style stoves—four iron sheets welded together with a top door to load firewood, and another below to remove ashes. Wilmer tells me that he built it in shop class at school. A similar stove heats the family home in the evenings, he explains.

"Wilmer, do the people of Quilotoa speak a language besides Spanish?" I ask in Spanish, since English isn't a language he uses.

"Yes, we speak Kichwa. It's closely related to Quechua, the Inca language spoken in parts of Peru."

"Which language are you best in?" I'd like to know.

"Kichwa. I still need to learn more words in Spanish," he says. At home, the family speaks Kichwa. In Chugchilán, just 14 miles away, most people understand only some of the Quilotoa words and speak a slightly different dialect, Wilmer explains (in Spanish).

Klever, the bright student, asks me if I can download onto Facebook the video I took of his mother, him, and his brothers. "No, I can't, but I'm so well-connected that I know someone who can," I answer.

I'll start the video with the 5,000 to 10,000-year-old stone axes and implements I shot in the museum where I found the postcard. I'll finish with the Pilatasig family and their vibrant Quilotoa culture, still living at 12,870 feet, 65 miles south of the equator. It's a culture maybe a thousand years old—*and counting.* This video, I realize, will demonstrate that the three missions have been completed successfully, and that the three strangers—the photographer, the Finnish-American from Minnesota, and the Quilotoa woman—are now uniquely connected.

• • •

I planned to take the afternoon bus from Quilotoa to Chugchilán, but it has left unpredictably early. Wilmer's brother Nelson, I learn, drives a car—transporting travelers hither and thither. Thus, thither, aka Chugchilán, is where Nelson and Wilmer say they'll take me. I'm wondering if Nelson has a driver's license, though, since we wait for Klever to signal from the road. Once he does, we take off out of town.

The postcard saga follows us to Chugchilán. Upon checking into my lodging at Mama Hilda's, I discover the postcard pasted to a wall! I call Nelson and Wilmer inside for a look. While visitors to Mama Hilda's have known about the card for years, only now do the Pilatasigs realize how popular it is. Nelson and Wilmer then return to Quilotoa with a little story to tell their family about the postcard that none of them had ever seen until this morning. They leave me in Chugchilán—but I'm not alone for long.

From Carnival to One Hundred Hours of Solitude
FEBRUARY 15-20, 2015

Today is Carnival Sunday in Chugchilán, a pueblo of 200 souls 55 miles south of the equator, elevation a less lofty 10,498 feet. The young at heart, laughing and shouting, chase acquaintances and strangers around the plaza, and once close enough, spray their faces, eyeglasses, and clothing—including mine—with shaving cream, called *lanza nieve,* or spray snow. Volleyball games run for hours. A miniscule café becomes a wild dance hall. A local band blares music late into the plaza's night.

Hesitate and protest as one might, I'll tell you, even a visitor holding a foreign passport cannot escape getting all mixed up in the joyful melee. The celebration lasts until I am fast asleep. Move over, New Orleans and Rio!

• • •

Is every village in these mountains filled with celebrating crowds? I decide to travel to Isinlivi to answer that question. To travel there from Chugchilán, most everyone says I'll be winging it out of town in the milk truck or in the back of a pickup. "Why aren't you hiking a few hours to Isinlivi?" someone even quips. I make the journey in two pickups.

On my second day around Isinlivi, where I will spend about a hundred hours, I find myself alone on a five-hour mountain hike. No crowds here. In fact, I meet just one person, an elderly farmer tending his cows by a stream near his hillside farmhouse—one I feel I could live in forever. I could have tried that, I think, the old farmer and I working side by side, as good friends, forever.

That night, back in Isinlivi, I dream that a hiking partner falls down a cliff into a rocky stream. I peek over the edge and see multiple leg fractures. At least that didn't happen to me on my five-hour hike—better that it happened to an imaginary fellow trekker in a dream.

My strange nocturnal adventure makes me wonder what dreams my would-be farm partner has as he works toward one hundred years of solitude so far away from every carnival in the world.

Toward the Galápagos Islands
MARCH 26, 2016

One year later, I am in Latin America again. My flight lifts off from the Pacific coast in El Salvador, Central America, takes a gander over the Caribbean Sea, and descends above the Panama Canal at sunset. After changing planes in Panama City, I fly over the Pacific forthwith, cross the Equator as a full moon rises just below the left wingtip, and descend into Guayaquil, Ecuador, South America.

Two days ago, I discovered a cut-rate, online, last-minute ticket for a cabin on a boat through the Galápagos Islands. It embarks tomorrow, for a week. I'd read two books about Charles Darwin in anticipation of a trip to the Galápagos last year, but instead spent all my time in Cuba. There's no internet on the boat, I'm forewarned, because these Pacific islands are "too remote."

I may have something to tell you after the visit, when I expect to belong to a slightly different species.

Back at 12,870 feet
APRIL 5, 2016

The multitalented Pilatasig family of Quilotoa. Maria, sons (L to R) Klever, Patricio, and Wilmer, and husband Jose (seated). Son Nelson not pictured. Maria is at the right in the iconic postcard, shown earlier.

From sea level—or a few feet below—in the Galápagos Islands, I jet to the hot, humid and flooded mainland at Guayaquil, Ecuador's largest city, then travel by bus past banana plantations, surging streams, and roaring waterfalls. The bus then drives past farm plots on the Andes Mountains, settled by indigenous peoples so long ago. Finally, I arrive at the Quilotoa volcanic crater, with an agenda that calls for no hike longer than 200 heart-rattling steps.

I'm visiting the Pilatasig family of six I met a year ago. You may recall that last year, I discovered an old postcard of three women sitting on the rim of this crater and successfully delivered six of the cards to them. This year, I carry favors of newspapers, imported apples I found in Guayaquil, and bakery treats from a remote lowland town, where the vendor girl inquired, "You are a gringo?"

Today, Jose, Maria, and their sons are building what is sure to be a wondrous shop, filled with apparel and the family's traditional paintings and masks—with signature streaks of modernism and magic.

Wait a minute! I won't blame you if you don't believe a word of this missive. For, as time goes on, you may receive a message swearing I am still in the ocean water around the Galápagos Islands, and will be forever.

Toward a Slightly Different Species
DATE: INDECIPHERABLE

Greetings now and forever from the Galápagos Islands,

Travelers on this boat—a young couple from the South of England, a retired couple from Australia, a German family of four living in Mexico with Dad working at a new Audi factory, a mother and her two sons from Maryland, two Israeli women, and two clinical molecular geneticists from the United States—are packed into two dinghies alongside the boat, ready for the first snorkel of the trip. It's 6:10 a.m. The dinghies don't motor away just yet, though, since the traveler from Northern Minnesota is still fast asleep in his cabin.

Fifteen minutes later, all of them, including the now awake but groggy one who missed coffee, somersault off the dinghies into the Pacific Ocean, right next to a 500-foot-high sheer cliff.

Thanks to coffee the next several mornings, everyone sidesteps around sea lions lounging on the beaches and avoids crushing the beautiful duck-like feet of the "blue-footed boobie" birds on the paths. Likewise, the gang successfully circumvents the long tails of grayish iguanas sunbathing on rocks on one island, and of their greenish cousins blending into the vegetation on another. Both species, the group learns, share a common ancestor that rode logs from South America's mainland, 600 miles to the east.

Several of the Galápagos Islands rest on one crunching tectonic plate, while several others sit on a different plate. The two sets of islands drift up to four inches farther apart every year. They appeared out of nowhere between 400,000 and four million years ago, born of lava flows caused by either magma rising from the ocean floor or actual volcanic eruptions.

"Charles Darwin's 17 species of finches in the Galápagos Islands all descended from a common ancestor," guide Sara informs the group. The Minnesotan barely holds back from blabbing out, "Let's wager on what comes first, the egg containing the 18th species, or the extinction of one of the first 17."

Sara has a penchant for challenging the visitors: "Do birds ever fly just for fun?"

"No, they're too busy with life's activities," the same traveler ventures, hyped up on nature.

"Correct!" Sara confirms.

"Oh," he murmurs with some surprise.

"If you saw a frigate bird circling over this beach, about to dive and kill a baby turtle, what would you do?" Sara queries the 16 travelers.

The busy-bird traveler with a heart of gold begins to explain what he would do, which involves rescuing the baby turtle.

"No!" Sara warns. "Let nature take its course! Frigates survive in part by killing baby turtles."

"Oh," sighs the murmurer.

"Out of one thousand turtle eggs that hatch, how many babies survive?" Sara now asks.

"Fifty!" declares the same heartfelt traveler with a love of numbers.

"No! One in a thousand."

"Oh, goodness gracious," groans the eager globetrotter, who now decides to stay quiet for a while—more in keeping with his Finnish-American reserve.

The giant tortoise stores water in a gallon-sized bladder and can go without eating or drinking for over a year, Sara tells the visitors during an afternoon on dry land. The fittest and smartest whalers, pirates, and other seafarers, eager to survive hardships between the 16th and 19th centuries, avoided starvation in part by capturing mostly female tortoises, which are smaller and easier to lift. They stacked the tortoises on their ships, alive.

The seafarers could thus consume fresh meat for months and drink water from the storage bladders. The 250,000-strong giant tortoise population of the 1500s, though, dropped to 3,000 by the 1970s, Sara explains, as her charges wander among the slow-moving behemoths that have survived.

Snorkeling in the Galápagos provides a week's worth of exercise every hour, the Minnesotan figures. He and the two young Israeli women, who are Red Sea scuba diving veterans, frolic in the deep ocean. They decide to swim into the shallow water of a volcanic crater called Devil's Crown, now mostly submerged. Soon, though, strong currents sweep them out of the crater and back into the ocean depths. When the Red Sea veterans and their pal finally run out of steam, the dinghy operator motoring nearby advises that they climb the ladder into the boat.

While many snorkelers focus on spotting a sting ray, tortoise, marine lizard, shark, or sea lion, the Minnesotan prefers floating above schools of thousands of glistening sardines or other fish so slender they are invisible, unless the sun's rays reflect off them just right.

This same traveler has long known how to cause an entire school of small fish to change direction simultaneously, again and again. He simply imitates Alan Gilbert, the conductor of the New York Philharmonic Orchestra at the Lincoln Center. Unlike Gilbert, however, he conducts thousands, not 106, and without Gilbert's look of the eyes or nod of the head. He just flails his arms or jabs his fingers toward the assembled mass. More nuanced arm and finger movements cause just 200—or 50—to turn in unison and swim a different way, as beautifully as any orchestra moves from adagio to allegro.

Is arm-waving and finger-pointing like this an inexcusable taunting of an innocent species? No! The fish conductor is in fact helping sardines practice their escape from a real predator. For, in a matter of minutes, waves of blue-footed boobies will dive-bomb at high speed, opening their mouths upon entering the water. They swoop and dive solo, in twos or threes, or an incredible five.

As a son in the Maryland family says, "It's an all-you-can-eat buffet for the boobies. I've never felt so in tune with nature in my life!"

Some boobies, however, are forced to cough out the sardines when accosted by robber-baron frigate birds. That likely tunes the Marylander in with nature to the *nth* degree.

The Minnesotan is becoming addicted to just floating or breast stroking in the Pacific, looking down through his mask with snorkel. What takes the cake for him, though, is witnessing a sea lion swim right at him upside down, a few feet below the surface. He soon imagines committing to a life spent in the waters of the archipelago. He vows to live out the rest of his years looking down into the Pacific Ocean, diving until his ears hurt, sometimes kicking his fins with the current, sometimes against.

Years pass. His old friends come to visit. They too take the plunge and never look up again. To pass time, they learn to take a perch and conduct schools of sardines. They are justly proud of their orchestras when Alan Gilbert of New York comes to observe.

Without preplanning or divine intervention, they form a new marine colony 600 miles off the coast of South America. Just miles south of the Equator, they occasionally foray over, under, or right through that very saturated, surprisingly thin line. Some feel vestiges of gills, fins, and scales itching to redeploy.

One bright day, Australian and Chilean marine biologists trail the colonists' wakes, tagging their ears with individual numbers. After a few more years, the colonists' past, present, and potential future is dissected by the journal *Nature Genetics* in a study titled "Toward a Slightly Different Species."

Two Continents, Two Conclusions
APRIL 17, 2016

The time of day is dusk. At $40 a month, the room above a smoky metal-working shop is no bargain. The rent has not been paid in 90 days. A lonely light bulb swings from the ceiling. It is burnt out, but there's no money in Alex's pocket to replace it. He won't have money anytime soon.

Coins have been collecting in Thomas's pocket. During a visit to Alex's room, he suggests that they go and buy a light bulb. They walk two blocks to a store and jostle with a crowd buying grains from sacks piled up on the floor. Alex elbows through. He buys a bulb.

Back at the room, the old bulb doesn't come out easily. The new bulb doesn't screw in very well either. Now Alex stands on the bed to get his arms around the problem. The socket gives him a shock. The new bulb doesn't work any better than the burned-out bulb. They give up. Alex grabs his keyboard from the bed. They leave the room in nearly evaporated daylight.

Alex and Thomas head toward a venue where Alex will sing. They come to a busy plaza where a hundred people mill about. As they cross the plaza, Alex motions to Thomas to look up. In the sky, a bright blue, yellow, and white object races toward the Pacific Ocean, a hundred miles away. It moves parallel to the ground, beautifully luminescent. It flies past in just a few seconds.

This is where Alex and Thomas stopped agreeing, in retrospect. To Thomas, the object flew only a few hundred feet above the ground. To Alex, it was very high. To Thomas, it was a highly sophisticated fireworks rocket. He has never experienced such speed, even though he's driven late at night on desolate highways with barely a police officer within radar range. He has never seen anything so amazing in the sky and could hardly believe his eyes.

To Alex, it was natural, as he kept telling Thomas over the next two days. Alex insisted that the object was an *estrella*—a star—or more precisely, a *meteorito*—a meteorite. He said local people see them occasionally.

"How can that be?" wondered Thomas. The multicolored object seemed to fly much closer, straighter, and faster than the monochrome shooting stars above his own continent.

But Alex and Thomas are near the equator, where more meteors enter the earth's atmosphere than in polar regions. And at high altitudes —as here in Latacunga—a surprising quantity of light rays travel from the retina to the brain each millisecond.

Thomas is not distressed about the series of events that ran from a burned-out bulb to the store to the reluctant socket to the electric shock Alex suffered, which he accepts as fate. These events led Alex and Thomas to the plaza right when the fabulous meteorite whizzed by at what Thomas believed was the speed of light.

But he concludes that, when on a continent different from yours, especially if 65 miles south of the Equator and 9,200 feet above sea level, it is best to believe what you are told about Mother Earth's phenomena by a native whose family has been living here for perhaps 10,000 years.

COLOMBIA

That Broken Line
SEPTEMBER 22, 2009

The line on my map between points A and B is a bit squiggly, and it is broken. If a broken line is significant, I'm in the dark, since I haven't found the key on the map. Point A is Villa de Leyva, nestled since 1570 in a remote valley, now reachable by long bus rides from Bogotá, the nation's capital. Point B is Medellín. The broken line seems to go from A to B through the mountains. It can't take longer than a day.

Tomorrow, I plan to travel from A to B, but today, here in Villa de Leyva, why not rent a bicycle and ride to the "Stonehenge of South America"? Since it's high noon, the guard leaves for his two-hour lunch break, closing the gate behind him. I'm alone now. I have a feeling that if I linger long enough, I'll learn when to plant crops by observing the shadows cast by dozens of stone pillars erected, perhaps, in the early years AD. The hang-up is that the bike must be returned in six hours. So I leave the pillars and their short midday shadows. I close the gate behind me.

I am now en route to see Kronosaurus Quensladicus. Schoolchildren, on their way to work in the fields, point me in a revised direction.

"*De dónde eres*? [Where are you from?]" one child asks.

"*Adivinen*! [Guess!]" I say.

They have ideas: "*Villa de Leyva*? *Medellín*?"

"*No y no*," I answer.

"*Venezuela*? *Japan*? *Africa*?"

"*No, no, y no!*" I exasperate. Finally, "*Sí!*" I'm indeed from the United States of America.

Soon, I'm face to skull with Kronosaurus—all alone with her (or him). I find myself calling her "Kronosaurus Rex." She's lying right where they found her 50 years ago, following 120 million years of rest. Kronosaurus was a mammoth reptile with a voracious appetite that lived in the sea. This alligator relative lives on as a fossil, as huge now as it was back then.

That evening in Villa de Leyva, I survey the townsfolk. "Can I go from here to Medellín on the broken line?" I ask.

"No" is the preponderant answer. Everyone tells me I must back-track to Bogotá, make a U-turn, and head to Medellín on a known route. "And why do you want to go?" one asks.

At 9 a.m. the next day, it's time to do it my way.

"Whoa!" I hear you yell. "Are you sure about this?" But now it's too late. I've already left.

Over several hours, I make it to Sáchica, Sutamarchán, Chiquinquirá, and Pauna. At each bus stop, I worry I may be heading into a dead end. At a small store in Pauna, I inquire if I can travel farther. They seem to say, "Yes, just wait awhile."

From my chair in the store, I stare out the door at the town plaza and the mountains beyond. A boy on a white horse rides back and forth. I believe he's just out for a ride, using his horse in place of the real thing—a four-wheeler, a dirt bike, a snowmobile, or a skateboard (of which there seems to be none in town).

I'm jarred back into consciousness by a family who tells me the bus has pulled into town. We all pile in. In a few short hours, we're in Otanche. The family informs me that if I show up in the town square at five a.m., I could "squeeze into that Toyota Land Cruiser over there."

I wake up just after four in my $7 room near the plaza. The town buzzes with people who've already started a new day—or never went to sleep. I order black coffee for 20 cents from a street vendor. At five, it's still dark. Four of us board the Land Cruiser and soon bounce up and down and out of town on that broken line. The four-wheel-drive had better not drift a foot or two off the line, though, or we'll fly head over wheels down the mountainside.

Soon, I'm able to write the map's key. A broken line means a one-lane gravel road through otherwise impassable but fertile mountains first traversed perhaps 10,000 years ago by hunter-gatherer-explorers. A broken line means bisecting an occasional farm and rare pueblo. It means beware of washouts and landslides but appreciate all the crystal-clear streams running across it. It means hitting a million neck-wrenching rocks that the vehicle was built to survive and entering fluffy clouds that reduce visibility to near zero.

The line also suggests there'll be people along the road who jump in for an hour or two, and others that reach in with money for the driver, who'll buy a specified necessity for them at the end of the journey, down at the Rio Magdalena in Puerto Boyacá.

Several people standing along the broken line now look into the back of our Land Cruiser as we move by slowly. They see 16 knees clattering against each other, kneecap to kneecap. More soon climb in, and we're at near capacity. The 11 of us with our 22 kneecaps and one live chicken bounce around in the back, three others do the same in the front, while two men standing on the rear bumper hang on for dear life.

The broken line foretells that the spare tires the driver has stocked will be employed—one for a tire that goes boom! and the other for one that deflates with nary a whimper. The line also means watch for an immobilized cow with one hind leg snagged on the top of a barbed wire fence—don't ask the 16 of us how that happened, but someone, please get out quick and help it.

Then the broken line comes to an end. We're at the bottom of the valley in Puerto Boyacá. It has taken us five hours to drive sixty miles. We work on our knees and necks. I tell the driver that the trip was an *aventura*—an adventure. He appears puzzled: "It was?" he asks. This route doesn't earn so much as a mention in any guidebook, even Lonely Planet's book for backpackers on a bare budget. I'm not saying nothing to no one.

Meanwhile, it'll be an easy journey up another mountain to Medellín. I've always heard that's where the drug kingpin of the world, Pablo Escobar, headed his cartel. He's dead now, and in a Medellín museum, you can even see a painting of him getting shot badly—like fatally. You might feel drawn to his gravesite, although you never know who you'll run into paying their respects.

I get ahead of myself, though. I'm still on my way to Medellín, in two days, not my one-day shortcut. Soldiers stop our bus. One climbs aboard, waving a small white flag. "This signifies peace and nonviolence," he explains.

The soldier orders all the guys to get out. Once outside, we each turn around, face the bus, stretch our hands up against it, and are frisked. None of us is carrying arms or bombs. Our luggage is opened. No weapons or explosives or cocaine are discovered; just clothes and an occasional toothbrush.

We're handed white flags to hold. "It's okay to smile," a soldier says. Another one snaps a group photo. Security forces will keep it handy, in case some of us decide to commandeer the bus or to cooperate with ambushing rebels farther down the road.

This is a country starting to see better days. I'll unfurl the white flag once back home, with good hopes for the world.

Luzmila and Her Tip of South America
SEPTEMBER 28, 2011

Tomorrow I'll venture with four other travelers and an indigenous guide to the tip of South America! Few journey there. We'll sleep in hammocks. And the water is swimmably warm, it's said. No penguins cavort within thousands of miles, though.

So, has global warming hit the extreme tip of the continent that points nicely to Antarctica? Maybe so, but this tip is not Tierra del Fuego, but the *northern* tip of South America, where a desert peninsula juts into the Caribbean Sea. Next week, I'll fly from Bogotá to New York City. Once there, I'm not planning to sleep outside in a hammock.

• • •

The time to venture forth is near.

A Dutch couple, a French couple, and I meet in Riohacha, the capital of Colombia's northernmost province. Once we leave, the driver of the 4x4 Toyota Land Cruiser must know the spot where Venezuelan gas is sold from 10-gallon containers lining the road, for no fuel will be found later. The driver must also know the rough gravel trails winding along the sea—and find the hidden cove where a boat captained by Cornelio will crest over the horizon toward us.

It's quickly apparent that Cornelio has boated these rough Caribbean waters before. We don't capsize! We just churn into the prevailing winds and slam on the surface a dozen times a minute. We're soaked from the beginning.

We're now advancing into what seems like the most remote place on earth. The coast retreats, then becomes closer, then farther. Mangrove swamps line the shore.

An eerily familiar site suddenly appears. Ahead are the dry, deeply colored mesas of Colorado, Wyoming, or Utah, aren't they? The only apparent difference is that water splashes against the mesas, as if global warming had raised the world's oceans thousands of feet, submerging much of the American West. The mesas look like desert islands in the ocean.

Cornelio beaches the craft at the bottom of a multilayered mesa. We cannot see the top, for its sides are too steep. One by one, we jump out in ankle-deep water, grab our backpacks from the boat, and slowly work our way to the top.

The top is flat. There, we find Luzmila's *ranchería*, where she lives with her husband and several children. Cornelio, his brother Hilario, and others from another family ranchería a bicycle ride away make themselves at home here too. In the open air but under a roof, they've hung five cotton hammocks for the five of us, each painstakingly knit over three months by women from this mesa top. The mesa is miles and miles long and a quarter mile wide. It feels like a long island—but one end is said to be connected to South America, which now seems a thousand years removed.

No clock hangs on the adobe walls of the few small buildings. Time is measured by sunrises and sunsets.

Lobster is our first lunch at Luzmila's, and we're unable to eat all that we're served. Our next meal is red snapper, caught just hours earlier. For breakfast, we have a choice of lobster, fish, and eggs. But why choose eggs?

A truck sits atop the mesa. It carries seafood away and hauls fresh water in. Where to and where from, I'm not quite sure. The truck, with us travelers as its cargo, now chugs to high, steep sand dunes that fall into the Caribbean Sea. We run with the breeze over the dunes. Cargo again, we jump down near a shoreline. I stand alone on a coastal rock. Of the 400 million people in South America, I am momentarily the most northerly of all. I stand alone on the tip of South America.

Over the weekend, Cornelio and Hilario carry us by boat to beach after beach, each unpeopled. We call these beaches our own— Bahia Honda, Bahia Hondita, and La Boquita.

"Hilario," I ask, "how many lobsters have you caught in your life?"

"On a good day, I catch 30 or 40," Hilario informs me. English words seem to amuse Hilario, so I practice with him, "Let's go, let's go swim, let's go up, hello, thank you, blue." I realize he doesn't speak fluent Spanish. I don't think he picks up my past perfect, "*Has viajado a Venezuela*? [Have you traveled to Venezuela?]"

Luzmila, family members, neighbors, and tall Daniel from Bogotá, on the family ranchería near the Tip of South America.

Daniel, a bilingual volunteer from the capital who assists the five of us, now chimes in, telling me that the language spoken on this speck of South America is their own. The Wayuu indigenous people, I learn, fought the Spanish tooth and nail. They were never subjugated. All sorts of oil people are now prowling the waters, however. The Wayuu raise goats and ship spectacular quantities of seafood to continental South America. Theirs is a matrilineal society, which means women own the land and gently rule the roost. Luzmila's family has lived right here for generations.

Meanwhile, the night wind whistles through our hammocks, celebrating its landfall. It's been traveling all the way from Africa, without touching so much as a rock on its journey.[2]

---

[2] The author's journey to the *other tip* of South America is recounted in his book *The Other Worlds: Offbeat Adventures of a Curious Traveler*. The accounts include "The Uttermost Part of the Earth," "Scientific Americans at Work," and "Lug Nuts on the Loose."

Bless the Forgiving Dog's Heart

APRIL 25, 2016

It's now a different year, and I'm in South America again.

After traveling from Ecuador to Southern Colombia, I soon ensconce myself in Popayán, a Spanish colonial city founded in 1537. Farther north, and hours off the Pan-American Highway, the town of Inza's market sizzles every Saturday. Few travelers—including me—would ever know to come here. But my seatmate on a jet to South America clued me in to the special, and especially remote, little town of Inza.

A pre-Columbian culture, I learn after arriving, flourished here from around 200 BC until the 17th century. Near Inza, an archaeological site known as Tierradentro is home to 162 underground chambers—where the elite were buried. Visitors are just beginning to venture to Inza. Most of those who do then climb down into the vividly painted, nearly hidden chambers that range from tiny to multiroomed.

On a quiet Sunday evening, as I sit in a café on a narrow street between the Inza plaza and the empty market, a man and woman whiz down the street to the café on their motorbikes. He carries a bag. The bag jumps around. After he opens it, the man twists the neck of the chicken inside until it is—well, it isn't dead yet, since its eyes still look around. He twists the chicken's neck again until it stops fluttering. He then hands the dead chicken to the café owner. Since I've already eaten supper, I finish my coffee and leave.

In Inza, soldiers man street barricades of cement barrels. Guerrilla attacks have rocked these mountains for decades. Three years ago, a bomb-packed truck parked close to the Inza police station killed six people. The station is now sandbagged. A peace accord is being negotiated in Havana, Cuba. Perhaps to show it is serious about rural development, the government seems intent on paving remote gravel roads in the beautiful Andes Mountains, even though a washout or landslide may be just around the next curve, paved road or not.

Back on the Pan-American Highway the next day, I see the fastest cyclist of my life. He's racing ahead of our van, right behind the loaded truck in front of us. As we pass the biker and truck, we see that the boy keeps just one hand on the handlebar. His "free" hand grips the back of the truck. He's found a way to ride 40 miles per hour!

I van-ride for hours toward Tuesday's weekly market in Silvia, elevation 8,685 feet. Silvia, like Inza, is a world away from the Pan-American Highway. At the market, one might fancy—and buy—a horse, saddle, wrench, sacks of grains, potatoes and more potatoes, fruits, vegetables, mango yogurt, hot soup and stew, coffee, medicinal herbs, tea from the *Amazonas*, and hundreds of brown paper–wrapped bricks of boiled and evaporated sugar cane juice. All the while hearing Spanish mixed with the indigenous Guambiano language.

Milling about are a hundred or more Guambiano men and women from a dozen rural communities, decked in traditional clothing. When school lets out at 2 p.m., some students join their parents at the market, including one who sits on a bench next to me. Early this morning, he walked an hour to town for school.

Adjoining the Silvia market is a restaurant. It has no name, but you can't miss it, with its wood-burning cooking stove, wooden benches that'll sit eight or nine, and tree trunk slices on the floor so two women can stand tall enough to reach the boiling pots and the sink. There is also the cat I stepped on and a dog that came to check the cat's condition—and to let me know this happens all the time, and we can still be friends. This is now without a doubt my favorite restaurant in Colombia —perhaps even in the world.

PERU

The Wet Desert Coast of Peru
JANUARY 30, 2015

I'm with Mario Tribeño Mar, who's been a friend since the 1980s.

Mario, I should explain, lives in Cusco. Mario has guided hundreds of visitors, including the president of Intel Corporation, to Machu Picchu and other destinations. One day last year, while he was pickaxing his yard, he pierced the skull of a mummy, then dug around it to look for gold, but just found three ceramics. If you visit Mario, you can hold the ceramics in your hands, but he reburied the mummy skull—"elsewhere," he says.

But today, Mario and I are exploring Lima, a city of 8.5 million. Before we can take off for the Caral Ruins to the north, a taxi runs over the edge of Mario's foot. It swells, but he assures me it's improving.

Since Mario and I are fit, we head to Caral, built 5,000 years ago. It's touted as "The Oldest City in the Americas" and "The Americas' First Civilization." For hundreds of miles, this Peruvian coast is a desert. Yet up in the not-distant Andes, hundreds or thousands of streams converge to form about 20 rivers that flow down through the desert lowlands to the Pacific. On the other side of the Andes, as many as 15,000 tributaries, originating in several countries, create a river that carries one-fifth of the world's fresh water. It's the Amazon.

By 3000 BC, inhabitants near the Pacific began to irrigate the rivers' floodplains and bits of the adjoining desert. The Sacred City of Caral —one of 23 settlements along the Supe River—was the elite's home and the ceremonial center. Today's people use these same rivers to irrigate fields of corn, sugar cane, asparagus, mangoes, peaches, and passion fruit.

From the Caral ruins, Mario now heads south, back to Lima and Cusco. I head north toward the still-distant equator in Ecuador. I will be stopping along the Pacific Coast at the Sechin Ruins near Casma—from a civilization that flourished in 1800 BC.

The Short Story of a Long Friendship
JANUARY 1, 2021

Mario Tribeño Mar was born into the Quechua and Spanish languages. He learned English in the United States in the 1990s. He's now a multi-lingual guide in Cusco, once the religious and administrative capital of the Inca Empire—the largest empire in the world in the 1400s. Back then, Cusco and Machu Picchu were separated by a three-day walk on the Inca Trail. Between these two sites was, and still is, Ollantaytambo ("o-yahn-tai-tombo"), where Mario was born.

How did Mario and I first run into each other? The story goes like this.

A boy of Incan descent, holding schoolbooks in his lap, sits on a stone wall in his hometown of Ollantaytambo. Behind him looms the 15th-century mountain fortress built by Inca emperor Pachacuti, along with ancient farming terraces and irrigation canals. It's a school day, but the boy has skipped out early. A backpacking visitor from Minnesota has discovered Ollantaytambo, the best-preserved Inca city in the world. He ambles over the cobblestone streets. The schoolboy and the Minnesota ambler meet and exchange one- or two-word greetings. Both with time to kill, they walk to the plaza, sit down in a café, and imbibe Inca Colas.

"*Vamos a Machu Picchu*," the boy suggests. It's just a two-hour train ride and a steep climb away. The visitor understands this simple sentence—but not a whole lot more. Try as he might, he can't get the Spanish words out for "I've already been there," or even "I went there."

"*Vamos a Machu Picchu*," the boy repeats—more than once. Facing an insurmountable linguistic hurdle, the visitor solves his problem by answering, "*Sí! Vamos a Machu Picchu la próxima semana!*"

And the following week, as the visitor promised, to Machu Picchu they go. Once atop Machu Picchu, the boy challenges the Minnesotan to go higher, much higher—to Huayna Picchu. And much higher they climb, but halfway up they confront an overgrown spot in the trail. A few climbing this trail in the past have eagerly burst through the bushy roadblock and rushed ahead—and fallen straight to their deaths, hundreds of feet below. Luckily, the novice is not hiking alone, and the boy tells him to follow in his footsteps. Just before the thicket, they turn left off the trail and squeeze through brush that hides the entrance to a tunnel. The tunnel leads the pair back to the open-air trail toward Huayna Picchu.

The boy explains in Spanish that invaders didn't see that the local Incas they were pursuing had suddenly turned left and into a tunnel. Pumped up, the invaders charged forward through the trail-blocking brush and plunged off the cliff. "The Incas patted themselves on the back for so cleverly designing the trail!" the boy explains.

The visitor, Tom, and the novice guide, Mario, safely reach the peak of Huayna Picchu. It's so much fun to clamber over the peak's boulders that they very nearly overstay their adventure, just managing to descend to Machu Picchu in the day's waning light.

Back in Ollantaytambo the next day, Tom follows Mario up the cobblestone streets and through a doorway in the 500-year-old stone wall surrounding Mario's home and corral. Tom meets Mario's mom and dad, Cerila and Cesar, sisters Isabel and Julie, and brothers Aristo and David. A meal cooks on a wood stove. A kerosene lantern shines its soft light onto each incredible Inca face. Tom doesn't yet know that this is the beginning of many new friendships.

• • •

Decades later . . .

On a special day in April of 2020, during the global shutdown caused by the COVID-19 pandemic, Mario dials a phone number from South America. A phone rings in North America. I answer it.

For years, conversations between Mario and me have been in English, not Spanish. Within a few minutes, our Easter Sunday and COVID-19 chat turns to the ancient day the two of us met.

"If you hadn't played hooky from school that day, we wouldn't have met," I tell Mario. I silently add to my inventory of wisdom: flaunting a rule for fun sometimes is highly beneficial—in this case, creating a lifelong friendship.

"It was a Thursday or Friday that we met," Mario figures. I wonder how he can remember that!

"I snuck out of school early because I had to start buying potatoes, corn, and other vegetables for the weekend," Mario recalls.

"I soon had big sackfuls of produce. On Saturday morning, I waited in the plaza where we drank those Inca Colas, Tom. A crowd of people waited with me. They had big sacks too, plus a child or two, a few goats, and sheep. We all waited for a big truck to appear."

"The goats, the sheep, the people, the sacks, everything got packed tight together in the back of the truck," Mario continues.

"Because I had a load of heavy sacks, I couldn't take much clothing with me. My father gave me a poncho to wear. The truck climbed up the rocky mountain road. It became colder and colder. We reached 4,000 meters [13,200 feet]. I really froze in the back of the truck!"

"Finally, the truck started to go down. We drove into a cloud forest at 2,500 meters [8,250 feet] and stopped in a village. Relatives of mine live there, and I slept at their house. Sunday is market day. At the market, I sold all the potatoes, corn, and vegetables I'd bought in Ollantaytambo when I played hooky."

"How did you travel back to Ollantaytambo?" I ask.

"By truck. The roads are too bad for any bus. And that trip each way takes six, sometimes eight hours."

"Mario, how'd you learn to buy bags of produce, journey to that village, and sell the goods?"

"My father did that and started taking me with him a couple years before I met you. I was 11 or 12. Soon, I could do that job all by myself."

"Where did you spend the money you earned?"

"I bought schoolbooks, shoes, and uniforms. Do you remember that the day we met, I had my school uniform on, and you asked if I was a student?"

"No, I don't remember that," I answer. "But I do remember you telling me later that you got scared when I talked to you. You thought I was a school official looking for kids playing hooky."

"I was afraid your job was to capture kids playing hooky," Mario explains, "and turn them over to the police!"

• • •

On Easter Sunday 2020, I thus learn, after all these years, that Mario wasn't playing hooky for the fun of it that day. He had a job to do—a job that enabled him to study at school on most school days. Freezing in the back of a truck was part of the job.

"Tom," I'm telling myself, "you're never too old to learn something new about a friend!"

Mario thanks me on that Easter Sunday, as he's done several times over the years, for inviting him to visit the United States three decades earlier, though it was harder than the dickens for him to secure a US visa. En route with the visa, Mario fell asleep at the Miami airport and missed his next flight. Upon his midwinter arrival in Minneapolis, he marveled at the twinkling lights in airport trees. He thought they were a very cool species of tree—one that grows lights!

One day, we visited my cousin Leah White, and her husband Ray led Mario onto what appeared to be a large, snow-covered field. Ray

Mario and Tom exchanged letters for years. Peru's hyperinflation in the late 1980s is demonstrated by this envelope Mario labored over.

drilled a hole through the snow, and deeper. To Mario's surprise and delight, water rose out of the hole from the lake below them. In short order, they were ice fishing on Lake Pokegama.

Come summer, Ray and Mario canoed through Minnesota's pristine wilderness, where a moose crossed their path. Back at Lake Pokegama, near Grand Rapids, Ray set up a target with a figure labeled "bandito." He handed Mario a revolver. Mario learned how to shoot that day. The young man from Ollantaytambo was seeing and doing it all! A few years later, Mario would return the favor, entertaining Ray as his guest in Ollantaytambo. Ray would have the adventure of his life, naturally, spending time at Mario's ancestral home and farmland, and riding a horse up the steep path to Machu Picchu.

During his visit to the United States, Mario enrolled in English classes at the Harry S Truman city college in Chicago, where I lived back then. His classmates were from Colombia, Japan, Russia, Israel, and the world as a whole. Mario's diligence earned him visa extensions worth a couple of years. It was long enough for him to learn to drive a car—and even to drive my mother 250 miles from Lost Lake to the Mayo Clinic, while I worked in Chicago. Mario became a good friend of my mom's, as he did with dozens of people he met in the United States.

Mario's mother and I have become good friends too. I've visited them several times—once for Mario's Western-style wedding to his longtime girlfriend Yolanda. The days before the wedding were spent in Quechua-style parties— enjoyed, too, by two other American guests: the chairman of the board of Intel Corporation and his jet pilot wife.

I hope to visit the Tribeño Mar family again, once the pandemic subsides. When I do, I'll hop in the back of a truck owned by Mario's enterprising brother David. I'll get packed tight with Quechua-speaking travelers, produce, sheep, and goats for a ride over the Andes Mountains. And I'll try not to freeze.

Cerila Mar, a lifelong resident of the 15th-century Incan town of Ollantaytambo, is the mother of six, including Mario Tribeño Mar. Cerila's grandson Maxwell snapped the photo when the two were hiking.

CENTRAL AMERICA

NICARAGUA

An Earful from Nixon

APRIL 4, 2007

While you and a stranger are a lonesome twosome contesting big waves off a remote Nicaraguan beach, should you risk gulping down a mouthful of saltwater by striking up a conversation?

And if you can get the right Spanish words out of your mouth before you work your way back to shore, might you suggest he and his friends meet you at a pizza joint for supper?

If Nixon—you've now learned his name—does show up with his friends for pizza, do you bid adieu on your way out the door, or ask if tomorrow he'd escort you to a swimming spot he's mentioned that's even harder to get to than the one where you two just met?

Nixon, speaking Spanish, seems to go along with your suggestion. It could be awhile before he learns his first words in English. If he did signal *sí* to go with you to a new swimming destination, you will discover that the "go" entails a bus up and away from San Juan del Sur on the Pacific Ocean, a taxi ride to a ferry boat, a boat ride to an island—and a bus that threads its way between two volcanic mountains to the island's far side, from where there is no more land as far as the eye can see.

• • •

The incoming wind is strong. White-crested waves crash into the island's Santo Domingo Beach, day and night. You feel you are standing by the ocean. Yet, look there! Horses stand offshore, drinking off the vestiges of ocean-sized breakers. Fresh water!

You really owe Nixon Alexander Mendoza a debt of gratitude for leading you to what's now your favorite swimming beach in the world, at Central America's biggest lake, on the far side of an island.

This island—Ometepe ("o-meh-teh-pay")—was settled one thousand to three thousand years ago by peoples such as the Mangues, Chorotegas, Nicaraguas, and Tiwanaco, or their predecessors. The bloodlines in Nixon's barrio may be a small mixture of some of these, added to a small contribution from African peoples and a predominant one from Europeans.

• • •

Nixon begins to learn English words, perhaps the first in his bloodline ever to do so. Playa Santo Domingo is now "beach fantastic." One shortcoming as an English teacher, you realize, is your failure to insist on proper word order. You have a completely ad hoc approach to the profession.

Between countless swims in huge waves on a beach fantastic, you sandwich beach soccer, volleyball, jogging, card playing, and riding bikes to the base of a volcano where 20 natural springs create pools for more swims. Since you've now decided to convert your general tour of Central America into a swimming tour, you have no problem walking a mile in the hot afternoon sun to an island stream that's dammed— for another exquisite swim. And repeating all this the next day.

The powerful waves may still captivate you on your last day, and you ferry out of the island so late that you miss the last bus to your next swimming destination. In that case, Nixon may invite you to his house for a night in a remote barrio. You don't say no.

A flag in front of the house signifies support for new President Daniel Ortega and the Sandinista heritage. All manner of relatives welcome you. You're treated to your own room, with a bed a foot shorter than you, a dirt floor, outdoor toilet, and neighborhood dogs that bark all night—except for their three a.m. naps.

By day, Nixon rides a horse through the village, visits friends, and throws rocks into fruit trees. You watch the rocks go up and come down, then realize fruit you've never heard of has fallen into his waiting hands. Later, Nixon comes from his kitchen into the yard, opens a hand, and offers you an iguana egg, which you eat—and then enjoy another.

Since a swimming tour wouldn't be complete without a look at the other coast of Nicaragua, you and Nixon make your way to the Caribbean Sea, board a boat to Big Corn Island, and then a smaller one onward to Little Corn Island. The beaches are fine and almost empty. Little Corn has no roads or vehicles but is dressed with sandy paths that wind their way through the jungle-like interior.

Time is on your hands. You walk the trails. You come across no one but a brother and sister selling their mother's gingerbread from a pail, which you make significantly lighter. Come evening, Nixon teaches you how to play the Loco Ocho card game. You listen to him sing songs with all words in Spanish—except for "beach fantastic."

Nixon gives you an earful of stories that he says are of different genres, such as "vulgar" and "scary." You're sure US historians have classified Richard Nixon's White House tapes into the very same categories. When Nicaragua's Nixon recounts one of the scary stories, you learn that if you find a book on the street of his barrio or of yours, do not read it, and by all means, don't tuck it under your pillow. This may be the book of the devil. Violating the rule will leave you and yours suffering all sorts of afflictions forever thereafter.

When it's time to leave, walk back across Little Corn's sandy paths to the spot where the panga boat awaits. On the way, you may see a crab shell moving near your foot. It's not just any crab shell. You have to know your shells. The crab in this shell, when crushed and mixed with like crabs, may be rubbed on your stomach every day for a week to alleviate gastritis. And don't forget the power of flowers, leaves, roots, and stems that you've heard about from Nixon on Little Corn.

Back at Nixon's barrio across the country, another swimming hole shows up on your list. It's a mile's walk. Thoughtless and in a hurry, you and Nixon slip through a barbed wire fence surrounding a lush banana plantation. You sense that this isn't an authorized shortcut. A bicycle approaches. The plantation guard, armed with a machete, confronts you. Alas, the confrontation turns to smiles, since Nixon and the guard know each other.

At the swimming hole in a river, you meet men and boys from the barrios. In the water, they make a tall, muscled human pyramid of bodies of many sizes but few shapes. The stranger among them happens to have a camera. Each will receive a photo sometime in the future.

Regrettably, you've missed what is touted locally as the "finest swim" in Central America: a 650-foot-deep lake in a volcanic crater. *Fumaroles* seep into Laguna Apoyo from the bottom, it's said. That makes you curious, but your dictionary is at home, gathering dust.

A fumarole might be a warm stream of gas, just from the sound of the word. If you pay a return visit next year, you and Nixon may be determined to see for yourselves. Upon arriving at Laguna Apoyo, you may challenge him to dive to the bottom to inhale a fumarole. After disappearing for some time, he may come back up with a scary story—one he will recount in his barrio. It will surely turn into a legend—one you too may tell again and again in your own country.

What You Get for $20
APRIL 11, 2007

The jacket I've carried on this six-week trip out of Guatemala has seen no use, so I'll pack lighter on future jaunts to hot spots in Nicaragua, Honduras, and El Salvador.

One finds the highlands of Nicaragua a relief from the 90- to 95-degree afternoons below. I am thus alert enough to spot a coffee cooperative in Jinotega, and more alert yet after sampling the co-op's expresso and cappuccino in quick fashion.

We all become talkative. The coffee entrepreneurs suggest I venture by bus to one of four distant destinations, three unpronounceable. I agree to visit Pueblo Nuevo. The co-op folks forewarn me to step down from the bus when I reach the pueblo, then walk a mile or two up a dirt road to Flora and Antonio's place. It's one of 650 small farms under the cooperative's umbrella.

"They'll be expecting you," I am told.

"You will phone them?" I inquire.

"No. They are always there."

So off I go, and indeed, there they are. For $20, I get a bed, three meals, coffee, a three-hour hike with Antonio, and a candle for my room.

Passing a certain kind of tree on the hike, Antonio instructs me how a wound can be healed. "Pull out your knife and cut into this trunk. Press your finger on the blood-red sap that oozes out. Watch as it turns creamy. Rub the cream on your cut. Presto!"

Refreshed from the three-hour hike, I spend a like amount of time helping the 13-year-old daughter babysit the cook's two-year-old— while we piece together a jigsaw puzzle of the United States. Some of the pieces, like Montana, are missing—fallen, perhaps, through cracks in the floor. For all I know, the sun doesn't shine like it used to on Big Sky Country.

Rather than hit the sack at 8 p.m. like the others, the daughter, son, and I play a board game under the kerosene lamp. The game cards quiz us on Nicaraguan places and hot spots. I answer most of the questions correctly, since I've just sweated my way through them. During breaks in our game, the 13-year-old answers my questions about coffee production and school. (She walks down to Pueblo Nuevo for school every morning. It takes just 40 minutes. Coming back up takes an hour.)

After breakfast the next day, Antonio saddles up a horse for me, and we head toward Pueblo Nuevo, where buses come by. Antonio follows on foot but halfway there says something—I believe he says he is going home.

I've never felt so free in my life. For the first time, I have my own horse and am on my own!

I conjure up visions of riding my horse straight through Pueblo Nuevo and not looking back. I may ride for weeks through the Nicaraguan and Honduran mountains, hunkering down in pueblos with unpronounceable names.

If, during my long travels, I happen to case a bank that needs robbing—but I get ahead of myself. First, I'll choose a name for my horse. I'll practice riding at getaway speed. I'll buy myself a cowboy hat, a six-shooter, and boots that I'll scuff up—this 1870s American outlaw is no city slicker.

Alas! Cold water is thrown all over my exciting life to come. I notice Antonio catching up on foot as my horse and I approach Pueblo Nuevo. I'm obliged to dismount, bid farewell to my horse, and wait for a bus.

• • •

A new Nicaraguan hot spot is Cerro Negro, the "newest volcano in the Americas." It erupted out of a cornfield in the 1850s. Every seven years or so, it rises in stature. Nothing grows on it because it's just a conical mountain of black sand and black cinder pebbles.

If Cerro Negro had erupted in a land with a wintry climate, people surely would have started skiing at breakneck speed down its slopes decades ago. So wouldn't you think a crazy visitor, like an Australian, would envision sliding down it, say, on an upside-down coffee table? Or a refrigerator? After telling himself he would never try those again, he designed a one-person toboggan.

The Australian's business now tells people like me, "You should fork over $20, hop in a pickup over rough country to the bottom of the volcano, lug a darned heavy board to the top, and ride it like a go-cart over the cinders and sand 1,400 feet to the bottom."

"What if I start going too fast?" I ask, fearful of the answer.

"Not to worry. Just dig your heels into the volcano as you're jetting down," the office advises. (Gals, no high heels, please.)

Cerro Negro's peak is windy, I'd say 30 or 40 mph. The guide in her 20s can't hear me say much, but enough to conclude what state I must be from. She's from Hutchinson, Minnesota.

Nor can I hear her say much—just the words, "90 percent of all our accidents happen when you—" and the wind then spikes to 50 mph. Thankfully, a minute later she repeats: "Accidents happen when you brake with just one heel, because you'll swerve and take a tough tumble."

I brake with two heels dug in hard, not just a little here and there, but the whole way down. Until just before the bottom, when I notice the only anomaly on the volcano: a little lump in front of me, too near to avoid. I take my tumble after all, head over two heels.

• • •

Before leaving Nicaragua for the Honduran capital of Tegucigalpa, I bed down in Somoto town. The hotel clerk suggests I offer the owner $20 and travel with him in his four-wheel-drive pickup to a canyon that the outside world never visited until four years ago. The canyon is deep and narrow, I'm told, and a river runs through it. This year is, I believe, its 13 millionth year, give or take, of digging itself deeper.

After splashing back and forth through the river in the pickup, and seeing farmlands strewn with boulders carried by the floodwaters of horrific Hurricane Mitch in 1998, the chasm looms before us. A canyon owner's two sons and I jump in a rowboat, and later the pair instructs me to sit on an inner tube while they swim behind, pushing. That's the program, since visitors have a camera and can't paddle.

Portaging the tube over rocky spots, we find ourselves deep in the canyon. After conversing about their days of swimming and fishing right here while growing up, we extract ourselves the same way we came in. The canyon entrance fee is $3, which includes the boat and the guide-propelled tube ride. That's how families here make a living, aside from working their now rocky farms.

The next time someone suggests I invest $20 to experience a coffee farm, volcano, canyon, or other hot spot, I'll remind myself not to dig in my heels, but just go for it.

HONDURAS

Lazing My Way from Guatemala to Honduras
FEBRUARY 12, 2004

I'm lazing back in the Guatemalan Caribbean town of Livingston, inhabited not only by the Maya, but also by the Garifuna people, who are descendants of shipwrecked, rebellious African slaves and indigenous people of Arawak and Carib origin. The Garifuna are a people rich in history, language, traditions, music, and dance.

After a few days, I'm inclined to head south to Honduras.

But—and this can happen to a traveler—I meet three guys who twist my arm into staying longer: a Maya, a Garifuna rapper, and a former East Los Angeles gang member of Spanish descent exiled back to Guatemala. They show me a splendid time. The next day, the dreadlocked rapper inquires whether I'd like to see his "bird sanctuary." Since I never say no, we're on our way. First, though, we laze our way through Livingston's streets, buying vegetables, chicken, and other makings for a meal. We head for the bird sanctuary on a trail and come to his secluded Shangri-la shack in a jungle. The other two friends wander by and join us for hours. Tropical birds call the jungle their sanctuary too.

We think we'll resume our festive and peaceful passage of time a year from now. Their twisting my arm left no bruise marks, and they swear they'll twist it again next year.

• • •

A feast for the eyes meets me in Honduras: cowboys herding cattle, a dead horse with rigor mortis in the middle of the road that forces the bus to swerve, and long construction rebars trailing out the back of a pickup, leaving sparks on the pavement. A guard at a hotel reception counter works on a 12-gauge shotgun; the safety, he says, is stuck (hopefully in the off position, I feel, in case robbers show up).

From Honduran beach towns, I move inland to the Maya ruins of Copán. A new pyramid temple was often built on top of an existing one, thus destroying it. In about 800 AD, however, a ruler developed a construction technique that preserved the prior temple (which itself had covered up and destroyed an earlier one). Archaeologists have discovered the hidden temple and dug tunnels to parts of it.

The guard is not around to take my tunnel ticket, but noticing that the padlock on the entrance gate is askew, I let myself in. If a number of off-shooting tunnels hadn't been locked up tight, I might still be wandering in the hidden temple.

Emerging from the tunnels, I travel to do a little business in the Honduran capital of—here's a mouthful and I always gulp at the end—Tegucigalpa. For the first time in my life, I now hold a ticket to Cuba! I'll leave on Monday for 25 days. Most of my 940-page Cuba travel book describes what not to miss—like remote Baracoa at the eastern tip of the island. Five centuries have passed, the book observes, but the place has lost none of the exquisite beauty that so impressed Columbus.[3]

The Circus Is Still in Town
FEBRUARY 6, 2008

Four years later, I step off a bus in the Caribbean coastal town of Tela on a Friday afternoon. By 9 p.m. I've found two friends—twins—I met on a trip some years ago. Soon we sit down on a plank in bleachers

---

[3]You'll read messages and stories about Cuba between 2004 and 2020 a little later, in the Cuba chapters of this book.

under a big tent, watching the traveling circus from Mexico—comedy acts, gymnasts, singers, an acrobat, a lion, a hippo, a cobra, a monkey on a galloping horse, popcorn, a fruit cup, Pepsi. Then, because it's the only show in town, we do it all over on Saturday night, when the bleachers are packed with a thousand people. By the look of it, I am the only foreigner.

In the meantime—Saturday afternoon—the twins arrive at my hotel with a cousin. The twins laugh when they tell me their cousin's nickname. I inquire, "What's so funny about '*Cadejo*'?"

"When he was young, he tried to pronounce *congrejo*, the word for crab, but it always came out cadejo" ("ka-DAÝ-ho"), a twin explains. "Cadejo," I'm told, "has a meaning of its own—it's an animal that resembles a dog. It's seen only in the dark of night around the inlet lagunas of the Caribbean Sea. It's an evil spirit!"

Now, still in the light of day, we walk to the beaches and inlet lagunas that run for miles. Garifuna villages lie along the shoreline. I realize that dozens of people know the twins. Their acquaintances call both of them the same name, *guapo*, rather than their given names. They call each other guapo too. While guapo almost always means "good looking," it can have other meanings in some Caribbean-tinged locales, but I neglect to inquire why these twins go by guapo. One works in construction, and the other is unemployed because he has tumors near each eye, Cadejo tells me.

Late on Sunday evening, I wander into a dilapidated beach bar with no apparent name. The waitresses tell me Miss Gloria owns it. I find gaps between floor planks, a jukebox whose song titles are hand-written in pencil, and a beer for 75 cents.

I keep real quiet, trying not to stick out like a sore thumb. The cops come in. They attempt to wrestle a cell phone away from a waitress. Looks like she refuses to give it up—though I don't know for sure because I don't stare, except out at the sea. The cops hang around and keep pestering her. She's not scared of them. Me neither, because I've already smiled and mumbled a greeting over my beer. Hopefully, they understand I'm not up to no good—unlike, apparently, Miss Gloria's bar waitress.

Circus workers now appear outside the bar. They want to walk down the street, but the cops stop them. I'm thinking the officers tell the workers they're not allowed on this street since they're not of drinking age. One by one, the boys pass some test and advance. The whole block is lined with low-class beach dives frequented by whomever—and one foreigner.

As far as I know, the circus is still in town. When it leaves, I'll just hang out at Miss Gloria's. If I close up the joint, like I did tonight, I'll help the waitresses jam nails and scissors into latches to lock the wooden windows on the inside so no one can bust in for a beer before they get the place open at nine the next morning.

I may come back at 9 a.m. tomorrow to help Miss Gloria's waitresses yank out the scissors and nails. Then we'll have all the time in the world to just stare out at the sea.

EL SALVADOR

Barred Entry: URGENT
MARCH 2009

Several immigration officers at the El Salvador border are debating about me. Finally, one who refuses to give me his name and whose badge obscures it as well, walks back to the office window where I have been waiting and renders the final verdict: "Leave!"

I ask if I may use the office phone to call the US Embassy in San Salvador. "Call them when you go back to Guatemala," he snaps.

And with that, I am refused entry and unable to join my 249 international colleagues whose mission is to observe a historic presidential election. I trudge back over the remote border bridge into Guatemala. I suspect there'll be nary a phone nor computer within miles to make a plea to my election observer contact at the *Centro de Intercambio y Solidaridad*, or CIS.

On the Guatemalan side, however, inquiries lead me into a store whose floor is covered with piles of used clothing. The owner beckons me through the sea of garments, parts a curtain, and invites me to sit down in front of a secluded computer. I send out my plea from behind the curtain.

email to CIS, san salvador
Subject: *Barred Entry: URGENT*
MARCH 6, 2009, 3 P.M.

I am on the Guatemala side of the border and have been barred entry into El Salvador. I do not have the El Salvador election authority's accrediting document, immigration officials tell me. What can I do?

The store owner refuses to accept any payment for my use of her computer. She is sympathetic to my problem. She tells me she also owns a cell phone but has run out of minutes. We solve that problem when I hand her 25 quetzales ($3). She runs out and returns quickly.

Relying on the phone's brand-new minutes, I connect with Leslie Schuld of CIS in San Salvador. Leslie will fax me an accrediting document—if I can just find a fax machine. Since the stars are lined up to assist observers working for a fair presidential election like the country has never seen before, the next-door business at this border outpost owns a fax machine. This owner, too, insists I use it for free.

Within minutes, the El Salvador immigration officers across the bridge stare at the faxed accrediting document I now present. They seem stunned. The senior official, whom I am now dealing with, demands to know how I obtained the document that I did not have an hour earlier. "It is not an original," he then declares, arguing it is thus invalid. He can't call CIS, like I request. He can call his *jefes*—bosses—but he tells me his jefes are unavailable, currently in *corte* with a judge.

At long last, he seems to understand that I will not trudge out of the country and back to Guatemala again. Like most immigration employees, he likely owes his position to the country's ruling party, ARENA, which has been in charge for the past twenty years.[4] Finally, he walks to the back of the office and dials up his jefes. He and the jefes discuss the matter on the phone—for 25 minutes. He shuffles back to the office window where I am planted and hands me back my passport. I think I hear him say "Tomás," in a soft voice. I say nothing. He then adds, "*Disculpa por retraso*," which I understand as "excuse me for the delay."

Ten minutes later, I'm in a van riding toward Ahuachapan. I meander in this small country for three days, then arrive in San Salvador to join observers from a dozen countries who have come to determine

---

[4] ARENA is the acronym for Alianza Republicana Nacionalista, or Nationalist Republican Alliance.

whether or not the presidential election will be conducted according to the rule of law. Many of us have volunteered for CIS, a rugged component of El Salvador's emerging democracy.

a historic election

A few days before the election, 250,000 citizens turn out at a San Salvador rally to support the candidate of the opposition FMLN— the Farabundo Martí National Liberation Front.[5] The FMLN grew out of the revolutionary movement against the entrenched El Salvador establishment. Between 1980 and 1992, more than 75,000 people died during the civil war, most killed by the government's regular and extra-military forces. Three of the dead were American nuns whom, along with a Catholic lay worker, the military murdered. Before coming, I read a book about US policy in El Salvador by Raymond Bonner, a *New York Times* reporter,[6] which has left me aghast at the callousness of US involvement.

Peace accords signed in 1992 led to several presidential elections. The powerful ARENA candidate prevailed over former revolutionary fighters the first two times. Now it is 2009, and a former wartime journalist, Mauricio Funes, is the FMLN candidate.

Over several days, we observers are trained in election procedures, visit both parties' offices, and are treated to one or more excursions. We are not there to put a finger on the scale for either candidate.

I write a note to friends:

I'm one of 250 election observers. This morning my group of 15 traveled to a semi-illegal village. The people once lived elsewhere, but earthquakes and Hurricane Mitch rendered them homeless. They staged a take-over of this government land in 2005. The police and the ARENA mayor of the large

---

[5] Or, in Spanish, the *Frente Farabundo Martí para la Liberación Nacional.*

[6] Raymond Bonner, *Weakness and Deceit: US Policy and El Salvador* (New York: Times Books, 1984).

municipality that encompasses the village have tried to eject the people from the land, and refuse to provide electricity and water. An FMLN candidate was elected village mayor last month, and the formerly homeless people are hoping for an FMLN presidential victory on Sunday.

Fifty of us Americans visited the US Embassy yesterday for a question and answer session. Today, we visited the Archdiocese of San Salvador's legal clinic, opened by Archbishop Oscar Romero before he was assassinated in 1980 while saying mass in the chapel. The legal clinic has investigated wartime massacres, kidnappings and disappearances. I understand the military death squads have not yet been entirely disbanded! I wanted an explanation. The clinic personnel then described some incidents.

Tomorrow, a group of us will travel to a town whose name I can't pronounce. That's where we'll observe the election. Later, we'll watch the vote tabulation on television. It should be fast since the presidency is the only contest, and only two candidates are in the running.

election day

Sensuntepeque is a provincial capital not many miles from Honduras. I'm assigned to one of several outdoor voting centers on the streets that circle the central plaza. It's 4:50 a.m. The election workers open a sealed cardboard box and borrow my flashlight to examine the ballots and instructions. At 7 a.m., the first voters appear. They stream to the voting centers all day long.

The officials know why I am here. I watch all day but don't observe any irregularities, which in the past were rampant in some voting centers. I decline to give my opinion on a procedural question the officials have. I am only an observer. I stand, I mill, I grab coffee from the nearby bakery.

A homeowner welcomes our group of observers into her house after 7 p.m. We watch the results on TV. The vote is close, 51 to 49 percent. FLMN's Mauricio Funes will become the new president. Pickup trucks full of cheering FMLN supporters drive through the streets of Sensuntepeque.

We observers can now go back to our respective countries or continue our journey. I'll return to my shack near Lake Atitlan, in the mountains of Guatemala. I believe my border crossing will be problem-free, as it had always been until two weeks ago.

A Journey to See Two Presidents
MARCH 2011

"That tube of Colgate is $1.25 . . . Here's your change," one of two girls tells me—not in her native Tzutujil language, but in Spanish. The two are sisters, working at their family store. I am at Lake Atitlan, Guatemala, once again heading to neighboring El Salvador, where I observed the presidential election two years ago. But this time, I am on a different mission.

"If you were journalists and could ask President Barack Obama one question, what would it be?" I ask the two sisters as I prepare for my mission.

"We're trying to answer your question. It's a puzzling one," one of the girls says. "Okay, we'd ask, 'What can you do about the hunger that children of the world suffer?'"

"*Adiós, muchachas*," I say in Spanish. "I hope to see you when I get back to Lake Atitlan from El Salvador."

Next, I head to a law office in San Pedro to continue my mission's groundwork. "I'm studying to be a lawyer," the young woman tells me. "How do you say that in English? . . . I work in this office. The woman at the desk is the secretary . . . You say you aren't leaving until we answer your question. Well, here is what we would ask President Obama if we were journalists. 'What is your plan to reform US immigration laws?'"

Then I see Geovany on the shore of Lake Atitlan. "I remember talking to you here at the lake years ago," he says. "You listened but didn't speak much Spanish then. Have you been practicing the Tzutujil Mayan words I taught you? You can use them on any street in town."

"I told you then that the wise old men and women in town, *los ancianos*, say that settlements are submerged and lost in the lake," Geovany recounts. "I think you believe me now that you've seen the recent newspaper articles. They're even looking for volunteer scuba divers to expand the search. Don't believe the German mathematician who claims his analysis of an ancient Maya script reveals that $300 million in gold tablets are buried in another Guatemalan lake. No, the only buried treasures will be found in this lake right here!"

I ask Geovany what he would ask President Obama.

"I'm not surprised by your question, Tomás," Geovany continues. "We're both *loco*. Well, I would say, 'Mr. President Obama, what can the United States do to assist Guatemala in uncovering and preserving Maya monuments—in terms of engineering, anthropological expertise, and economic assistance?'"

"By the way, Tomás, what is the probability of you ever being in a room where people ask President Obama questions?" Geovany intimated that it is unimaginable. Regardless, I am hopeful.

Having left the mile-high and 1,200-foot-deep Guatemalan lake, this journey now moves, bus by bus, into El Salvador.

"I'm Francisco," my seatmate tells me. "I've been on buses for four days and nights straight. I don't sleep much. This bus will get me to within an hour of my land in El Salvador." To my delight, he describes how he began his journey. "I started out in San Pablo, Minnesota. It's called 'St. Paul' in English," Francisco explains.

"I live in a senior apartment on Tedesco Street," he continues. "The United States has good services for seniors. I'm 70. I take these buses from San Pablo to El Salvador every year. I have four kids living in the US. My other two children were killed in El Salvador's civil war. I fled in 1982 and took asylum in the US. I have a permanent resident card. Here, take a look."

"The war was tragic, wasn't it, Francisco?" I say.

"Yes, government planes bombed many towns," he says. "Everything was destroyed. Nothing was left—*nada, nada, nada!* Except for some cats and dogs. Many people were killed—*muchas personas, muchas, muchas!*"

I ask Francisco the question I have for one and all.

"I would ask President Obama, 'What will you do to help the people who've been legally living in the US on an annual visa for many years? What can you do to help them become US citizens?'"

The bus arrives in the capital, San Salvador. Francisco and I part. I hop into the front seat of a taxi.

"What kind of music do you like, *señor*?" I ask the driver after a minute or two.

"I was a big fan of Pink Floyd, Alabama, the Archies, Donny and Marie Osmond. I went to some of their concerts. I lived in California decades ago."

"How did you find tickets for all those concerts?" I ask in English, since the taxi man knows it well.

"It was easy," he asserts—and seems inclined to confide in me. "Once a month," he reveals, "I drove my car from Tijuana to San Francisco. The police in San Diego and Los Angeles sometimes stopped me. They searched my car but found nothing. They asked if I was running drugs. 'Who, me?'

"I kept driving north—to a 7-Eleven store in San Francisco. When I went back to my car from 7-Eleven, I found $10,000 in it. The bag of drugs hidden in the brake system was gone. I returned to Southern California. It was easy paying $1,000 for a concert ticket. I spent my time drinking, smoking, and doing drugs. I made a trip from Tijuana to the 7-Eleven every month. Every time, I found $10,000 in my car.

"How old was I when I made those trips? I was 18. I was bad, *muy malo*. Now I'm good, *bueno*. I haven't smoked or drank for 30 years. I'm a Christian."

I now ask the taxi man, "Does your family know what you did at age 18?"

"No, they don't know a thing about my life at age 18. Here, sir, is your stop. *Mucho gusto. Adiós*." I get out of the taxi and walk off, only then realizing I was so engrossed in his story about life in California that I didn't ask what question he'd pose to President Obama.

The next day, I walk into San Salvador's Hotel Sheraton Presidente. I'd noticed from a map in a newspaper that the Sheraton Presidente is the bull's eye of a circular "security zone" that will be in effect next week. I'm curious if the hotel has any room specials for me at that time, since I'd love to hang out in the lobby to catch glimpses of history.

"We have no space at all," the receptionist answers, deflating my balloon. I don't ask more questions because I bet she's been instructed not to divulge nothing to no one. Before leaving, I take a minute to check the spot in the restaurant where a brazen, mysterious gunshot killed a CIA agent during the civil war.

Just outside the hotel entrance, sitting at the ready is—at first blush —a metal detector like those used in most of the world's major airports. With all its bells and whistles, though, it must be a new age whole-body scanner. Near the hotel, on Avenida Revolución, a barbed wire barricade sits, ready to roll. I saunter down the avenue. I see a work crew and stop. (If you want to become better informed, a truism of travel is to stop to visit work crews.)

"I'm Armando," says one. "What are we doing on this sidewalk?"

"Yes," I say, continuing in Spanish, "what are you doing with that rectangular manhole cover?"

"I am welding it down," he tells me.

"What on earth are you doing that for?"

"For security," he answers.

"You mean the visit—"

"*Sí, la visita del Presidente Barack Obama.*"

"What's down there?" I'm curious to know—and I might even jot this down sometime.

"All the cables for television, phones, communications," he answers.

"Is this the only cover you're welding down?"

"No, this whole route!" and with a wave of his arm he indicates a distance of kilometers. (Arm waves are in the metric system, not in feet, yards, or miles.)

"Will you break them all loose after *la visita*?"

"No, only as needed."

"Just how many are you welding?"

"One hundred and twenty," he answers.

I begin asking another question—but withdraw it. I fear I've already set the whole security operation back by a whole manhole cover, maybe two.

Thinking about Armando's 120 manholes over kilometers, the wave of his arm was in the direction of the national cathedral. That's where the body of Archbishop Oscar Romero is entombed. He was the cleric assassinated during the civil war while saying mass in a small chapel next to the Hospital Divina Providencia.

The archbishop had been an outspoken critic of the government's murder and torture of its own people in the war from the 1970s to 1992. He'd also confronted Pope John Paul II over the Vatican's support of the military government. The United States also supported the regime with a whopping $4 billion—no doubt contributing to thousands of deaths.

This week marks the 31st anniversary of Romero's death. Every year, millions of El Salvadorans commemorate the archbishop. Those affiliated with the ARENA party voted out of the presidential office two years ago after a heinous history, however, don't seem to celebrate.

President Obama will visit the cathedral and tomb one day before the anniversary. Presidents, I think, rarely make visits of such great symbolic importance to a people in a foreign land. A TV commentator has compared the lives of Martin Luther King Jr. and Archbishop Romero, equating their philosophies, dedication, life work, and assassinations.

You may approach the chapel next to the Hospital Divina Providencia, walk through the side door near the altar where the archbishop's assassin entered, and sit in the chapel alone. You can then walk across the street and ask a nun to let you visit the sparse quarters where Monsignor Romero lived.

You may also enter the hospital, turn left to visit a ward of seriously ill cancer patients—mostly children—and listen as they chat to a new visitor, a foreigner! Two years ago, when I was an election observer, this is where I met Jessica (pronounced "Yesica"), a most beautiful 14-year-old girl too weak to hold her head up, who didn't let me say goodbye without a *beso*, a kiss. This is also where I met Rudy, who described his hometown in the distant east of the country, as other patients listened with their heads turned toward us.

A year ago, I wanted to see Jessica's beautiful smile and hear her beautiful voice again. I returned to the hospital. Jessica had returned to her hometown and died. I asked about Rudy, too. He also had gone back to his hometown and died. At Hospital Divina Providencia yesterday, I visited new children in Jessica and Rudy's ward.

• • •

The president of the United States and his family flew from Chile to El Salvador yesterday, March 22. They are staying at the Sheraton Presidente. It just so happens that I reserved a room in Hotel Florencia —on that welded-up Avenida la Revolución. The Florencia is situated just a couple blocks down the street from the Presidente. I picked room no. 1 because it looks out on the avenida. Who knows, people might not be allowed outside at crucial times, so at least I'll be able to peer through the window.

Security forces surround the Sheraton Presidente and the avenida. President Mauricio Funes will host a state dinner for the Obamas at the presidential palace at 8 p.m. this evening, a newspaper informs me. "I need to find out where the presidential palace is," I convince myself. I pull the city map from my back pocket. The palace is on the other side of town, I learn.

A chance conversation with the Florencia hotel clerk an hour later reveals that my map is wrong. A new presidential palace is a mere three blocks down the avenue. That's magic!—which happens quite often to curious travelers in faraway lands.

At 7:30 p.m., I walk ever so slowly past the lush grounds of the presidential home, turn around, and do it again. A hundred guests, it seems, are showing up in cars, all invited for dinner. I am the only pedestrian. Only I lack an invitation. I am the hungriest of anyone, I'm sure, having missed lunch. A figure in the dark shadows just inside the fence doesn't see fit to toss me an invitation. He cannot see my mouth watering—for food and history.

Those armed soldiers, those motorcycle police, those machine gunners in turrets on armored vehicles, do they think I am wandering around aimlessly? No, surely they must take the measure of me and decide I am a super-undercover agent sent in to inspect the security operation. I would have lingered at the fence during dinner if the display of armed might hadn't intimidated me—super-undercover agent or not.

I start to inch my way up Avenida Revolución, away from the presidential palace. It is eerily silent and dark, with no one else on the avenue except a few select soldiers. It is now 8:01 p.m., time for the feast of the decade to start. Yet the two presidents have not yet arrived from the cathedral, where they've been paying their respects to the late Archbishop Romero.

Suddenly, a string of police motorcycles now speeds down the dark avenue toward me. Two black Cadillacs, one of them carrying two presidents, follow. Other vehicles loaded with secret service agents and accredited journalists, as well as an ambulance, tail the Cadillacs.

I press the Record button on my Flip video camera and point it at the limousines as they roll by me. I should have waved to the two presidents instead. Since security forces have displayed such might, I am the only civilian who has ventured to the *avenida*, and thus the only one to wave to them. Through the five-inch-thick dark windows of the limousine, I couldn't see if Presidents Obama and Funes were peering out at lonely me—with questions in their minds.

I only knew that I was hungrier yet. I walked up Avenida Revolución, ducked into Wendy's, and ate a hamburger.

• • •

Now it's Wednesday. Air Force One has left El Salvador and must be flying high over Cuba on its way to Washington. I just left partially excavated Joya de Ceren, a town buried since 650 AD under volcanic ash, Pompeii style. I tried to get into the nearby San Andres Maya ruins, but it's closed all day. Why? Michelle Obama and daughters Malia and Sasha visited the ancient site before speeding to Air Force One.

I'd envisioned that people I met the last two weeks were journalists who could ask President Obama a question of their choosing. Not that I foreclosed the possibility of my own presence—with an abundance of questions—in an audience where President Obama would speak and listen. Truth be told, I had sent a compelling email to the US Embassy in El Salvador three weeks ago, pleading my case for a spot in an audience if the president were to give a speech in this country. The request was dynamite! Who in their right mind could say no?

President Obama did not, in the end, give a speech in El Salvador. The embassy never said no to me—it just never saw fit to answer my plea.

I'm going home to sit in my shack in Guatemala.

GUATEMALA

I hang out at Lake Atitlan in Guatemala every year. That's where I own a tin-roofed shack in a Mayan town that lies at the base of a volcano, in maize- and coffee-growing mountains.

Last year, I related stories of Guatemala, like "Kite on a String Without End," "The Fisherman and My Dog," "Voyage to My Private Island," and "Voyage to My Private Sauna."[7]

This year, I have more to say. Let's begin far from my shack— almost clear across Central America.

Back to the Stone Age of Hot Water Showers and Ancient Dugout Canoes
APRIL 11, 2007

A nine-hour jaunt begins when my friend Carlos informs me that "we'll go for a walk on the beach." We begin by climbing the hill to his house in Livingston, a town on Guatemala's Caribbean Sea that you can't get to from anywhere in the world—except by boat down the Rio Dulce River, or on the Caribbean Sea from Puerto Barrios or the coast of Belize.

While Carlos sharpens his machete, I relax in a hammock in his thatched-roof, plank-walled, dirt floor home. Before Carlos, his puppy Londres, his 10-year-old nephew Reiner, and I leave, we humans eat a fish each and corn tortillas.

Carlos says goodbye to the elderly—not in Spanish, but in Q'eqchi'. As we walk past neighbors sitting in front of their houses, Carlos

---

[7] Pick up *The Other Worlds: Offbeat Adventures of a Curious Traveler.* It's readily available online and at locations noted on the author's website, www.TomsGlobe.com.

greets them with "adiós." That seems odd, but perhaps he is saying, "We're on our way." Another day, when we were just heading downtown, he greeted them with "adiós" too.

It's 10 a.m., and I'm sure I'll be back in my Rios Tropicales Hotel room by noon today to catch up on my sleep. After all, we're just going for a walk on the beach. The only diversion will be when we stop for a drink.

After we shuffle a mile down the beach, Carlos eyes a good tree. He climbs up, throws down coconuts, and then slashes them open with his machete. Once refreshed, he asks if I'd like to ride in a *cayuco*. "Yeah, of course," I say. "Why not?" The cayuco, I see, is an ancient dugout canoe Carlos's uncle beaches there.

Carlos glances at a cell phone he pulls from his cutoffs pocket.

"Carlos, you have a nice cell phone," I remark.

"It wasn't mine two weeks ago," he responds.

"So how's that?" I inquire.

After fishing in the ocean, he explains, he beached the cayuco right here.

"When I started walking home, I heard a phone ring," he says. "I moved toward the sound and found a phone half buried in the sand. I answered it. A secretary was calling all the way from Guatemala City. 'Thanks for answering my phone!' she said. She had lost it while visiting this beach, she told me.

"The secretary was so happy that I'd email her the 30 names and numbers in the phone that she told me, 'The phone is yours to keep!' I saw she'd called her phone 20 times, and no one had answered. The 21st time, I heard it ring in the sand."

We now yank the cayuco into the choppy water and hop in. Puppy Londres has never before seen the ocean, and he's palpably apprehensive. Reiner appears calm, though. While Carlos paddles, I bail water—it's leaking in at the rate of five gallons a minute.

Londres and I expect to capsize at any moment. Carlos assures us we'll get to calm waters soon. "Soon" comes in a mile. We find ourselves at the mouth of the Quehueche River. We turn into the mouth and sail in silence under a footbridge.

While Carlos paddles with our only paddle and I bail, Reiner takes care of the puppy. We make our way up the slow-moving Quehueche for half an hour.

"Here's a place we can swim," Carlos informs Reiner and me.

What happened next is a scientific puzzle that would have baffled me forever if I hadn't yelled for Carlos and Reiner. They wade over to where I stand—on a super-warm rock at the bottom of the cool river. A layer of real warm water nestles just above the rock. A hot spring in the river! I conclude.

As I move out of the way so they can stand on my discovery themselves, I step on another rock—warm too—and another. It seems the bottom is filled with hot springs! No wonder Carlos loved to swim here with friends when he was growing up.

"Can dozens of hot springs erupt out of earth right here in this swimming hole?" I incredulously ask myself. "So, tell me! Why is the river bottom so warm?" Yes, I'm asking *you* right now, just like I'm asking Carlos. Let's stop for half a minute and consider this.

Carlos's explanation surprises me and may surprise you too. "The water on the bottom of the river is actually warm saltwater from the Caribbean Sea," he explains. "It flows upriver during high tide!"

I'll have more questions for Carlos when I see him next year. Questions sometimes don't flow out of my mouth fast enough, like, "Hey, Carlos, what happens at low tide? Does the warm layer get flushed out to sea? Does it return to our swimming hole at every high tide, or just the highest of tides?"

Now you have a few moments to think.

• • •

Meanwhile, I must add that a small house stands near our swimming hole. We see no one around. Wouldn't you think these jungle river dwellers might have—quite inventively—installed a pipe at the bottom of the river to pump water to their house for warm showers? As luck would have it, right above a hot rock, my feet find what I unmistakably deem to be a pipe! It's parallel to the river bottom. I do, of course, call Carlos over. He seems baffled by it.

"Where does the pipe end up?" I wonder silently. "Does it run to the outdoor shower stall that's beside the home? Can the people who live here take oh-so-soothing showers only during the Caribbean's high tides?"

Meanwhile, while Reiner and I are swimming, Carlos finds a rag laying on the riverbank. Next, he picks up stones, one for pounding and others that are wedge shaped and sharp. Early peoples must have made use of this river's stones too. Hep to living in any century, Carlos tears the rag into strips, wedges the strips into the canoe's long cracks with a sharp stone, and softly pounds the strips in.

Does Carlos successfully plug the five-gallon-a-minute cracks? Yes—to a 2.5-gallon-a-minute degree. On the way back, I bail only half as furiously as I did on our expedition's outbound journey.

I may draw a map so you can find Carlos Pop Xol if you want to co-lead your own scientific expedition to these parts. Just remember, practice simulated bailing exercises before you leave home. And bring a puppy if you wish.

• • •

I think I dreamt that I sent the message above to an esteemed ocean hydrology journal. I fear, however, that if it is printed, a critique may follow. The very next issue of the journal, I'm embarrassed to say, will probably read like this:

To the Editor
Journal of Sea Hydrology
Miami, Florida

I write to comment on Tom Mattson's erroneous and incomplete "scientific" observations in last quarter's journal. Having studied and lectured on river-ocean hydrologic interactions, and already planned a vacation to the beautiful Caribbean beaches in Livingston, Guatemala, I sought out Carlos Pop Xol ("pope shoal").

Mr. Pop Xol was only too happy to set Mr. Mattson's conclusions straight. For starters, the "pipe" that supplied "hot water showers" for riverbank residents was no pipe at all. Mr. Pop Xol said he looked at Mr. Mattson's "pipe" and found it to be a long stick stuck in rocks on the river bottom. He believes he did mutter as much to scientist Mattson in Spanish. Mattson probably lives such a cushy life in the US that he assumes people living in the tropics must pamper themselves with warm showers.

Had Mattson's "scientific" mind inquired just a little further when he was on his "expedition," his friend Carlos would have told him much more about the phenomena Mattson "discovered." For starters, the warm ocean water moves up the Quehueche along the riverbanks, whereas the faster-moving freshwater moves down the middle. (Is that why, Mr. Mattson, when Carlos paddled upriver, he did so close to the riverbank?)

Quite understandably, much more saltwater moves upriver at high tide than low tide. When it rains heavily, the rushing river blocks out most of the saltwater, and the warm water condition at the swimming hole disappears. More warm water, of course, collects in the swimming hole during weeks without rain.

Mr. Pop Xol never experiences the same condition twice, he reports. During Mattson's lark, the rocks were covered by a couple inches of warm water. Mr. Pop Xol had not experienced that precise condition before. Other times, the warm water layer is much thicker, of a warmer or cooler temperature, or nonexistent.

Mattson was also ignorant of the underlying reasons for Mr. Pop Xol's vast experience. Beginning when he was about 10 years old, he and two or three friends would tell their mothers they were "off to the jungle," and off they would go—with their homemade slingshots. At the swimming hole, they hunted for parrots and for birds whose names they did not know. They barbequed what they killed. After lunch, they swam—and learned far more about river-ocean hydrologic interaction than Expeditioner Mattson could ever hope to comprehend.

Others, very knowledgeable too, could have added to the report. You'd have to go no further than Carlos's brother Felipe. True, Felipe did not spend part of his childhood killing birds, since he preferred to study, work, play soccer, and protect nature. He brings a slightly different perspective. Felipe Pop Xol reports that 90% of Livingston's people have visited the site, called Mujer Vuelve. Some visit to swim or bathe, while others think or meditate. Thus, only some of the visitors have experienced the warm water phenomenon.

Felipe also explains that the river hosts a large fish population. Saltwater fish like barracuda, sardina, palometa, and siera swim in the parts of the river where ocean water predominates. River shrimp thrive in the very clean river waters and taste even better than lobsters. They command a price of $25 in a restaurant.

Mr. Mattson might have mentioned that people with different heritages visit Mujer Vuelve. Livingston is among the most diverse communities in Central America, being comprised of the Maya indigenous people (like Carlos, Felipe, and their several siblings), a large population of African-Caribbean Garifuna people with an amazing history all their own, and ladinos.

Mr. Mattson can confirm what I report by calling Felipe, or Carlos—who'll answer on that "nice Samsung phone" he admired so. I'll give him this much: First, the canoe in which he agreed to travel might have indeed been tipsy, but ancient it wasn't, having been made in about 1990, according to Carlos (does Mattson really think they last forever?). Not to further deflate him, but the canoe—although homemade—was not carved from a tree trunk (or "dugout"). Finally, he did ask Carlos questions, albeit a woefully inadequate number.

Mattson can expect a good-natured ribbing from laid-back Carlos sometime soon. Carlos says the US visitor shows up at the Caribbean out of the blue, and Carlos is quite willing to take off with him on spur-of-the-moment adventures.[8]

As for acquiring basic facts, better luck next time.

—James "Langostia" Hernandez, PhD
Acme Hydrological Consulting of South Florida

[8] A Carlos-inspired diversion for Tom Mattson was a ride along the Caribbean beach—on the back of Carlos's motorbike. You may go along on this joyful ride! Check out Tom Mattson's Virtual World Tour YouTube link (Episode 2) on the author's website blog page—at www.TomsGlobe.com.

The Cultural Consultant
FEBRUARY 20, 2012

This year again, I've reached the town where I own a shack—San Pedro la Laguna, established in 1550.

Most residents speak the Mayan language of Tzutujil as their mother tongue, and most speak Spanish, too. My friend Geovany, who is my cultural consultant, or "informer," tells me the Tzutujil ("tzoo-to-heel") spoken in each neighboring town is different than the version spoken here. The people of Santiago speak a pure Tzutujil and talk faster than others, I'm told. The people here in San Pedro mix in a little Spanish and may only understand 85 percent of that next town's talk. Two towns the other way, the Tzutujil seems to have gotten mixed up, and the people of San Pedro may only understand 65 percent of what they say.

Residents on the other side of the lake speak the Kaqchikel Mayan language, and someone on this side—a 25-minute speedy boat ride away—may understand only 15 percent of that language, I'm informed (in Spanish). Spanish is often the go-between language when people from towns of different languages meet.

The informer also says he knows from which town a woman or girl is by her traditional clothing. He claims he can often tell an older man's hometown by his Tzutujil intonations and by the size and style of his sombrero. Facial expressions are also a clue to where one lives, and some people in San Pedro are taller than those of neighboring pueblos.

Most younger men don't wear sombreros, the informer points out, but he often knows where a young guy is from—even if wearing Western clothing—by how modern his garb is, how he speaks, how he acts, and how he walks.

"What does a young guy or girl from one or two towns away think about the young people here in San Pedro la Laguna?" I ask the informer.

Mile-high and unfathomably deep, Lake Atitlan is home to a dozen Mayan pueblos. Here, departing San Pedro la Laguna by boat.

He thinks for a minute. "They may feel young people here are extroverted," he answers, "like in freely talking to someone of the opposite sex, in joking and playing jokes, and in being more daring to take physical challenges."

If you have a question for this informer, let me know. I'll get the answer back to you. Then, of the 6.993 billion people in the world who are not native to this lake, only you and I may be privy to the information.

The Plot Thickens
MARCH 4, 2012

As I begin to digest all that I've learned about how people from neighboring towns speak, dress, and even walk differently, a question zooms in from San Pablo, Minnesota—or perhaps it's called "St. Paul" back there.

"Do people from two different towns ever get married?" Dave Fadness asks. "If so, does the informer know—by meeting the couple's child—*which two towns* the unseen parents are from?"

I immediately check with my informer, breath abated.

"Yes, people from different towns do get married," is his instantaneous answer to the first question.

Hearing the second question, words roll off the informer's tongue. "The wife moves to the husband's town. The children grow up exhibiting the characteristics common to the people of his town, and their language will be distinctive of that town. They'll likely wear the clothes of that community. They may act—and walk—like those people."

Thus, an observer will probably assume both (unseen) parents are from the husband's town.

"The mother," the informer adds, "will probably keep wearing the clothing distinctive to her hometown, at least for a while. She cannot, of course, lose her ingrained speech very easily. Over time, however, she'll likely adopt many of the attributes of her new community."

Now here is a zinger. If the mother is from San Pedro la Laguna, she may be influential in her adopted town. Her neighbors or other good friends may follow some of her practices, like making a meal distinctive to San Pedro, or preparing tortillas like she does.

"Why?" you might ask. The answer: San Pedro la Laguna is bigger, has more businesses, and has more schools. It's better off. More outsiders, even a lot of foreigners, visit it. The man delivering my *Prensa Libre* daily paper informed me today that he delivers 250 *Prensa Libres* and tabloid *Diarios* in San Pedro (including a *Libre* to my shack), but only a fraction of these numbers in nearby towns.

Thus, a San Pedro woman who marries a man from a neighboring town may have an outsized influence there. Who among us would have thought? I've checked with Interrogator Dave in San Pablo, Minnesota. *He* would not have thought.

Now that we're on a roll, let's discover a little more.

The young woman who serves me coffee many a morning explains what towns the passersby outside Las Cristalinas Coffeehouse are from, based on their clothing. Now I sometimes rest my *Prensa Libre* on the table and study those passersby through the open-air windows. Many walk from the dock up to the town center to shop, sell goods, work, or even go to school.

This informer–coffee server now turns the tables on me.

"Where are those women on the street from?" she asks.

"From Tzu'nuná?" I say.

"Yes! And where are *those* women from?" she asks, pointing to the next group.

"From Tzu'nuná!" I'm sure.

"No! From San Marcos."

"They look the same to me," I insist.

"No, the women from Tzu'nuná wear headbands." Now I'm clued in.

A curious traveler can't have too many sources of information and opinions, I feel. So I hop in a boat bound for San Marcos, the third town away.

The young woman running the bakery does, indeed, offer more factual information: the slick "gelatina" hairstyle is also a clue to which town a boy is from. She adds that some older people in San Marcos, like her grandfather, do not speak Spanish, and that some children have not yet learned it.

Off I go in a tuk-tuk to San Pablo, back toward San Pedro. I promised a gang of kids I'd bring them the photos I took one day as I sat on a curb eating vendors' snacks. I approach a boy, asking in Spanish where the kids in the photos live. He laughs, seemingly embarrassed, and runs. He doesn't seem to understand Spanish. His father tells him, in Tzutujil, that he is to take me to the house of two of the kids.

I now use the Tzutujil word I finally learned how to pronounce hours earlier. It means "let's go." It's a one-syllable word, but I can't spell it for you—sorry. The boy leads the way. I manage to coax a few words of Spanish out of him. At the house, I hand the photos to the mother and four daughters who have come to the door. I look at their traditional ankle-length skirts and blouses—and conclude without a doubt that they live in this town.

• • •

I now ask my original informer, "How many foreigners who hang out around Lake Atitlan know what you and others have told me?"

"*Cero* [zero]," he answers.

You and I are thus in the super-know—in large part because of the question that flew in from San Pablo, Minnesota. You might be ready to ask about the distinctive characteristics of people who don't live around here, but in Mayan towns on the other end of the lake. Don't even go there.

What the Ancient Winds Are Blowing
FEBRUARY 13, 2014

I've reached my otherworldly destination again this year, my shack town in Guatemala's Western Highlands. Today, a north wind rushes over us from Mexico, cooled by a US cold wave. A foreign publication claims that a north wind means a person who has drowned in Lake Atitlan is being carried away, the lake having just taken his or her soul, while a south wind carries away people's sins.

I now have a burning question: "Do people today believe in the old meanings of a north and south wind, or are they just myths?"

To hear the answer, I didn't even have to leave my shack. It blew in on a light westerly wind in the form of a friend, Mario, who's helped save my orange tree from parasitic vines and once tossed our made-from-scratch pizza into my brick oven. He informs me of Maya beliefs he's learned by talking to the wise.

If I'd asked Mario yesterday morning whether he'd ever heard the beliefs about the winds, he would have said, "No, never." It just so happens, though, that about the time I was writing those earlier sentences, Mario and his wife were conversing with his wife's 87-year-old grandmother. The grandmother had declined to move into a new concrete block room built for her. She explained that she prefers a traditional room with plenty of air moving through it—from every direction.

The grandmother then educated them of certain beliefs, born out of wisdom. A north wind means someone has drowned, she explained, that the depths of the lake have kept his or her soul, and that big waves might wash the body onto boulders along the shore. She also explained that while a north wind brings some illnesses like a cold or a cough, a south wind is purifying and carries away illnesses.

"Does the grandmother really believe this?" you might ask Mario.

"*Believe* is not the right word," he'll tell you. "She *lives* the words of wisdom of the Maya people."

"Do you have any idea how she learned about the winds' meanings?" I inquire.

Mario says he wanted to know too. So he asked her, just like he's asked questions of many *ancianos* over the years.

"When I was 17 years old, my grandfather told me this," she answered. "I asked him how *he* learned," she continued. "He said he learned about it from *his* grandfather, and that grandfather learned this lore from *his* grandfather."

Mario and I counted the generations that passed down this folkloric wisdom in his wife's family. It is seven. And perhaps it was handed down through many more generations for centuries before that.

Knowing Mario, I believe he'll teach his children and grandchildren in 2030, 2040, and 2050 what he is learning every day from *los ancianos* in his community.

Another sure bet is that Mario will teach the next generations in his lineage where their ancestors stepped 10,000, 30,000, and even 60,000 years ago. The footsteps of about 3,000 generations were imprinted on three continents before they even appeared on Guatemala soil.[9] I wonder what these ancestors thought of the different winds that blew on their shores and through their mountains, forests, and plains over the last 60,000 years.

Snapshots

APRIL 29, 2015

I am back at Lake Atitlan. This is visit number 12 in as many years. I'll zero in on a handful of experiences impressed into my mind this month:

A boy pushes his toy truck into a small store where I'm spending a few minutes buying a beverage and chocolate Kisses. He places a one-quetzal (or 13-cent) coin on the counter, much higher than his head. He asks for a roll of toilet paper. The girl behind the counter tells him toilet paper costs two quetzales. With another long stretch of his arm, he coughs up a second coin. He jams the roll into the cargo bed of his truck—the better to avoid ejection when he makes a sharp turn.

"Does your truck go *rápido*?" I ask the boy in Spanish.

The boy tells me nothing but gives his truck such a hard push that it flies out of the store. He follows it across the street, then pushes it into the store again—the toilet paper still securely embedded.

"How old are you?" I ask the young truck driver.

---

[9] This DNA-based account, "Ancestral Walks," was released in the author's first book, along with a global ancestral route map. The same type of *National Geographic* DNA analysis uncovered the migratory routes of 3,000 or so generations of the author's matrilineal and patrilineal ancestors. See *The Other Worlds: Offbeat Adventures of a Curious Traveler*, 112–15 and 236–41, for the accounts of the incredible journeys of Mario's and the author's ancestors. The book, and the author's website, www.TomsGlobe.com, both display the unique map of these ancestral movements across the globe. Perhaps it's the first such map to appear in any adventure book!

The boy still says nothing—but he unfurls one finger of a hand, then a second and a third. The fourth is slow. The fifth is so tentative I don't believe that one at all.

Now I bend down and press a foil-wrapped Kiss into the tube of the toilet paper roll. Last I see, the boy is pushing his sweet truck home —with toilet paper and a Kiss. Will the cargo bemuse his mom and sisters?

• • •

"What the heck is happening?" I ask myself after I finish a morning swim and start climbing Lake Atitlan's volcanic rocks. Out of the corner of my eye, I glimpse a boy jump off a high boulder toward the lake. When he is halfway down, I see a silent explosion of—of what? Items of clothing have just exploded outward from his jumping body, everything falling into the lake around him. His friend then jumps off the boulder, and he too lets loose an explosion of clothing.

This calls for an explanation! Boulder by boulder, I climb over and ask. Had they ever done that before?

"No," they answer.

"When did you first think about doing it?" I tell them this might be a first in the world.

The first boy decided, on the spur of the moment, to grab his clothes and fling them everywhere on the way down. The second boy followed suit.

"Do you have a name for this?" I inquire.

"No, we don't," one responds.

"*Explosión de ropa*—explosion of clothes," I suggest to them. I may never see such an explosión take place again. Am I right in swearing that only the two boys and I have ever witnessed such an event? Let me know if you did it as a youth or as a spaced-out adult.

• • •

Alaskan students from the Christian School of Anchorage hauled their band instruments here for a visit. Yesterday, they joined a parade through town. This morning, they congregate on the dock, about to leave.

"What is the most surprising thing to you about this town?" I ask an Alaskan girl.

Upon reflection, she answers, "The people are so loving."

To double the scientific accuracy of my poll, I ask the same question of an Anchorage boy who's standing on a different part of the dock (thereby ensuring the gender and geographic diversity of the random sample).

"The people are so nice," he answers without hesitating.

My unanimous polling results confirm that Lake Atitlan might well be among the best destinations on earth.

• • •

Entry to the Catholic church in the middle of town is granted by steps on the left and right, or by a long stone ramp in between. As I walk by the bottom of the ramp, I see kids doing something like kids in Minnesota have done beginning perhaps thousands of years before statehood: they are sliding down the incline. (I did a double take, since at first I could have sworn there was snow on that "hill.") These Maya children use, as a sled, the hard skin of a large plant—it's shaped just like the bottom of a canoe, curved up front and back.

"What's the name of the game?" I ask the kids.

"*Huse-huse*," they inform me.

"What plant do your sleds come from?" I want to know.

"*Ah-toot*," they answer.

I realize they are answering my Spanish-language questions in their language of Tzutujil.

Later, I ask the women who live across the path from my shack how to say these words in Spanish. Huse-huse, they tell me, is *resbalar* and means sliding. The women don't know the Spanish word for ah-toot.

I guess they've never needed to use the word for that plant when speaking their second language.

Someday, I'll ask a few of the thousands in town how to say ah-toot in Spanish. From there, it'll be a quick hop and skip to discover how to say ah-toot in English. For now, though, you and I are not in the know—and it's just one of the many unanswered questions a curious traveler amasses.

The Venomous Butterfly
MARCH 25, 2018

As I step on the bottom of the 1,200-foot-deep lake near shore, strewn with boulders from a volcanic eruption one eon ago, a fluttering in the water catches my eye. A large insect! But what exactly is this creature with beautiful colors wingtip to wingtip?

Other than its beauty, the only thing I know is that it will never again take flight if it remains in the water. It is condemned to death by exhaustion, or by a ravenous bird eating a tiny critter on a boulder, just 25 beak lengths away. The intriguing bird is a *zanate* (pronounced "sa-ná-tay").

I know what to do, due to a swimming experience last summer in a now ice-covered Minnesota lake. One day, I'd carried a waterlogged bee, flailing about in the water, to a dock, and thence to the top of a clover.

I pull this Central American insect out of Lake Atitlan and drop it on a rock, where it joins my towel, sneakers, and mangoes. It lands upside down. Surely, it knows how to right itself. I will not interfere any more in its born-again life!

But right itself, it does not. Finally, my index finger and thumb gently pinch a wing and lift the creature, righting it. Surely it will fly, now that it's upright and dried from the spring equinox sunshine and the mountain breeze.

Meanwhile, I realize I've never seen a body and wings so colorful, so beautiful. The design of one wing blows me away. My quick-on-the-draw imagination sees a running deer with no hind legs but a rear quarter and tail tapering away into the distance. No automobile, airplane, or running shoe company has ever (yet) dreamt up a trademark so amazing!

I need a photograph to learn the name of the animal later and to immortalize the design of that left wing. My camera, though, is up the cliff and a hundred meters away in my shack. If the insect dies right here on the boulder, I'll certainly take it home. It doesn't die, though, and doesn't move at all—unless I touch its wings.

It's time for me to leave and climb the cliff. Would I kill the insect by transporting it home? Could be. I do it anyway. I wrap it in the black Calvin Klein T-shirt I bought off-season in Minnesota, put the Calvin-Klein-with-creature in my knapsack, climb up, and stride home, just as satisfied as if I were carrying a stringer of fish.

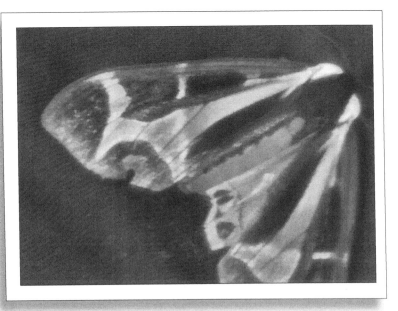

Motionless, the mysterious butterfly lies on a Calvin Klein T-shirt at the author's shack.

Outside my shack, I open what I've carried. The wings still display nice designs, but by virtue of my having wrapped the insect up, they have contracted. Now the design is not quite like the one I hoped to peddle to Nike to replace the swoosh for the next 50 years.

Awhile later, neighbor Ventura Matzar stops over, perhaps to practice his English, following up on his rise and shine at 3:00 a.m. every Saturday to endure a mountainous bus ride to study English in Quetzaltenango.

Ventura hears my story exactly as you've heard it. I then show him the creature. It clings to the Calvin Klein so tightly with its antennae/antlers/pinchers/legs that our loving pulls on a wing do not dislodge it. I do wonder, however, about a coating of a pollen-like powder on the shirt, right around the clinging creature.

"What is the insect?" I ask Ventura.

He thinks it may be a butterfly.

"What is the probability that your father or mother knows what it is?" I wonder.

"Sixty percent," he figures.

• • •

Two days later, I put that 60-percent probability to the test. Ventura's father Pedro stops over.

"Pedro, look at this photo."

"This is not a *mariposa* [butterfly]," he tells me, "but similar to one. You seldom see it in daytime. They come out at night and fly around a light bulb. They devour mosquitoes. A *zanate* bird might love eating it, too."

Pedro doesn't know its name in Spanish, but it's called a *gahiz* in the Mayan language of Tzutujil.

"Ventura knows how to write in Tzutujil, so I'll ask him how to spell 'gahiz,'" Pedro advises.

Pedro now tells me a story that will have me examining my fingertips for days.

"When I was little, my father told me to never touch a gahiz," Pedro recalls. "'If you touch it, the powder on its wings will hurt your fingers real bad,' my father warned me. I was six years old. And curious! So one night, when I saw a gahiz, I touched it. Within a few hours, my index finger started hurting bad."

"The next day at school," Pedro recounts, "I snuck away during a 30-minute recess to talk to a doctor I knew. By then, my finger was all swollen. The doctor injected something into my finger. When he squeezed it, yellow liquid oozed out. He put a Curita Band-Aid on my finger. I pulled the Curita off before I went home that day. I never told my father. The doctor didn't either. I might've gotten spanked."

I tell Pedro that my shirt from the lake still has powder on it. I haven't yet worn it again. I'll triple wash it in a bucket in my yard, I decide, and then purify it in the mountain-bright sun.

The next morning, like every morning, I'm at Las Cristalinas Coffeehouse. I tell my story to the workers. "G-a-h-i-z" is a fine way to spell its name in Tzutujil, they say, adding that it *is* a mariposa—a dangerous one. "Ohh!" they exclaim with some alarm. "You touched it?"

I'll ask Ventura if he's felt numbness in his fingertips. I didn't mention to Pedro that his son and I had our fingers all over the gahiz's wings.

Meanwhile, I can almost hear a reader asking me:

"Tomás, whatever happened to the gahiz that you rescued from death? Did you kill it by wrapping it in your braggadocio'd Calvin Klein and sticking it in your knapsack?

"And, Tomás, it seems you never even asked yourself why the gahiz was in the water in the first place. Think a little! There's a strong probability that it was chased by the zanate bird and plunged into the lake. The zanate had it right where it wanted it and dined first on a little lake critter it saw, keeping one eye on the gahiz. Then you had to come along and wreck nature's order of things. Are you paying for that with swollen fingertips?

"One more minor detail, you flubbed. Your anecdote's title is not apropos. 'Venom' is injected into prey. The powder you describe is *poison*. More apropos would be 'The Poisonous Butterfly' or 'How the Gahiz Poisoned Calvin Klein's T-shirt.'"

I'll answer this diatribe in a few words. The gahiz was still clinging to the shirt outside my shack that evening at my bedtime. But in the darkness of night, the venomous butterfly flew away to freedom! And my good deed left only a slight numbing sensation in my fingertips for a couple days.

Do you, avid reader, know the name of the species in English, Spanish, or Latin? And if you can learn more about it, submit it and this anecdote to the *Journal of Insect Science* so that another of the world's 20,000 butterfly species can have its due. Send the same information to me via the TomsGlobe.com website. I'll post it in a blog. I may even title it "The Venomous Butterfly."

MEXICO

MEXICO

Stepping Off a Bus into an Emerging Pandemic
APRIL 29, 2009

What happens when a flu epidemic hits a city of 20 million people and authorities fear a pandemic?

Sunday—Before I take my second step in Mexico City off the bus inbound from Acapulco, a police officer hands me a face mask. And before I can decide whether to put it on—since only 20 percent of people are wearing them—I accidentally drop it on the floor of a nearby subway station. Should I strap it on my face now? I must pick my poison. I stick the mask in my pocket, figuring I'll keep five feet away from everyone else. I hadn't foreseen getting crowded together with my share of the city's 20 million inhabitants.

That evening, 12 of 20 passengers in my subway car wear masks of one style or another. I can't see most people's faces, only their eyes. They see my whole face. People are looking at each other closely— likely wondering, "Who among us has the flu?"

Churches still have masses. Movie theatres are open. But all schools in this capital city are ordered to close for 10 days, starting tomorrow.

You might have seen news of two brothers on the street selling, for $4, face masks that have a 30-cent wholesale value. Following a popular outrage, they and four others are arrested and charged with obstructing a public way.

Monday—I visit the Mexico City tourist information kiosk in the huge Zocalo central plaza, a block from my $15-a-night hotel. I'm told the museums are closed. I'd planned to go to the best museum in

Mexico, the National Museum of Anthropology. In previous years, my visits for a few hours at a time weren't enough.

I'm seated in the megachurch-sized cathedral facing the Zocalo. I need to sneeze real bad, but I'm sure everyone would start praying for me—and themselves. I suppress the urge. Outside, police hand out face masks. I accept one. I'm now wearing it in this internet café, like all the other customers. My face is hot. By yesterday, the swine flu was suspected to have killed 50 people. This morning's paper says the number is 103. The internet reports it is 150.

I decide to treat myself to a Starbucks coffee. I sit down inside to drink it. The security guard tells me to enjoy it on the open-air patio next to the sidewalk. A young man dressed for business asks if he can share my table, since no one may sit inside for fear of spreading the disease.

Tuesday—The TV news is 100 percent focused on swine flu: "Wear your mask. If you don't, at least cover your coughs and sneezes with your forearm or bent elbow. Don't greet anyone with a handshake or kiss. Wash your hands often." The schools in all of Mexico are closed, not just those in the capital. At Starbucks, I may no longer sit on the outdoor patio. I go to McDonalds and do sit inside—under speakers blaring loud music. I ask the manager to turn the volume down. He turns it off. No one else is there to enjoy it.

I'm now used to the mask hanging around my neck when it's not on my face. I go to Sanborns, an exclusive department store, to buy pastries to take out. As I enter, I pull the mask up over my face. "Why is it all wet?" I wonder. I suppose when I hopped in the shower an hour ago, it was dangling around my neck. At least it's clean. Maybe it'll last double the usual two-day life.

Wednesday—The government orders all restaurants, except those serving take-out food, to close. A line of masked customers stand outside a Burger King, waiting to order takeouts. They're allowed in two or three at a time. I walk into Café Santo Domingo, next to the awe-inspiring Santo Domingo Church from the 1600s, but after I purchase coffee, I'm on the street again. People snack on the city's few benches. I share mine with a homeless man. I don't think he's eaten today.

Banamex, the megabank, urges customers to use its website. And, it says, please don't come into the bank unless you're wearing a mask. (This is the right time for the likes of Jesse James.)

Now 17 of 21 passengers in my subway car wear masks. The hundreds of Cineplexes, Cinemexes, Cinepolises, and other movie theatres are closed. The bars have long since been shuttered and all music concerts cancelled. The churches no longer say mass. Life in the city seems to be slowly melting away.

Tomorrow, I'm making a beeline for the US, with early stops at the Louisville Slugger baseball bat factory and the Louisville Bats Triple-A stadium, with its 12,000 flu-free fanatics. Soon afterward, I'll be home in Minnesota, where the closest I'll come to the distant swine flu epidemic will be daily reports on the news.

• • •

Several years later, a research team reported that this H1N1 swine flu, which started as an epidemic in Mexico and became a worldwide pandemic, originated in pigs from a very small region in central Mexico. Apparently, this was the first time the origin of an influenza pandemic virus was traced in such detail.

The virus, they found, was a mix of two swine viruses that had been circulating among Mexican pigs for more than 10 years before one emergent strain became infectious to humans. The 2009 pandemic lasted over a year, even though a vaccine was developed in just a few months.[10]

In the meantime, this virus continues to circulate as a seasonal influenza in many parts of the world, including the US and Mexico.

---

[10] "2009 Swine Flu Pandemic Originated in Mexico, Researchers Discover," June 27, 2016, Science Daily, http://www.sciencedaily.com.

All Because of the Pope—and Other Christian Traditions
APRIL 5, 2012

The Mexico I've never been to is the Mexico I go to now: Spanish colonial cities northwest of Mexico City—Morelia, Pátzcuaro, Querétaro, Guadalajara, San Miguel de Allende, and, despite the pope, Guanajuato. If any were founded after 1530, it wasn't by much.

The Camino Real—or Royal Road, a colonial trade route that ran all the way to what is now New Mexico—runs out of Mexico City and through some of these towns. San Miguel de Allende, for example, was established as a waystation for the silver shipped from distant mines to Mexico City, and later into the chests of the Spanish royalty (if not the chests of pirates or the bottom of the deep blue sea). Millions were invested in San Miguel de Allende's churches and mansions. They're still there today, together with the nearby rolling, dry cowboy country punctuated by prickly pear cacti, whose nopal leaves provide food and drink.

• • •

The Sunday before Palm Sunday in San Miguel, the alarm clock rouses me at five a.m. Predawn, I maneuver through the crooked streets toward fireworks that will blast for another two hours.

The night before, many residents had taken buses to the Santuario de Atotonilco church, which houses the figure of a beaten and bloodied Christ—a statue credited with miraculous powers. At midnight, the travelers departed Atotonilco and silently marched the eight miles back toward San Miguel. They bore the much-revered statue of Christ, as well as those of the Virgin Mary and the Apostle John. Each of these figures was wrapped in dozens of silk scarves as protection during the journey. This procession is known as Our Lord of the Column, or *Procesión del Señor de la Columna.*

Well enough rested, hundreds of us silently greet the marchers at sunrise on the edge of San Miguel. We watch several marchers slowly remove the silk coverings, one by one, from each figure. Belatedly (it seems to me), the procession starts anew toward a San Miguel church, still some distance away. Having joined as reinforcement, I'll march with the procession for that last stretch.

As we shuffle through the streets, we step on the flower petal–covered "carpets"—or *alfombra*—made of sawdust saved up over months. The marchers' horns blare, as if on cue. Several small groups of people sing, each group with its own single well-worn hymnal. Each group appears oblivious to the others, but all are moving together at the same slow pace.

The singers are mostly old men in cowboy hats and women in clothing not bought at any modern apparel shop. The song of the group close to me is sung only this one morning of the year, I learn. Perhaps it has been sung just once a year for a century or two.

It is a profound experience. Not that it is my first of the week. In the World Heritage City of Morelia, I had met a young man carrying a guitar who mentioned that he would perform at a church that evening. To me, live guitar music in one of the magnificent stone churches built two or three centuries ago would qualify as a once-in-a-lifetime experience. The guitar player gave me the church's address. I looked forward to an acoustical treat.

That evening, I hunted for the church, certain that its towers would soar into the clouds. The closer I moved toward the address, though, the fewer were the buildings that soared even 15 feet upward. At long last, I came to a nondescript building. It was packed with decidedly non-Catholic parishioners, some of whom were kneeling, heads to the floor, sobbing, while a woman moved from one kneeler to the next, covering each with a small sheet. The guitar music was nearly imperceptible, with the weeping and the amplified sermon growing louder by the minute.

The deafening sermon soon exploded out the door and through the windows of vehicles driving on the street. How good could this be for the ears of the children skirmishing on the church floor with toy guns or playing hide and seek? It might all be worth it, I thought, if someone were born again—and by gosh, that is what seemed to happen.

• • •

Let's return now to the Sunday in San Miguel that, for me, didn't start 'til near daybreak. I leave the procession and its aftermath at 10 a.m. to grab an hour of sleep in my hostel bunk. At noon, I join a Sunday excursion headed by expatriates, mostly Americans, who started to trickle into town in the late 1940s. We're soon enjoying a garden and home tour, different every Sunday. The ticket revenue benefits the remarkable public library and the local children, who are taught about computers and English from volunteering expatriates. (This historic *Biblioteca Publica* is billed by one traveler as "the coolest public library in the world.")

My tour group first motors to an organic garden and a nature preserve on the chaparral where cacti predominate. (Now I love cacti just as much as penguins. What I never saw in childhood, I treasure as my years advance.)

The final stop is a three-level home (or is it four or five?), built by the architect-owner and his artist wife. Her paintings fill the home, together with antiques from around the world. We—two busloads of us—are allowed a free run of the house. I'm the first one in and the last one out. I probably could've stayed and lived in half the house for a week before the owners realized I was there—but I had my heart set on Guanajuato.

• • •

I leave San Miguel on this packed-with-excitement Sunday, since I've reserved a room three hours away in Guanajuato. The newspapers, I read later, had informed timely readers that Guanajuato was blocked to all traffic from the outside world by 1,200 security guards. On the way to the San Miguel bus terminal, the taximan emphasizes that all bus service to Guanajuato has been suspended until Pope Benedict leaves in a day.

I tell the taximan I'll go toward Guanajuato on a different route and sleep in a town that's partway, if need be.

"That's what you'll have to do," he informs me.

"All because of the pope!" I exclaim, not quite fuming.

"Yes!" he agrees. (Laughter in the taxi.)

Once I make it to my partway destination, I learn that a bus will head to Guanajuato, despite the pope. Apparently, the 1,200-strong security force hasn't blocked off the back route into town. It is a beautiful ride through the mountains at sunset. One on the bus would have to be very forgiving of the pope for the delays, given this treat of utter beauty.

As I check into a bed and breakfast in Guanajuato, a face mask covers the face of homeowner Carmen. She explains that because the pope is in town, her voice is all hoarse from shouting.

And that's where my day ends. I am too late to see the pope. The day's sunrise procession with the once-a-year hymn sung by seemingly ancient people, the organic farm, the myriad cacti, and the multilevel house of which I was ushered out filled my plate. Shouting for the pope, though, would have been icing on the cake.

the friday of sorrows—san miguel de allende

Four days later, I return to San Miguel from Guanajuato. One and all recall the *Siete Dolores de María*—Seven Sorrows of Mary. It falls on the Friday before Good Friday—the Friday of Sorrows. The first of the Seven Sorrows was not finding a proper place to give birth to her son; the seventh was the burial of Jesus, and her solitude. Building an altar of sorrows on this day is, I'm told, unique to Mexico. This tradition dates back to the 1500s, interrupted only during periods of civil strife.

What will we experience here—on this day only—and nowhere else in the world?

Dozens, if not hundreds, of San Miguel families erect an altar to recognize the Seven Sorrows and to comfort the Virgin Mary. The altars display images of the Virgin of Sorrows and Christ. They're decorated with white flowers (symbolizing Mary's purity), a purple cloak (pain and penitence), bitter oranges (the Virgin's sorrow), fresh chamomile (the colors representing humility and beauty in body and soul), and sprouting wheat (Christ as eucharistic bread). You do have some leeway, though, in your design. Altars also pop up at dozens of churches and public fountains.

The real action starts at sundown. Bands of roving friends and families search the 400- to 500-year-old back streets for altars erected in houses' open windows or doorways, or even living rooms. Don't just enter and make the sign of the cross. No! You accept what the family offers you and move on to the next altar further down the street. And accept what is offered there, too.

You frenetically continue paying respects until your feet are sore or you are too full to continue, for by now, you've consumed any number of *paletas*—fruit-flavored ice cream on a stick—and your share of drinks like the sweetened milky rice *horchata*. The ice cream and drinks, as well as burning pumpkin candles, represent the Virgin's sweet tears.

I recommend this centuries-old celebration in San Miguel de Allende—a town that, a year after I visited, was voted the number one city in the world in the *Condé Nast Traveler* magazine's annual readers' poll. Just don't make the mistake I made of sitting down in an all-I-could-eat buffet restaurant just before I busted out onto the streets and joined what seemed to be mob melees—except we all understood it was a sacred evening.

To top off this experience, I'll be in Havana, Cuba, this coming Easter Sunday, hot on the heels of Pope Benedict again.

Seven Things We Learn, and Who May We Thank?

MAY 6, 2013

querétaro, mexico

1. A nearly complete human skeleton was unearthed a few years ago near Mexico City. It dates back to 10,000 BC. It's about the earliest evidence of humans in this area. Who is responsible for educating us about this?

2. Indigenous inhabitants opened a mine in 15 AD near Querétaro, northwest of Mexico City. The mine operation was labor intensive. The miners dug tunnels, hammered at walls to loosen valuable minerals, hauled away findings, and traded the product in distant communities that weren't mineral fortunate. Mining was also a religious and magical endeavor, courtesy of gods of the underworld. Who is responsible for discovering these treasurable facts and passing them on to us?

3. If you were ready to leave the nomadic life in 500 BC and become somewhat sedentary, where would you start farming? Why, for sure, as one of Mesoamerica's first farmers, you'd search for a spot where it is easy to grow nutritious foods. Pick out fertile soil near a river! Plant corn! Harvest! Oops, after neighboring farmers nearly go under, you'd learn to get smart with calendars so you don't plant too early or too late. Or you might talk to the budding calendar experts. (Sorry, this may condense 10 books detailing calendar and agricultural development into one paragraph.)

    You've also learned, by virtue of 2,000 generations of ancestors, how to fish and hunt by several means, how to select wild fruit from trees and bushes, what roots are ideal over the fire, what wild vegetables are the most nutritious, and how to treat a myriad of medical conditions. So, with all your farming, hunting, and gathering, you wouldn't be all that sedentary after all. Who is responsible for un-covering this and turning it into learnable form? Hang in there, the answer will be revealed very soon.

4. After your descendants do quite well for the next 1,500 years (with ups and downs), for some reason the agricultural communities you founded in North Central Mexico start disappearing. Around 1000 AD, nomads and seminomads from the north retake the land. Some of them live in groups as large as 100 to 400. They confederate with neighbors to defend against threats. Who says this?

5. Then the Spanish Conquistadors arrive in the early 1500s. Your descendants and many other indigenous peoples fight them until after the 1850s.

6. In 1806, fighters from a Spanish hacienda ranch, under the direction of the hacienda manager, attack your descendants, who live in a small village. They burn the villagers' homes, cause stillbirths, and force everyone to flee. To the surprise of many, the judicial system prosecutes the hacienda manager. Burial grounds are dug up and prove the deaths of fetuses. The defendant, though, appears to get off with light punishment. Who dug up this information and passed it on?

7. Casting a glance back at ancient history, we learn that a mammoth died near today's Querétaro in 7000 BC. Its fossilized bones have been dug up. Today, two gloved and masked women painstakingly scrape, hammer, and chisel the fossilized skeleton. One of the women periodically sweeps the floor, gathering up fossil dust.

Who may we thank for educating us on these seven things? The Querétaro Regional Museum! The museum and its active paleontology laboratory occupy the cloister and some of the inner courtyards of the old Convent of San Francisco Grande, which was constructed in Querétaro in the 1530s.

This information is just the tip of the iceberg in a single museum. More than 55,000 other museums have been painstakingly created and are open to the public in 202 countries. This may be a record unmatched by any other of the possibly one million intelligent-life planets in the universe.

So much to learn about life on earth. So few years to learn it.

CUBA

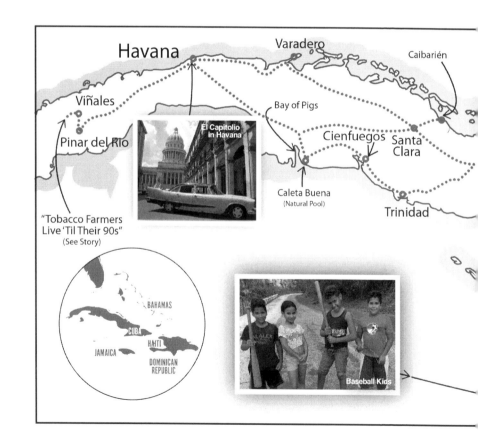

Havana

Varadero

Caibarién

Viñales

Bay of Pigs

El Capitolio
in Havana

Pinar del Río

Cienfuegos Santa
Clara

Caleta Buena
(Natural Pool)

Trinidad

"Tobacco Farmers
Live 'Til Their 90s"
(See Story)

BAHAMAS

CUBA

HAITI

JAMAICA

DOMINICAN
REPUBLIC

Baseball Kids

CUBA

First Messages from Cuba
MARCH 2004

I'm venturing to Cuba for the first time, walking in cities founded by
Diego Velasquez between 1511 and 1515. Here, in the city of Trinidad
(1514), people are meandering on cobblestone streets carrying birds
in cages. Why? Perhaps because it's a leisurely Sunday. I get involved

CUBA

Cayo Guillermo
Cayo Coco Resorts

Morón

KEY:
Routes traveled
between 2 and 20 times

Misael
and
puppies

Camagüey

Gibara

Holguin

Alejandro de Humboldt
National Park

Bayamo

Santo Domingo

Baracoa

Santiago
de Cuba

Guantánamo

in some discussions and hear talk about American foreign policy (*malo*, or bad, I am told). My Spanish is improving, but Cubans drop off word endings, so my mind adds sounds to figure out what they mean. I find few internet locations but music everywhere.[11]

april 2006

Cuba is probably the most interesting country in the world for me to visit right now, and I'm in a minor state of shock after experiencing it for 23 days. The economic and social support system is nearly the polar opposite of the United States's; the nation's history is momentous, and its people are especially expressive, to say nothing of the wonderful museums, pre-1520 cities, and beautiful beaches; there's music everywhere—a sign on the door of a great little live music hall in Santiago, translated from Spanish, declares *Entry Prohibited With a Bottle of Rum*. I've also climbed a steep learning curve figuring out how to travel from place to place.

And more. A friend got hauled off by a cop for, I guess, talking to me. I didn't see him anymore. I think he slipped some money to the Havana officer on a dark street corner and was told to vanish. I'm hoping, anyway. In Cuba's second largest city, Santiago, the police questioned people I was talking to but said not a word to me. Might I, or they, be counter-revolutionaries?

The first World Baseball Classic was just played in seven locations from Puerto Rico to Japan. Fans enjoyed seeing Cuba topple the USA in a game televised from Puerto Rico. A young man on a bicycle raced around downtown Santa Clara after the game, yelling "Cuba sí!, Yanquis No!" Cuba lost to Japan in the finals, though. Rather than

---

[11] My first book offered readers four accounts of Cuba, from "The Shots Maribel Heard" to "Advance Man," which cover journeys between 2010 and 2016. The entries here date from my earlier Cuban visits, right up through this century's second decade. For all I knew, my adventure in 2004 would be the one and only time in my life I would see Cuba. Returning to Cuba became a habit, though. I'll write a report on each *future* Cuban journey I may make in my life—follow along on the blog page of my website, www.TomsGlobe.com.

expressing disappointment, as in, "We just lost the Super Bowl, so our season had a dismal end," Cubans were thrilled and proud of their team and its performance. Fidel Castro threw a celebration. Fidel is, by the way, still going strong at 79 or 80. (People don't expect big changes if he dies.)

Baseball games à la Cuba are played in streets. They're usually played crosswise, not lengthwise, and not with a ball but plastic bottle caps. The batter sees the twisting and looping pitch come at him at non–Big League speed. He gamely swings. If he connects, the cap may fly, or roll, into someone's open door across the street. It is then fetched.

february 2009

I head east out of Havana on a three-hour bus journey, then embark on a planned one-hour taxi ride on a lonely road going south. When the taxi breaks down, I hop in the back of a passing ambulance, jumping out at the Bay of Pigs. That's where CIA-supported Cubans from Miami and elsewhere invaded Cuba in 1961, aiming to overthrow Fidel Castro. A museum in Playa Giron, at the vast mouth of the bay, describes the Cuban victory. Castro got wind of the "secret" invasion, I learn, stood at the ready with his armed forces, and unleashed a withering counter-attack. One may visit a Bay of Pigs museum and meeting hall in Miami, I would discover a year later, and listen as veterans describe their escape from the bay into a nearly impenetrable jungle thicket, and their arrest days later.

Renting a bicycle, I pedal five miles along the ocean from the bay's mouth to a natural, long "swimming pool" parallel to the ocean, called Caleta Buena. The pool is beautifully wavy, since the ocean is always squeezing in and out through a narrow channel. The pool has tides, too. I could live near Caleta Buena for years and never be heard to complain.

Two days later, I rent a motor scooter in Cienfuegos and ride 12 miles to an expansive botanical garden established by a sugar baron in 1899, and later managed by Harvard University. Over 2,000 species of tropical plants thrive here, including 230 species of palms and 400 of orchids.

Now I'll head to the Cienfuegos bus station for a ride to Santa Clara, the site of Che Guevara's historic 1958 victory, when he derailed an incoming train full of dictator Batista's troops. Che's mausoleum can be visited too, since Bolivia sent his body back in 1997.[12]

march 2010

This year, my adventure in Cuba is a month long, half still to come. Julio Muñoz's house, where I'm staying in old Trinidad (1514), was built quite recently—think 1800—and was featured in a 1999 *National Geographic* spread. I spent this morning at the house in conversation with two professional photographers—Julio himself and the British Keith Cardwell.

Keith has visited Cuba 42 times and was a good friend of famed Cuban photographer Andrew Korda. Korda took one of the most famous photographs in history: a serious-looking Che Guevara in his beret. I've seen this image thousands of times, most often on T-shirts in countless countries. Korda told Keith that on the day he took the photo, Che was suffering from an asthma attack. That gave Che the unforgettable look now burned into the memory of hundreds of millions.

During one of Keith's stays in Cuba 10 years ago, two years before Andrew Korda died, Korda was upset that Smirnoff was using his Che photo to advertise a liquor. Keith soon engaged British lawyers to sue Smirnoff on behalf of Korda. Korda later traveled to London to open a photo exhibit, and at that time Smirnoff settled the lawsuit for $2.4 million. Korda told Keith he would donate the money "to Fidel Castro and Cuba." Korda borrowed Keith's phone and called Fidel in Cuba to give him the great news—Keith paid a big phone bill!

---

[12] Che Guevara's unparalleled stature in the history of Santa Clara is described in more detail in the author's first book. Check out the chapter "Che's Mausoleum or Bar La Roca?"

On Keith's subsequent visit to Cuba, Fidel hugged him for helping Andrew Korda—and Cuba! The day before I left Trinidad, I looked for Keith to give him a goodbye hug, so I'd forever be just one hug removed from Fidel Castro. I missed Keith, however, and still long for that hug.

Snapshots of Ice Cream, Love, and Soccer
2010 AND 2012

The vendor who operates the soft ice cream machine on Obispo Street in Old Havana sells 600 to 700 cones a day, she tells me. The price in pesos is equal to a US nickel. The government is subsidizing the cones, I theorize, as well as the coffee at run-in, run-out counters, which cost much less than a nickel. Many patrons, like me, often order two cones or two cups of coffee at once, since we've had to stand in line and jingle the change in our pockets.

• • •

Disregarding a travel guide's opinion that the city of Bayamo is a "low key, unexciting sort of place, where tourism is of little importance," I journeyed here yesterday. Parque Céspedes is now the most soothing plaza I know in Latin America. No vehicles are within earshot—they're prohibited on the streets that enclose the downtown plaza. Bicyclists must dismount.

Yesterday, I caught the tail end of a plaza ceremony that honored the victorious Bayamo veterans of the Bay of Pigs. A heavily medaled soldier and other veterans thought it cool I'm from the United States, the enemy in 1961.

A nickel-and-dime ice cream sundae parlor on the nearby corner was irresistible to my ice cream–crazy taste buds and the brain cells wired to them. A local couple joined me at my table, as is the custom. Their anticipatory faces told me they have the very same neural setup.

As we talked about the Cuban victory at the Bay of Pigs, the wife studied my face. I remember it happening, I told them, and recently read a book by a British historian about what the hell was going on inside the Kennedy White House in the run-up to that disastrous CIA-sponsored invasion.

Cuba's baseball playoffs pit Sancti Spiritus against Bayamo in the local stadium this evening. One of Cuba's millions of baseball fanatics gave me the lowdown on the best players tonight, including the current home run leader. Hector, a bicycle taxi operator, will drive me there. At his suggestion, he'll park his bici-taxi, come in on my dime, enjoy the game with me, and then drive me back into town.

Retract! My remark that tickets to the playoff game will be on my dime is wrong—a ticket costs less than three cents!

• • •

If you visit Bayamo, hopefully you'll see my favorite couple—an odd couple, I thought the first time I saw them. Not odd because he is dark skinned and she light skinned (all combinations are common in Cuba), but she looks some years older and has lost many teeth, perhaps from smoking nonfiltered cigarettes down to the quarter inch. Judging from his rugged body and his clothes, I was sure he was a hard laborer.

The odd couple sat lovingly close to each other on a plaza bench. I had nothing to do but watch. After awhile, they broke out in a duet of songs for all those around to enjoy. The next morning, I saw the "hard laborer" again. He was playing chess in the plaza. The day after that, he was drawing a portrait.

Later, as I nursed a one-cent shot of coffee in the stand-up coffee shop, the couple had a little spat. I took it they weren't married and didn't always live together. Everyone in the shop watched with concern. The two made up, though, and walked out together. I could feel everyone applauding in their hearts.

If you find yourself in Bayamo, you'll quickly recognize them. They might sing a duet for you. You'll have nothing to do but listen— in this "low-key, unexciting sort of place."

• • •

After settling down at my favorite place in Camagüey, I wondered, "How would I describe my feelings about this spot in 25 words?"

It wasn't hard: On an ancient cobblestone plaza in the middle of Cuba, I'm sitting at night on the church steps, never desiring to leave.

Just then, a boy of about 12 walked by and spoke a few engaging words. The next day in the same place, the boy and his friends approached me again. They needed player number six for two teams of three each to play soccer in the plaza.

"No," I demurred, wanting neither to ever get up nor embarrass myself. I finally relented, though. They made me a goalie. I left my post on occasion and joined an offensive attack. Doesn't everyone want to score and be a hero? That's not how the game is played, however, and we didn't do too well.

Afterward, the players sang a popular Cuban song with gusto. They even shed a few (fake) tears. It's all tucked inside my video camera. When I saw them again six years later, they remembered meeting me in their San Juan de Dios Plaza, but did not remember singing the (sad) song.

Now I still see two of them every year or two. All of us seem to feel it's a treat, and we don't sing any sad songs—or play soccer.

Avoir du Culot and Not Looking Back
MAY 5, 2012

Truck and train carried me all day long from Bayamo in eastern Cuba to Morón in the center. Why in the world did I come to such an out-of-the-way place? Oh, yes, now I remember.

It goes like this. First, stay with Santiago and Alejandra near the Morón plaza. They've got bedrooms. In the evening, phone taxi man Eduardo to negotiate a day trip to an offshore island, the famed Cayo Coco, which looks north toward the Bahamas. A 10-mile-long causeway runs from the mainland to exclusive resorts along miles of Cayo Coco. I hope I can find a beach to relax on for a couple hours. I wouldn't think about paying the price of staying on the island—even though every hotel's rate includes unlimited food and drinks, swimming pools, water volleyball, aerobics, disco, an ocean beach with bars, and name-that-tune contests.

In our phone call, Eduardo suggests that he drive me to a more fantastic, more remote beach. It's past Cayo Coco, at the end of another causeway. That island is Cayo Guillermo (but don't spread the word).

In the morning, three Frenchmen want to join me. They're staying at Santiago and Alejandro's home too. I'm game. At the 9 a.m. departure time, two of the French adventurers are searching for the third. They can't find him. They apologize and back out. Before Eduardo and I can pull away, though, the missing man comes running, waving his arms.

"Just like a movie—an American movie!" the ringleader, Michel, declares.

Are more such scenes yet to come? Could it be a French-American movie shot in Cuba? We may find out in short order.

We take off in Eduardo's smooth-running, 1980s-era Russian Moskvitch sedan. We hit the causeway. It's sure to fly by in a blur. But something isn't kosher. Eduardo doesn't have the necessary permit. Guards manning an international-style checkpoint stop our vehicle. Eduardo quietly instructs us that, if the police ask, we are to tell them that we are not paying customers, just friends of his. The Frenchmen tell me that the day before, when the police quizzed them on a different taxi trip, one of them was the "husband" of the taxi driver's daughter.

Today, we don't get quizzed, but the guards study our passports inside the guard shack for quite some time. Perhaps Eduardo tells the guards that we are his friends, or even relatives (Cubans are generally prohibited from crossing this checkpoint unless they work at a resort). We are allowed to proceed.

Once on Cayo Coco, my French cohorts instruct Eduardo to drive toward the Five Star Meliá Resort. One of them urges Eduardo to request permission at the Meliá guard shack for us to peek inside the hotel grounds for five minutes. We are damned curious. Permission denied!

The Frenchmen now direct Eduardo to reconnoiter the situation at the *fabuloso* Hotel Tryp. It looks like five stars and counting. Again, Eduardo asks for permission. Permission granted! For 10 minutes! Nonguests seldom get even a 10-second view. In fact, no one is supposed to be on hotel property without the blue wristband identifying wearers as guests entitled to all manner of food and drinks.

By the time I snap a couple pictures of the open-air lobby and make my way to the maze of interconnected pools, the three Frenchmen are swimming. I happen to like swimming too. A plunge into the warm sea follows the swim through the maze. After this, we're out of the hotel (all wet) and back at the taxi at 11:30 a.m., just five minutes late. No penalty is assessed for our infraction.

Son of a gun! The Moskvitch is giving Eduardo a carburetor headache. He suggests we adventurers go back and wait in the lobby. Now that we have a head of steam built up, we tell him, "Find us by the pool!" Swims in the pools, swims at the beach, and sun, sun, sun on the lounge chairs make us hungry and thirsty, no fault of our own. We have money to burn, but it is not accepted at prepaid resorts.

There happens to be a saying in French, however: *avoir du culot*. Michel educates me on this pivotal philosophy. In our case, it means "Don't be afraid to ask for something even though you've got no right to have it."

As *avoir du culot* would have it, the other two Frenchmen, Ahmed and Hussein, soon appear. They carry four hamburgers. The waiter didn't notice they lacked wristbands. Michel now leaves and returns with four more to share. *Avoir du culot!*

"I notice you didn't look back once you left the restaurant with the hamburgers," I tell Michel, adding, "You're demonstrating a companion philosophy to *avoir du culot* that I learned on Saipan Island in Micronesia."

"Really? What's that?" he asks.

I explain that one evening on a Saipan beach with a group of friends, one of them, Antonio, suggested to me, "Let's go to a family party for a few minutes. I have to show my face." Antonio and I motored a few miles to his huge family party on the edge of nowhere. When we were partway down the long row of end-to-end tables filled with delectables, he came up with a bright idea, blurting out, "Let's really pile it on our plates and bring them to the beach for all our friends." We then methodically worked our way to the last table. Carrying two fully loaded plates, we headed straight for the car. "Is this OK?" I asked Antonio.

"Don't look back and you won't be embarrassed," Antonio answered.

• • •

The four of us are really enjoying Cuba's Hotel Tryp now, and we're thirsty. But it is time for a pool swim again. A few minutes later, Ahmed wades toward us from the swim-up bar, holding a cup of juice in each hand. I discover that I, like the French, can swim to the bar (time and again), each time keeping my wrists under water as I order. Michel notices that once I turn and head toward them with my hands full, I never look back.

"This time, I'll make it rum and Coke," I tell Michel before my next excursion

"No, just juice," he answers. All three Frenchmen are Muslims and do not drink alcohol, I learn. Michel's mother is from Morocco, as are both of Hussein's parents. Ahmed's parents are from Algeria. All three were born in France. All will graduate in civil engineering from a Paris university this year. Two want to land jobs in oil and gas, the other in nuclear energy.

Ahmed and Hussein now leave the hotel to check on the taxi in the parking lot. The guard bars them from reentering. Hussein waits at the hotel entrance, while Ahmed sneaks in from the beach. Eduardo is still working on the taxi, he informs Michel and me. Ahmed says he and Hussein will stay out and help Eduardo fix the carburetor.

Sauntering around the edge of one of the pools, I spy a broken blue wristband under a lounge chair. Stealthily, I pluck it up but have no intention of actually wearing it. Some words immediately come to mind (and you can probably add more): "obtaining property under false pretenses," "theft of services," "trespass," "deportation," "international incident." Michel (bless his heart) disagrees with my decision not to sport the blue wristband. In fact, he's downright happy for us.

I decide I won't wimp out on a good friend like him. I stick the broken strip partly under my Mexican wristband so it won't drop to the floor and condemn us. We barhop to a food counter. I, of the blue wristband that keeps coming loose, order five Cokes and five ham and cheese sandwiches (the only kind they have). I take the ham from Michel's sandwich, since he is Muslim. He takes the cheese from mine, since I live near Wisconsin cheeseheads and their kilos of cheese.

I pack the other three warm sandwiches in my knapsack to take to the three at the taxi. (Is absconding with food for nonguests another chargeable offense?) Ahmed, Hussein, and Eduardo, however, are nowhere to be found. The taxi is gone too. Have they all been arrested? Are the police going to throw the book at us?

I manage a flawless hotel reentry, thanks to my wristband. Michel and I treat ourselves to the three sandwiches I could not deliver—double ham in each of mine, double cheese in his. I catch myself thinking that an ocean-view room might even fall into our laps for a couple weeks.

We decide to patronize a high-class bar for juice and coffee. A woman from Quebec, who's vacationed at this hotel 27 times, strikes up a conversation. Then a young New Brunswick casino worker says he's stayed at three hotels on this beach—and our selection is his favorite.

"And you?" he asks us.

"Us? Ahh . . . it's virgin territory," I answer. "But we got into the swing of things this morning, within the first 15 minutes."

"See you at the disco tonight," the New Brunswikian tells us, thrilled that he seemingly has found friends he can party with late into the Cuban night.

• • •

It's 7 p.m. It'll be dark soon. Did Michel's "American movie" script include being marooned on an island? Where does the script have us bed down? Michel says if we lie on the beach, critters will bite us. If we sleep in the hotel yard, guards will jar us awake in the middle of a paradisiacal dream.

So, deciding to take one more stab, I walk to the lobby. Hussein and Ahmed are sitting there, waiting, barred from coming in even for a minute to look for us. They had pushed the taxi out of sight. It's still broken, but Eduardo has found another taxi for us. He'll have his towed back to the mainland.

Outside, a hotel guard hovers around us like a hawk as we climb into the replacement vehicle. The guard is not happy—until he sees us disappear into the sunset.

Last I saw of the three Frenchmen, they were hopping into a 1954 Ford the next day, leaving Morón for Cayo Coco and Cayo Guillermo to search for that elusive beach where we were heading in the Moskvitch. We wished each other well.

If you travel to Cuba and follow in the footsteps of Michel, Hussein, and Ahmed, you may discover that they're still making movie scenes. Involve yourself! Just remember: *Avoir du culot* and *Don't look back*. It'll seem like *déjà vu* all over again.

Tobacco Workers Live 'Til Their 90s

APRIL 3, 2014

A photographer, this Jasper of ours, sometimes shows up out of the blue, such as in "A Glimpse through the Window" and "A Glimpse Above," earlier. He is on another mission today, yet he doesn't plan to snap a single photo. But oh! could he, for he's plotting an adventure in Cuba's most picturesque locale.

Will his mission end in exuberance, or utter failure? Jasper is as eager as anyone to find out.

He rents a bicycle, hush-hush, in the city of Viñales in Western Cuba. It's hush-hush because the capitalist-leaning bicycle owner is seeking a little cash flow without government permission to do business. Jasper tends to get caught up in such schemes, without an ounce of intent. (If officially questioned, he's told to say that the bicycle is *his* and not that he rented it from *someone*.)

The photo from 2004 that drew the roaming photographer back to Cuba's tobacco fields in 2014. He searched for these men, hoping to deliver the picture. In the center are brothers Armando (L) and Dundo (R). On the far left is the father-in-law of the young farmer on the far right.

He pedals the high-quality bike out of Viñales, heading west. He rides past fields growing world-famed tobacco. Karst mountains with sheer cliffs topped by nature's finest greenery captivate his photographer's eye.

Jasper does not stop, though. He is on a mission, clutching four prints of the most wonderful photograph ever taken of farmers working in a tobacco field. None of the four men who are pictured has ever seen the photo. They'll see it today if—and only if—Jasper finds them!

A decade ago, Jasper had gotten off his rented 50cc motorbike, slithered through a field of tall tobacco, chatted with the farmers, and motioned the question of "foto okay?" Jasper didn't ask the farmers for their names. Now, ten years later, he has only a mild recollection of the whereabouts of the field.

Before departing Viñales today, Jasper decided to show the photo to two women.

"The two older men are brothers," they said, "but the brother on the right, he died three months ago."

West of town, Jasper lays his bike down. He walks into an unplanted field to ask a man who walks in circles, holding tight to a plow pulled by a plodding ox. The farmer stops and eagerly examines the photo. The two younger men in the picture, one the other's son-in-law, live at the end of a long trail running south from the road just a few minutes from here, the man informs Jasper. Upon shooting the man and his ox with his camera, Jasper feels he has another prizeworthy photo.

Jasper soon turns off the road and begins biking up the long trail. It becomes an obstacle course. A rope with barely any slack lies across the path, one end staked into hard ground and the other attached to a mean-looking bull. Jasper pauses and surveys his predicament.

"If I continue on my mission, the bull might charge me," Jasper tells himself. "If it doesn't charge, it may yank the rope tight just as I ride over it, throwing me for a loop." He wonders for a second who would win in bull against bike. Unfortunately, no one is within yelling distance to advise him what to do.

Jasper takes the easy way out, surprised at how smart he is to think of it. Moving off the horse cart and oxen trail, he lays his bicycle in a thicket. He broadly circles the bull. "If the bull charges, the rope will yank him back," he figures. The bull seems to know Jasper is taking the wise way around. Jasper can now walk toward the house set against the hills.

Upon hearing a soft knock, a woman comes to the door. Jasper shows her the photo, which delights her. She calls to her son-in-law. As he looks at the print, he smiles too.

"These two photos are for you and your father-in-law," Jasper tells the young man, who's a decade older now. One of the two older men who are brothers died three months ago, they confirm. The brother who died, though, wasn't Dundo, the one pointed out by the women in town; it was the other, Armando.

Armed with general directions on where he might find Dundo, Jasper retraces his footsteps down the trail. Empowered by the success of his mission so far, he stays on the trail and steps across the rope, speaking softly to the bull the whole time. It sure does stare at him every second, though.

Fifteen picture-perfect bicycle minutes later, Jasper spies an older man working in a tobacco field. A quick look tells Jasper it is none other than Dundo, now in his 90s, still hard at work in the field where he was a decade earlier.

Upon seeing the photograph, Dundo is much surprised. He remembers when it was taken. He even recalls that Jasper gave the men a couple of pesos so they could later relax over a few rum drinks. Jasper does not recall.

A man on horseback now comes down the road and pulls up at the edge of the tobacco field. It's the son-in-law whom Jasper met earlier. An unlit and unfiltered Cuban cigarette in his mouth, he asks Jasper if he happens to have a lighter. Jasper doesn't. Dundo chimes in, "I don't smoke." Jasper finds it curious that Dundo, a lifelong tobacco farmer, does not smoke. Fortunately for the smoker, another horseback rider pulls up to visit. He has matches.

The Cuban men, smokers and nonsmokers alike, pose for more pictures. They now have a question for Jasper: "Is that your [high-quality] bicycle?"

"Yyess," Jasper says. Hemming and hawing, he reverses course, though. "Ah, no, it really isn't."

Jasper's mind flashes back to the day he rented the 50cc motorbike and first met the tobacco men. He'd left his Minnesota driver's license in Guatemala, but the government motorbike agent in Cuba told him not to worry. "But if a police officer stops you and asks for your driver's license," the agent added, "pretend you don't understand Spanish."

This time, Jasper is supposed to pretend he owns the bicycle. What will he be asked to pretend next time, he wonders.

"You should buy a place around here; it's legal now," are the tobacco farmers' parting words. "We have beautiful views, as you can see. Don't wait 10 years to come again. We'll roast a pig and throw a Cuban party you'll never forget."

The next time he visits Cuba, Jasper will pack today's pictures and a camera. And he'll have a fresh reason to rent a motorbike or nice bicycle and ride into tobacco country.

A Cent Well Spent
MARCH 15, 2018

I'm in Cuba again this year—my dozenth time. On a peninsula in the city of Cienfuegos, I'm about to hop aboard municipal Bus No. 1. I figure it will whisk me uneventfully the 17 blocks to an 1819 Cuban downtown.

Later, I'll return to the 1950s Southern California–style Casa Juanchi in Cuban suburbia. Juan Sanchez and his wife Norma park a white 1957 Chevrolet in the driveway. The car's been in the family for

60 years. My spacious bedroom—with exquisite midcentury furnishings—faces an aquarium- and bird-stocked backyard. On a bench here, among birds, I once read Gabriel García Márquez's *One Hundred Years of Solitude.*

Might I find a few minutes of solitude on this bus ride? A few minutes will be telling.

Through the bus windows on the left—far across the Caribbean bay—I observe three oil-refinery smokestacks belch a by-product or two of crude oil that steams in by tanker from Venezuela, Russia, Algeria, and Iran—and never from Houston.

While I am correct about the general direction of Bus No. 1, it is in no hurry, detouring off the classy Calle 37 marine drive that begins near the peninsula's tip. The bus carries us through a workaday neighborhood and past the Cienfuegos Elefantes baseball stadium. This stadium is where Cienfuegos-born Yasiel Puig played Cuban ball—he's now a sometimes-phenomenal outfielder for the Los Angeles Dodgers, the reigning National League champions. He was known locally to have a quirky personality, a view now shared by some across the *Grandes Ligas*—Big Leagues.

Hopping on the bus are many peppy passengers from three younger generations, who'd spent this Sunday afternoon at the beach park on the peninsula tip, Punta Gorda. They're now on their way back to their neighborhoods, if not yet to the doors of their homes. Those on the afternoon outings faced a strong north wind "from the Continent" (being North America) that lowered the temperature noticeably—three or four degrees—almost instantaneously.

More ride seekers flood on at each stop. The voices, louder by the kilometer, fill the few remaining air pockets. Music louder than the voices blares—until the driver orders young riders to lower the volume on their boombox. One could ride Buses No. 1 through 50 in most of the world's cities and not be treated to this Sunday's cacophony, I tell myself.

New thrill seekers squeeze aboard through the rear door by me, not paying the fare. Lumbering up through the back door, too, is a young couple carrying a large midcentury-style baby stroller. It fits in crosswise at the extreme back of the bus—except I'm now standing with my back pressed against the rear window.

Looking down at the stroller in front of me, I see no hint of anyone inside, for a fresh fabric bordered in white lace lies atop the unseen child. (The fabric is protection against feared diseases mosquitoes transmit, I later learn, though Cuba arms door-to-door attack teams with fumigation equipment and fumes.)

Within a few minutes, the mother seems to ask me to perform some task at the foot of the stroller. Among all the passengers, only I am in a position to reach it, and yes, only I (and possibly the baby) are sometimes confounded by the peculiarities of Cuban Spanish. (A Cuban remarked yesterday that Cuban Spanish is a "disaster." Some who see me flailing in a disaster zone come to the rescue.)

I bend over toward the foot of the stroller, stretching my arm gently downward. I notice a wooden clothespin holding the fabric to the stroller frame. Now touching the clothespin, the mother encouraging me on, I release it. Standing at the head of the stroller, the mother slowly pulls back the covering over her precious, beautiful baby for all whose necks can crane to see.

The father stands beside the mother. He bends over and puts his face upside down to the baby's, a connection the baby does not want broken. The mom or dad, not a stranger from afar like me, surely belongs in the one-person spot I occupy alongside the wide-eyed baby. I nudge sideways bit by bit toward the rear door.

I don't know where, *if anywhere*, the route of Bus No. 1 will end —I might stay on and be treated to 100 years of solitude intermittently broken by cacophony. I'm not sure that I want to pursue that future, so a minute later, I step out into a downtown that is a mere 199 years old.

A thought goes through my head as my feet hit the pavement: *That trip was worth the one-cent fare!*

----○

El Café del Viente Pasos, or The Twenty-Step Coffee
MARCH 3, 2018

I've returned to the village of Santo Domingo along the River Yara in the mountains of Cuba.[13] For years, I bedded down in a cabin whose door could not close at Casa Sierra Maestra. That shack is now history, and in its place sits a spacious, spanking new room. But conveniences some travelers take for granted—a TV, radio, telephone, alarm clock, water hotter than lukewarm—are all in a future that hasn't yet arrived.

A bit later, I'm at the *casa* of my friend Yorbanis Viltres Mejía. I'm sitting at his two-person kitchen table, gazing out through open Brazilian wood shutters at the lush gardens, steep above the Rio Yara. Yorbanis, a well-known character in some of my stories, has not yet been consigned to the annals of history; nor have critics' wild supposition that he might be a fictional figure been proven. But don't be too surprised if someday he appears in a graphic novel.

Yorbanis is *real* and will soon serve me the cup of coffee I've been waiting two years for. It's *his* coffee, in that he pulled from rich soil 200 Arabica coffee seedlings growing haphazardly from unpicked beans at a mountain *cafetal*, and carried these seedlings to his premises for replanting. And now, short years later, he crushes beans from maturing trees with a wooden mortar made from a hollowed-out tree trunk, thence brewing the coffee in his particular manner.

Unmentioned here are all the steps in between, so that we can get right to one of my two questions: "Yorbanis, of all you know about the many steps needed to produce coffee, what percentage did you learn yourself, and what percentage did you learn from others, or from books or classes?"

---

[13] Adventures in these mountains are also described in *The Other Worlds,* on pp. 17–37.

Yorbanis explains that, most of what he knows, he's learned from *sabiduría popular*—folk wisdom passed down through generations, including his grandparents. He's learned from experience, too, especially sun-drying beans on the road that runs past his hand-built cabin up to Fidel Castro's still elusive command center from 1958. Other times, he dries beans on the soil in his yard, giving the coffee flavor a hint of *la tierra*—the earth. Experience has also taught him how to roast the beans in a pot over a small wood fire.

When pressed, Yorbanis says 80 percent of what he knows, he's absorbed from sabiduría popular, while 20 percent he's learned himself.

"Yorbanis," I remark, "the 38,000 different products in a Minnesota supermarket have traveled an average of 1,100 miles to get there—and some travel half full of preservatives and other chemicals. A study at Iowa State University revealed that the various ingredients in strawberry yogurt sold in Des Moines supermarkets travel a total distance of 2,216 miles. So, how far did the beans for the coffee you're brewing travel from the trees to your kitchen?"

Yorbanis seems to be calculating the distance in his head (unlike the Iowa State analysts at the Leopold Center for Sustainable Agriculture). Within a few seconds, he answers: "*Veinte pasos*"—20 steps. Not one of these 20 steps goes *up* into his house, for the house floor is just an inch above his yard. He or his friend Marbelia sweep any in-blown debris right out either door. Chickens are predilected to walk right in, as is a visitor from Minnesota.

Meanwhile, I've offered to search for new guitar strings for Yorbanis's three-string and acoustic guitars when I visit the cities of Bayamo, Sancti Spiritus, Trinidad, Cienfuegos, Havana, and Santa Clara. I wonder how many steps that will take—20, 2,000, or perhaps 20,000?

The Boy Who Saw It All
JANUARY 2020

The boy lived in the mountain village of Santo Domingo. He had a ringside seat to history. He was not yet nine years old. But there he was!

He observed the one-time law student from a land-rich family, who now led a revolution among *campesinos*, urban workers, and students. And he watched the personable, one-time doctor who had joined the revolution—even though he was a foreigner from Argentina.

The boy had a good vantage point for watching and listening—for he lived with his grandfather Lucas. His grandfather risked everything by inviting the revolutionaries into his house, arming them with information about the mountain terrain and logistics, and funneling mule-load after midnight mule-load of food and medical supplies to the growing rebel army based in a secret hideaway up the steep mountains.

The fight—against all odds—pitted the rebels and their supporters within the population against a corrupt dictator and his powerful army and air force. The village became a dangerous place to live. Many villagers—the boy among them—fled, hiding in a mountain cave for weeks. When the boy returned to the village, he found the tortured body of his grandfather, Lucas, with bayonet punctures throughout his torso.

Others survived to fight another day. One was the revolutionary leader, who had sometimes slept overnight at the boy's house. He was Fidel Castro. Another was the physician-turned-revolutionary, Che Guevara.

If you have read the first volume of my adventures, you may feel you know the boy, whose name is Juan Gonzalez Castillo.[14] In fact, Juan and his wife Maria extended an invitation to President Barack Obama and his family to visit their home, days before the president

---

[14] Juan was a central character in the stories of Cuba published in *The Other Worlds: Offbeat Adventures of a Curious Traveler*, which includes some of the author's journeys in Cuba; North, Central and South America; Asia; and London.

made his historic visit to Cuba.[15] The invitation to the president was offered in "Advance Man," the author's spontaneous, yet detailed, report about the track the president ought to follow through Cuba to get the best and most enjoyable adventure of his presidency. It even included a Top Secret/Eyes Only map.[16]

Recognizing that the president may be "engrossed in other causes" and unable to reach the mountain village in the following couple years, the author resolved that he would interview Juan himself and produce a gripping historical microdocumentary.

Did I, the one-time advance man, keep that promise? Yes, I did. Juan Gonzalez Castillo, his son Miguel Gonzalez Garcia, and I sat for hours plumbing Juan's fascinating memories in April 2019. I later committed it to "film"—just in case you or Barack Obama never make it to Santo Domingo and have a chance to hear Juan's stories firsthand, before they disappear with him.[17]

How I Got into America from Cuba
MAY 12, 2014

In Miami, the US immigration officer and I take turns clutching my passport. I try not to think about how shifty-eyed and fidgety I must look. Upon my departure from Cuba, an immigration officer in Havana had accidentally stamped one of the pages with "CUBA." It was 6:30 a.m., and perhaps that officer was not fully awake yet. Due to decades of US restrictions on American citizens keen to travel to our

---

[15] *The Other Worlds*, 36.

[16] Ibid., 25–37.

[17] Slimmed down portions of the video, *Eyewitness to a Revolution at Age Eight*, may be viewed by checking out the author's blog at www.TomsGlobe.com. An English-only, Spanish-only, or bilingual DVD is available by inquiring at the website's Contact button. And check out a three-minute YouTube clip about Juan's family, through the link on the website blog page; it is Episode 4 of "Tom Mattson's Virtual World Tour: Cuba's Santo Domingo Village." For more background and family photos, check the December 2019 photo-blog on the website.

southeasterly neighbor, Cuban officers typically know not to stamp American passports so their holders can go back home without facing uncomfortable questions.

So, as I hand over my passport in Miami, I am nervous. Luckily, I am also well prepared. For that, I can thank moviemaker Francis Ford Coppola, who owns a resort in Belize. I'd flown from Cuba to Mexico, and then made a side trip to Belize, for the first time in my life. I parked my rental vehicle at the beautiful tropical grounds of the director's resort, wandered the gardens, and paid a visit to the bar. During a friendly discussion with the bartender, I asked this Coppola employee to play the role of immigration officer in Miami, where I was soon headed. The bartender, a fan of "Mr. Coppola's" movies, was more than happy —and, it turns out, skilled—to oblige. He demanded that I answer tough questions about whether I (a patriotic American) had visited Cuba. He also warned that the nice officer I might first encounter at the immigration booth may be a prequel to a tough officer sitting in a back office. The bartender kindly played both roles.

But perhaps the immigration officer in Miami is as sleepy as his colleague in Havana. Or perhaps this is my lucky day. Sometimes US Immigration asks me what countries I have visited, but the Miami officer doesn't. They often flip through my passport, glancing at the stamps. He doesn't. They usually look at my answers on the immigration form to questions like "What countries did you visit?" He doesn't. If he had, he might've noticed that the form does not give multicountry travelers like me enough space to list each and every last little country, especially if the traveler, like me, happens to have writ large.

If you need to practice for similar situations sometime, stop in for a drink at Mr. Coppola's Blancaneaux Lodge in Belize. No problem being sweaty and nervous: the overhead fan will keep you cool—the very same fan from the opening scenes of *Apocalypse Now*, according to your bartender/immigration officer(s)/accomplice.

I may visit Blancaneaux again, since I'm planning to return to Cuba—and more than once. You and I may meet at Blancaneaux, where the bartender will teach Americans who've recently visited Cuba an in-your-face course titled, "How to Get into America from Cuba."

A JOURNEY
IN AFRICA

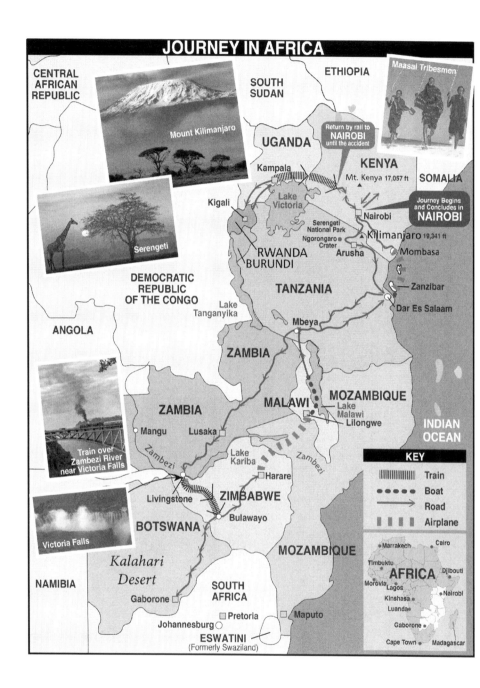

JOURNEY IN AFRICA

CENTRAL AFRICAN REPUBLIC

SOUTH SUDAN

ETHIOPIA

Maasai Tribesmen

Mount Kilimanjaro

UGANDA

KENYA

Return by rail to NAIROBI until the accident

Kampala

Mt. Kenya 17,057 ft

SOMALIA

Kigali

Lake Victoria

Nairobi

Journey Begins and Concludes in NAIROBI

Serengeti

Serengeti National Park

Kilimanjaro 19,341 ft

Mombasa

RWANDA
BURUNDI

Ngorongaro Crater

Arusha

Zanzibar

DEMOCRATIC REPUBLIC OF THE CONGO

TANZANIA

Dar Es Salaam

Lake Tanganyika

ANGOLA

Mbeya

INDIAN OCEAN

ZAMBIA

MOZAMBIQUE

ZAMBIA

MALAWI

Lake Malawi

Mangu

Lusaka

Lilongwe

Train over Zambezi River near Victoria Falls

Zambezi

Lake Kariba

Zambezi

KEY

Train

Harare

Boat

Livingstone

ZIMBABWE

Road

Airplane

Victoria Falls

BOTSWANA

Bulawayo

MOZAMBIQUE

Marrakech

Cairo

Kalahari Desert

Timbuktu

Djibouti

AFRICA

NAMIBIA

Morovia

Lagos

Nairobi

Gaborone

SOUTH AFRICA

Kinshasa

Luanda

Pretoria

Maputo

Gaborone

Johannesburg

ESWATINI
(Formerly Swaziland)

Cape Town

Madagascar

A JOURNEY IN AFRICA

Mr. Thomas Mattson
. . . Berkeley, California
USA.

Dear Sir,   25-1-1979.

With reference to your letter of 27th December 1978, we would advise that our India/Africa passenger service has long since been discontinued. We regret that we are therefore unable to furnish you with any information.

Yours faithfully,
Mackinnon MacKenzie & Co. LTD.,
V.M.Kothare
As Agents For
P&O Steam Navigation Company
Bombay, India

Thwarted in my dream of "steamer India to Africa," I failed to set foot on that continent in 1979. Not until 1986 would it be feet and steps in Africa, by virtue of a cheap London to Kenya air ticket via the Moscow and Cairo airports.

Let's move to Africa now.

Kenya and Uganda: A Spectacular Introduction to a Beautiful Continent

Low-budget safaris at Kenya's equator and later in Tanzania's Serengeti open my eyes to a fact little-known to me: zoos don't even begin to portray animals in their natural habitat. How can so many different kinds of animals mix together at random? And they roam with no fence within any land-bound or airborne animal's eyesight! The number and variety of deer-like creatures alone knocks my socks off.

One evening, we see that no one attends to a giraffe hobbled by a serious leg injury. A lion, the continent's primary predator, always thinks twice about attacking an adult giraffe because the giraffe—though lacking claws and sharp antlers—can kill a lion with one kick to the head. The limping giraffe we see at dusk, though, will likely be devoured by dawn.

As my feet step on the soil of the Rift Valley here in East Africa, little do I know that my ancestors, and those of the five billion other people alive today, may have lived right here 60,000 to 70,000 years ago —part of a population of perhaps just 10,000. Thus, without knowing it at the time, I am likely the first person in my matrilineal or patrilineal line to set foot in Africa since my early ancestors walked, boated, or rafted out of Africa to the Arabian peninsula about 60,000 years ago. It would not be until the 21st century that I'd learn major details of my "deep ancestry."[18]

• • •

Within days, I find myself in Uganda, Kenya's neighbor to the north. Dictator Idi Amin has recently been ousted. The Air France jetliner highjacked in 1976 with its 248 passengers is still on the tarmac at the

---

[18] Analysis of the author's DNA by *National Geographic's* Genographic Project is the basis for "A Brief History of Traveling Genes." This story is found in *The Other Worlds: Offbeat Adventures of a Curious Traveler*. A map of the circuitous ancestral journey from Africa to Finland (and on to Minnesota's Iron Range) appears in that book (pp. 240–41), as well as on www.TomsGlobe.com, where it's in wondrous color.

Entebbe airport, never moved since Israeli Defense Force commandos ended that hostage crisis. The jet is not a tourist attraction, though. Only later would books be written and movies made about that nail-biting tale.[19]

In Uganda, I hope to obtain a visa for neighboring Rwanda. I've planned to visit some of our relatives in the wild—gorillas and chimpanzees. But learning it would take quite some time to get the visa, I return from the border town to Kampala, Uganda's capital. The city is short on hotel rooms. A student, very light skinned, befriends me and helps me search for a vacant room.

We wander about the city in the evening. My friend introduces me as his "father" to his acquaintance, who turns to me and asks, "Are you his father?" I could say "no" and make my friend out to be untruthful, or say "yes" and tell a lie. I give a fuzzy, noncommittal answer and manage to leave it at that. I wonder if that "son" of mine has ever met his father, perhaps a foreigner, and felt he had a father for a day.

It's now time to head back to Kenya, where I've stowed belongings that I might need in India and countries that would follow. The best way to travel from Kampala to Nairobi, I hear, is by train. And doesn't everyone love an overnight train journey? This one, though, is not to end as expected.

Sitting in our seats in early evening, a couple of sharp bumps jolt all of us before we come to a fast stop. People stand up, walk around, and even get off, though we are not in any town. The locomotive, which I can see since I am now walking alongside the train, is lying on its side. A truck (or "lorry," as they call it here) has been crushed while crossing the tracks. Someone murmurs that the engineer and the truck driver are in the wreckage and are both dead.

Not seeing any injured person, I snap pictures of the wreckage on the inexpensive camera I travel with. Young men who tell me they

---

[19] See, for example, the book by Saul David, *Operation Thunderbolt: The Entebbe Raid— The Most Audacious Hostage Rescue Mission in History* (New York City: Little, Brown and Company, 2015).

work for the railroad accost me. They order me to march down the railroad tracks to a town a mile away. They follow. Now I'm standing across a counter and facing officers in what seems to be a county sheriff's headquarters. I stick my hand in my pocket, hoping to open the camera to expose and ruin the film. Since the camera is new, I fail to execute my plan. I am given a new order: "Follow me!" I'm led into the corner office and instructed to sit down across from what appears to be the county sheriff.

When he finds out I am from the United States of America, I immediately find out a little about his life. "I went to the United States," the sheriff tells me. "I visited Los Angeles. We drove to Nevada on the freeway. The United States has the greatest expressways! I enjoyed visiting your country."

The sheriff calls for a lieutenant. I must follow him. "Hurry!" I hear and step up my pace—but realize it is the sheriff's order to the lieutenant. This time, I won't have to walk. Police officers open the back door of an American-sized automobile that then motors me back to the accident site. I plan to stay overnight on the train, but an American hospital nurse who lives nearby and heard the train smash the lorry strikes up a conversation. He invites me to stay at his place. He says he can take me all the way to Nairobi the next day, where he is going anyway.

The next morning, I enjoy a car ride to Nairobi, the first time in a couple months I am in a private automobile. Eager to see how my accident pictures turn out, I find a Woolworth's store and leave my roll of film to be developed. As I walk the streets, it occurs to me that the store personnel will see my photos of the crash, which is now on the front page of the newspaper but without photos. Will they call the police? I hurry back. My developed photos are ready for me, with no police around nor, apparently, on their way. Whew! I didn't want to get hauled to a police station twice in different parts of the country for the same photos.

Before long, I'm off to neighboring Tanzania—by bus.[20] This time, no one tells me the best way to travel in these parts is by train. And doesn't everyone love an overnight bus journey?

Tanzania by Day and Night

In the vast savannah plains of the Serengeti, two million wildebeest, as well as hundreds of thousands of gazelles and zebras, migrate every year, seeking fresh grazing and, perhaps, better quality water. Lions, leopards, cheetahs, hyenas, and wild dogs follow, seeking meat. Other land animals also call this ecosystem home, as do 500 species of birds.

Here, too, is the 2,000-foot-deep Ngorongaro Crater, formed by an exploding volcano that collapsed on itself. Nowadays, when the spectacularly lush rainy season unfolds in February and March, wildebeest arrive at the crater to give birth.

I'm out of Tanzania's Serengeti to the city of Arusha, and then in a back-row seat on an all-night bus—soon passing sunset-draped Mt. Kilimanjaro. A sharp jolt from a pothole every twenty seconds, all night long, limits my sleep to a dozen 10-second spells. Stretching outside and buying gum and candy from a boy at a 2 a.m. stop is the only relief.

The bus lets me off, with my limbs gummed up, early in the morning. As I open my eyes, I find I'm in Dar es Salaam (meaning "Abode of Peace," in Arabic). I'll return later, but now I'm just passing through. I buy a bus ticket for Lusaka, Zambia.

Zambia's Eternal Downpours

The sky is a sunshine-brilliant blue. The downpour is mighty, though this rain does not come from the sky.

---

[20] Follow the author's African journey through seven countries on the map at pages page 130, and shown in color at www.TomsGlobe.com.

A minute earlier, each drop had been one of trillions in the tranquil Zambezi River that separates Zambia and Zimbabwe in southern Africa. Every drop in the sunny-day downpour suddenly—and quite violently—left the peaceful Zambezi and became part of the largest curtain of falling water in the world. The water hits the bottom of Victoria Falls with such a thunderous force that millions of drops rocket back up. Once they clear the top by 15 feet, they shower down on anyone standing, dumbfounded, on a lush trail along the cliff's edge. Among the delighted and dumbfounded were a brother and sister from Lusaka, and me. We enjoyed the eternal downpour so much together that we later exchanged letters still marveling about it.

Does it ever stop raining? I don't know—I just hope it pours forever on every traveler who wanders the mind-blowing trail in the future.

Southern Africa by Steam Locomotive and Bus

Just inside Zimbabwe from Zambia, a steam locomotive—on its last legs—powers hundreds of passengers halfway across the country to Bulawayo. The road out of Bulawayo to the southwest leads to Botswana. I jump on a bus heading in that direction. Within hours, I can see from Gaborone, Botswana's capital, the hills of apartheid South Africa, only a few miles away. I am tempted to go in that direction, but if "South Africa" were stamped in my passport, a number of strongly disapproving neighboring countries would bar me entry or reentry. Nelson Mandela has been imprisoned in South Africa for the last 24 years. He is serving a life sentence for advocating the end of the brutal apartheid system of racial oppression.[21]

To the west of Gaborone lies the second biggest desert in Africa, the Kalahari. Purists argue that it's not actually a desert, since it enjoys

[21] Nelson Mandela would remain imprisoned for another four years—and released only after decades of condemnation by the world's protesters and certain governments, and fears of a civil war. In 1994, he became the first president of South Africa to be democratically elected. He served as president for five years, and in retirement remained an active advocate for justice. He died in 2013 at the age of 95.

a bit too much rainfall—five to 10 inches a year. I'm told that the Kalahari is home to mammals like the oryx, leopard, and cheetah, many birds of prey, and the hoodia cactus—used by the San people for thousands of years to ease hunger and thirst.

As I sit in a Gaborone café, I overhear a conversation about "CIA" —apparently, I might be one of its agents. Elsewhere, I am told that the CIA likely dropped the AIDS virus on Africa from above.

In a bar, I am treated to a long evening's conversation by two Brits. They own a four-wheel-drive vehicle, good to make the several-thousand-mile journey north to Egypt. It seems they need a third person —me—and I am welcome (as long as I understand they are smuggling diamonds). Perhaps the diamonds are from the new, open-pit Jwaneng Mine, 75 miles to the west. It's the richest diamond mine in the world. But I don't pry.

On that journey, which could end in death on a highway or life in prison for all three of us, I opt not to go. Instead, I jump on a diamond-free bus bound for Zimbabwe.

Zimbabwe's Celebratory Day

Pulsing through the air of Zimbabwe's capital, Harare, is the jubilant excitement of a celebration about to begin. One and all are invited to the soccer stadium for the sixth anniversary of independence declared on April 18, 1980, following 90 years of British colonial rule and a period of renegade white segregationist rule. Robert Mugabe is president. Amid police sirens, a VIP visitor—Palestine Liberation Organization Chairman Yasser Arafat—is escorted through town. On the soccer field, two Zimbabwean brothers invite me to climb the stadium steps. High above the field, I sit, yell, laugh, and cheer with them for the independence that was so long in the coming.

A Restless Night Atop Bulky Cargo

A short flight from Zimbabwe over Mozambique lands near Lilongwe in Malawi. A good way to move farther north, my Lonely Planet guidebook tells me, is to hop on an overnight boat traveling most of the length of 2,300-foot-deep Lake Malawi, the southernmost in the East African rift system and the ninth largest in the world. A student heading home on vacation shows me the best place to sleep—under African stars on a canvas covering mounds of bulky cargo. Disembarking at 6 a.m. in Nkhata Bay, we are lucky to find a room for a couple hours of the kind of shuteye I grew up on.

The student now heads to his home an hour's bus ride away. My two-month journey in Africa will end in a week. I'll be in Nairobi in just a few days to pick up stowed belongings before I fly to India and onward around the world. Meanwhile, I'll head to Africa's coast along the Indian Ocean.

The Vibrations of Zanzibar

Once back in Dar es Salaam, Tanzania's capital, I like the sound of "Zanzibar Island." Zanzibar is a semi-autonomous state, having joined with Tanganyika in 1964 to create Tanzania. The islands of this Indian Ocean archipelago are famed for cloves, cinnamon, nutmeg, and black pepper.

I'll be assisted on my spur-of-the-moment voyage to Zanzibar Island, a man on the Dar es Salaam pier tells me, since his wife is traveling on the same boat to her birthplace. She'll accompany me and help if I have questions.

Each of us passengers sleeps on our backs, side-by-side, on the wooden deck. I'm not wise enough to keep my legs straight all night, and when I bend my knees, I lose the space where the knee-to-toe segments of my body had nicely laid. Other voyageurs' body parts nudge into that precious space and hold tight—until I finally manage to reacquire the territory in the wee hours.

On the Zanzibar dock in the morning, I bid adieu to the good Samaritan who'd given me a tip on a good spot on the deck to sleep and occasional updates on the progress of our trip. Very soon, two brothers befriend me. With my ready acquiescence, they lead me to their house, where I sit with their family around a coffee table. When I finish the cold bottle of Coke they give me, they offer another. I decline. No family member takes a sip of anything, not even water. It is daylight, and this is Ramadan.

One of us now refreshed, the brothers and I explore their corner of Zanzibar for hours. We wander Zanzibar's Stone Town, the best-preserved testament of the old Swahili culture—a mixture of East African peoples and the Arab traders who once sailed along these shores. It was in this enclave, I learn, that thousands of slaves were sold. In the years that followed, the brothers and I exchanged a few letters. One was to be wed, and I imagine the festivities were an event for a lifetime in that Zanzibari family.

Overshadowed by Maasai Tribesmen

A short flight carries me from Zanzibar to Mombasa on the Kenyan coast, 150 miles north of Zanzibar and 200 miles south of Somalia. After two days, I purchase a bus ticket to Nairobi. Once aboard, I find a man sitting in my assigned seat. Within seconds, I learn I won't have to deal with this problem myself. Three very tall young men sitting around my seat examine my ticket and his. They inform him that he's correct about the seat number, but he's wrong about the bus. He departs. I sit.

After sunset, our bus heads inland toward higher elevations. The three tall guys share a mysterious substance. They chew—and invite me to chew too. Why not, I think.

The darkness extends everywhere around our fast bus on the lonely highway. The only lights are those of a periodic oncoming vehicle. The four of us bob our heads into the aisle to engage those headlights—

time and again. It is the best entertainment around. We four are wide awake. Everyone else is fast asleep.

I don't ask my three companions what we are chewing. And why would I care? Later, when I become more knowledgeable, I conclude it must be *khat*, a flowering evergreen shrub native to East Africa and the Arabian Peninsula. It contains an amphetamine-like stimulant that may, says Wikipedia, cause "excitement, loss of appetite, and euphoria."

The next morning at dawn, the four of us—three towering over the fourth one—climb down from the bus. We're in Nairobi, Kenya's capital. I'll stay a couple days, but the three of them are not yet home. They'll soon take another bus to visit their families in Kenya's highlands, having worked in hotels on the coast performing tribal dances in traditional attire for tourists.

At a breakfast restaurant, the eyes of other customers focus on our table. Others watch, too, as we mill about town. Yes, three are dark skinned and one is white. People are not looking at me, though, and don't seem to find a white guy with three Africans curious. Rather, the capital city residents focus on my companions. Why? They are still dressed in their traditional red "shuka" robes and wear multicolored, intricate tribal necklaces, as well as wrist and ankle bracelets. They probably don't change to Western dress for anyone. They also carry long sticks. They are Maasai, a semi-nomadic people and one of the tallest ethnic groups in the world.

Thus would end a two-month trip in 1986, from Uganda north of the equator almost to the Tropic of Capricorn in Botswana. I still want to go back to the birth continent of all our ancestors, explore the endless gems it has to offer and meet many a person more.

EXPLORING AMERICA BY MOTORCYCLE

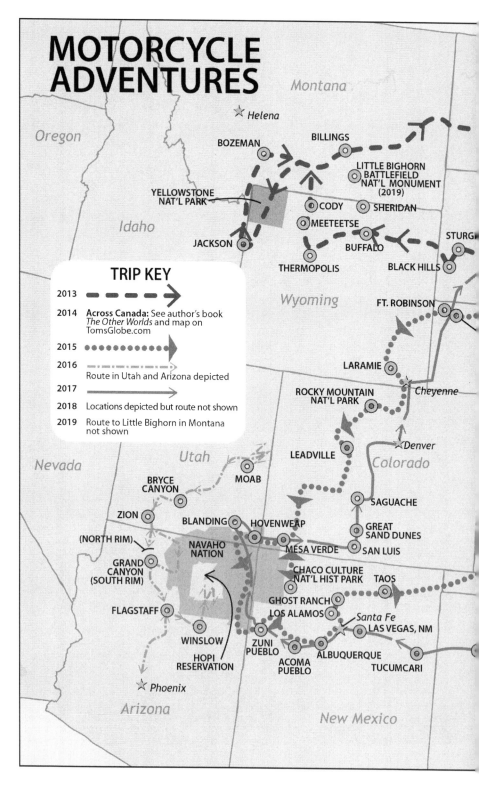

MOTORCYCLE ADVENTURES

Montana

☆ Helena

Oregon

BOZEMAN

BILLINGS

LITTLE BIGHORN BATTLEFIELD NAT'L MONUMENT (2019)

YELLOWSTONE NAT'L PARK

Idaho

CODY

SHERIDAN

MEETEETSE

JACKSON

BUFFALO

STURG[...]

THERMOPOLIS

BLACK HILLS

TRIP KEY

2013	➤ ➤ ➤
2014	**Across Canada:** See author's book *The Other Worlds* and map on TomsGlobe.com
2015	●●●●●●●●● ➤
2016	·—·—·—·—➤ Route in Utah and Arizona depicted
2017	——————➤
2018	Locations depicted but route not shown
2019	Route to Little Bighorn in Montana not shown

Wyoming

FT. ROBINSON

LARAMIE

Cheyenne

ROCKY MOUNTAIN NAT'L PARK

☆ Denver

Nevada

Utah

LEADVILLE

Colorado

BRYCE CANYON

MOAB

ZION

BLANDING

HOVENWEAP

SAGUACHE

(NORTH RIM)

NAVAHO NATION

GREAT SAND DUNES

GRAND CANYON (SOUTH RIM)

MESA VERDE

SAN LUIS

CHACO CULTURE NAT'L HIST PARK

TAOS

FLAGSTAFF

GHOST RANCH

LOS ALAMOS

Santa Fe

WINSLOW

ZUNI PUEBLO

LAS VEGAS, NM

HOPI RESERVATION

ACOMA PUEBLO

ALBUQUERQUE

TUCUMCARI

☆ Phoenix

Arizona

New Mexico

MOTORCYCLE ADVENTURES OF 2013

Not realizing I was capable of riding a motorcycle a thousand miles into the American West, I never made a plan to go. It felt overwhelming. One wintry day, though, an elderly woman in the Mesabi Family YMCA whirlpool told me she and her husband had traveled through the West on their motorcycle. And they loved it!

"What was your favorite place?" I inquired.

"We liked South Dakota and Montana," she replied.

Visions of a motorcycle adventure like that popped into my head that November afternoon. I'd often ride dozens of miles from home, and even 300 miles south to a friend's farm to sit on a tractor. Now I could go west, I started to believe. Yes, I *will* go west!

The next autumn, on my first trip, I wrote home about experiences I'd never have had but for a winter encounter in the whirlpool.

The Cowboy You Meet on the Next Stool
SEPTEMBER 2, 2013

It's Labor Day. Yesterday, after winding for hours through the Black Hills of South Dakota, I rolled over beautiful hills at 70 or 80 miles an hour to Buffalo, Wyoming. I woke up this morning in a hotel opened in the 1880s. The name of the place? Occidental Hotel.

• • •

"Ernest Hemingway wrote part of *Farewell to Arms* in your room," the desk clerk informs me in the morning. I'd picked that room not because I dreamed of a destiny as a writer, but because the room's back door opens just above a furiously fast, ice-cold stream.

It isn't coincidental that many a character have stayed at the Occidental. Calamity Jane drove freight wagons on the Bozeman Trail that ran out front. Robert LeRoy Parker and Harry Longabaugh (Butch Cassidy and the Sundance Kid) rode in from their hideout—I forgot to ask which of these names they checked in under. Presidents Theodore Roosevelt and Herbert Hoover also found the Occidental to their liking. Buffalo Bill Cody visited. None other than Owen Wister based characters in his celebrated novel, *The Virginian*, on gunslingers and cowboys he observed in the saloon and lobby.

So, I'll base this story on a character I meet in the Busy Bee Cafe at the Occidental.

• • •

I order a buffalo burger from my stool, all tables being occupied. I share the buffalo with a man I believe to be a cowboy who's just finished his meal on the next stool and still seems hungry as a horse.

If you're riding west and find a cowboy on the stool next to you, follow a tradition traceable to the 1870s: converse. This particular one doesn't live here in Wyoming but drove this way for a rodeo near Sheridan.

"Drove a pickup, right?" Surely I can't go wrong with this.

"No, I have a car," he answers.

"Do you like rodeos?" I inquire.

"I *love* rodeos," he wants me to know.

"Where are you from?" I ask.

"Polson, Montana. It's 12 hours away," he explains. "But I work on a ranch a couple hours from here."

"What's it like on the ranch?" I wonder.

"I'm the only ranch hand for the owner," he tells me. "The owner can't ride a horse very long at a stretch anymore. His kids have all left. They don't want that life. We've got 9,000 acres and lease 9,000 more from the government. We've got about 300 head of beef cattle."

"Do you keep the cattle in the barn in the winter?"

"No, they're outside. I ride a horse to check on them and round them up. A four-wheeler or a pickup wouldn't work on the terrain."

"Do you have more than one horse to ride?"

"We have a lot of horses. I ride five different ones. In the summer, the owner leases other horses to dude ranches. We get them back in the winter."

"When you pick one of the five horses to ride for the day, do the other horses feel bad?"

"Hmm, that could be," my new Montana friend says, "but more often, the one I'm on would like to turn around right away and go back to be with his pals. He misses them."

"Does anything else keep you busy on that 18,000-acre ranch?" I'm itching to know.

"I do all the mechanical. Our well distributes water to quite a few tanks. Each cow drinks 20 gallons of water a day, times 300 cows, that would be . . . (as he borrows the cashier's calculator) 6,000 gallons a day. I checked on the water before I left, and I gotta drive back tonight. It would be bad if there's no water. Something goes wrong with the pumps and the system a lot."

"Where do you get drinking water?" I query, since I now dream that I'm an Owen Wister dying to draw an original picture of a cowboy.

"It runs off the roof into a buried cistern," he says. "We use a hand pump in the kitchen, and it comes right up. When I go to town, like today, I have to load up on supplies."

"What do you do about eggs and bread when you run out?"

"We have chickens. And I've been baking bread for a year."

"Do you have neighbors?"

"Yes. Three within 10 miles. There's no town within 50 miles, and the 50 miles are gravel."

After a glance out the window, he laments, "Oh, look, it's dark already!"

"You gotta drive two hours?" I ask.

"Yes. I'm used to it, but I'm also used to going to bed early. It's already 9 o'clock."

"So you're a cowboy!" I say.

"Well, hmm, yeah," he answers.

We still have a minute for me to wonder what in the world he does at night 50 miles of gravel away from a one-horse town. "Like, do you have TV?"

"Yeah, but I think it's broke. I haven't turned it on for a long time. I read; have you heard of Dean Koontz? I play the guitar and sing. Sometimes I visit one of those neighbors who lives a few miles away."

"Do you have cell phone service?" I'm keen to know.

"It's not good from the house, but in some places on the ranch, it works."

"Well, Kerry"—we finally asked each other's names—"I can text you sometime."

"Yes, I like to text."

"Hey, Kerry, let's go out on Main Street. I'll show you my motorcycle." Outside we go.

"Can I sit on your Harley?" Kerry asks.

"Sure," I tell him.

He gets on. I feel he must be imagining riding day after day through his own American West.

But he surprises me: "Gee, I wouldn't want to ride this."

"Why not?"

"I think it would be dangerous," says the man who rides horses over rough terrain every day.

Then Kerry heads home, traveling the last 50 miles on gravel, getting to a place where he has three neighbors within 10 miles.

I sit here in Ernest Hemingway's old room—the back door opened to the roaring river Hemingway heard too. I believe Theodore Roosevelt, Herbert Hoover, Butch, Sundance, Jane, Ernest—not to mention Owen Wister and his entire cast of Western characters—would have enjoyed the stool next to Kerry, each in their own time.

Calamity Jane might entice hardworking and serious Kerry into driving wagons on the Bozeman Trail all the way to—ah, Bozeman, circa 1880.

Kerry's example might, I feel, lead Butch and his Wild Bunch out of the Hole in the Wall and onto the straight and narrow before they could become any more famous. I'd wager that Kerry wouldn't be mesmerized by Mr. Cassidy's intelligence and charisma and pulled into the Bunch's string of wildly successful robberies. And as a Dean Koontz fan, Kerry might be thrilled to become a good friend of Ernest Hemingway's.

It's easy, too, to envision that Kerry's impression of Teddy Roosevelt might draw him into the Rough Riders charging up San Juan Hill in Cuba in 1898. After all, Roosevelt recruited law enforcement personnel, miners, college athletes—and cowboys—for his volunteer regiment.

And like it or not, Kerry might've ended up in Owen Wister's *The Virginian* as one of the two men—their six-shooters about to be drawn—facing off on a dusty street. It was "the first 'showdown' in fiction," Britannica reports.[22]

Tomorrow, Kerry will be riding the horse he chooses for the day. And I'll be riding in the opposite direction, over Powder River Pass at 9,666 feet, down through Ten Sleep Canyon in the Big Horn Mountains, and into Ten Sleep town itself. I'll park my 760-pound machine about the same time Kerry dismounts from his thousand-pound horse.

---

[22] Britannica, "*The Virginian*, novel by Wister," https://www.britannica.com/topic/The-Virginian-novel-by-Wister.

Gunfire in Saloons
SEPTEMBER 6, 2013

Yesterday, inching my way through Wyoming, I was entranced by petroglyphs etched in a stone-walled canyon. The place was incredibly remote; in fact, I was the only one there. Native peoples created the etchings over millennia—between 200 and 11,000 years ago. The boiling-hot canyon sits between the dinosaur town of Thermopolis, with its prehistoric hot springs, and Meeteetse.

I'd slotted Meeteetse for a 15-minute stop on my mental itinerary. But since I like bullet-riddled saloons—like the Cowboy Bar, where Butch Cassidy was once arrested—I ended up spending the night.

• • •

This evening, I find myself in downtown Cody. Buffalo Bill Cody built a hotel and saloon here at the turn of an earlier century. I've selected a stool halfway down the bar as if it were mine every night. This way, those on the shady side of the law won't get trigger happy with me, I figure.

"Did you put any of these bullet holes in the walls?" I inquire of the man to my right. I'm in the habit, it seems, of gettin' to know dudes sittin' on stools in Western saloons.

"No, but a good friend of mine did," he answers.

"A gunfight?" (That's obvious to me.)

"No, a party."

I'm a bit deflated. "I noticed bullet holes in the saloon down the road a piece in Meeteetse last night," I tell him.

"The same friend of mine put some of the bullet holes in that saloon," he fires back.

"A gunfight?" (Surely.)

"No, a party!"

I wonder aloud if the other drinkers were surprised by the gunfire or knew it was coming.

He smiles. "Some were surprised."

Half the time, I stare at the bullet holes and at the extraordinary wooden bar in front of us, listening all the while to my new friend-for-an-evening, who could be a cowpoke or, I tend to believe, a gunslinger. He notices me admiring the bar. He tells me one of his gun-toting pals claims that Queen Victoria commissioned the building of this bar in France. She sent it to Buffalo Bill as a gift, the story goes, after having immensely enjoyed "Buffalo Bill's Wild West" shows in England.

Today, a visitor to the Buffalo Bill Center of the West in Cody can watch the early, herky-jerky, black-and-white moving picture recordings of the Wild West Shows. And spend hours more in this museum, one of the greats in the American West.

Another special place in America is Cody's original townsite, where Old Trail Town now stands, in late 1800s glory. Dozens of log buildings, from cabins and livery stables to general stores and a school, were disassembled in Wyoming and Montana, and reassembled here. Spend some time in a saloon—without refreshments—where Butch Cassidy hung out! I'm wondering if he and his outlaw bunch partied it up and left the bullet holes in some of these buildings.

An Original Place on Earth
SEPTEMBER 11, 2013

My friend Lee Mattson from Seattle and I met yesterday and drove round and round through Yellowstone National Park. Much wilderness has been preserved forever. The 1988 fire that burned 36 percent of the park, though, is still evident. Yellowstone must be one of the two or three most amazing original places on earth. Nowhere else has such magnificent colors, bubbling hot liquid, and pungent smells coming right out of our planet. Much of it is more accessible than decades ago when my family visited the park on an exploratory road trip from Minnesota.

I savor every piece of it, as I remember that in a certain number of years, perhaps 100,000, the greatest volcanic eruption in recent geologic history could blow the entire region sky-high, raining volcanic ash for thousands of miles across North America.

Raw Blues, Tinge of Gospel, Smattering of . . .
SEPTEMBER 17, 2013

Early this morning, the west wind blows me out of Montana. A café in small town Driscoll, North Dakota, serves up a morning Russian pancake and sausage. The three businesses that still exist seem to outnumber the homes.

Late this afternoon, in the homestretch, I detour through downtown Fargo. I just want to take a peek at the end of the earth, so to speak, since my friend Steve Wroe once told me that his hometown of Fargo "is not the end of the earth, but you can see it from there."

The Fargo Theatre's grand marquee announces that musician Jonny Lang is performing tonight. Jonny sings "raw blues, a tinge of gospel, a smattering of soul, and a dose of rock 'n roll," according to an industry insider.

I saw him perform when I lived in Chicago in the '90s. At the box office on Fargo's main drag, I now snap up a remaining seat in the distant, upper back row. Now of Los Angeles but as a native of Fargo, Jonny could say, "I see Grandma and Grandpa in the audience!" He plays guitar nearly as intensely as Jimi Hendrix, I believe.

So, I will be overnighting in downtown Fargo! The fog may hide Minnesota for the first couple of riding hours tomorrow. After 21 days and 2,853 miles, I'll be home by suppertime.

MOTORCYCLE ADVENTURES OF 2014

Since I spent a surprise overnight in Fargo and slinked through a fog-shrouded Minnesota the next day, I've imagined myself riding through the West again this year. In 2014, though, I'd ride 100 miles north to Canada, cross the Northern woods and prairies via Winnipeg, Moose Jaw, Medicine Hat, and Calgary, and then lose myself in national parks with names like Banff, Jasper, Yoho, and Kootenay. They'd be clustered together in Alberta and overflow into British Columbia. Home would be a day's ride south from Radium Hot Springs, British Columbia, and then three days' east through Montana and North Dakota. Major elements of that 3,619-mile ride in 2014 are described *The Other Worlds*.[23]

---

[23] The motorcycle route across Canada, and back across Montana and North Dakota, is displayed on the in-color map pages of www.TomsGlobe.com, as is the map of many of the routes described in this book.

MOTORCYCLE ADVENTURES OF 2015

Wow! Another late summer shows up, and with it, a new motorcycle adventure that had been gripping my calendar for 11 months. My Minnesota mind envisions riding the streets of Gallup, New Mexico, and through the vast Navaho Nation in Arizona. The first day, though, I discover the states that I'll have to go through between Minnesota and there. "Enjoy them all," I tell myself.

The Rapid-Fire Route from Fort Robinson to Leadville
AUGUST 31, 2015

Asleep in a 1906 cavalry barracks, I dream I hear a bugle's reveille. It's 6:30 a.m., and I struggle to arise. But barracks it is no more—instead, it's partitioned into small rooms for visitors. Fort Robinson is now a 22,000-acre state park in the far northwest of Nebraska.

The US Army was encamped here in 1874 during the "Indian Wars." Over the years, the base became one of the largest military installations of the northern plains. Meanwhile, in 1877, Crazy Horse surrendered 889 members of his Sioux tribe at the fort, before being stabbed to death by an army private while "trying to escape."

A year later, troops based at Fort Robinson captured 149 Cheyenne people—led by Chief Dull Knife—who were fleeing back to their northern homeland after they'd escaped from Indian Territory in Oklahoma. Because they refused to return to Oklahoma, they were denied food and water. The Cheyenne broke out through windows, grabbed guns they'd hidden, and attempted to escape, in what became known as the Cheyenne Outbreak. The last of the Cheyenne were killed or captured two weeks later. Some had holed up on a nearby butte, 600 feet higher than the fort (which proved to be a good lookout for a jeep driver and me today).

The rapid-fire history of Fort Robinson continued for 65 years after the Cheyenne Outbreak. An all-black cavalry regiment, whose members the Plains Indians called "buffalo soldiers," was stationed here beginning in 1885, long before the army was integrated. Hundreds of dogs destined to participate in World War II were trained here. In 1943, the first of 3,000 German POWs arrived at Fort Robinson. Only one of the prisoners ever escaped, making his getaway on a freight train. The jeep driver informs me that when the POW was nearing Lincoln, Nebraska, he climbed off the train, found a bar, and had to settle for what he considered watered-down American beer. Still wearing his prisoner pants, he was captured.

The driver lets me in on a historical incident about Crow Butte that he and I spy from atop Cheyenne Butte. Crow Indians, he said, once stole Sioux horses from a plain near a fur-trading post where 1,000 or 2,000 Sioux sometimes camped with up to 5,000 horses. The Sioux pursued the Crow. The Crow released the horses and took refuge on top of "Crow Butte." The Sioux assembled at the bottom, the capture of the Crow seemingly assured.

That evening, the Crow lit a ceremonial funeral fire on the butte top for a mortally wounded comrade. The Sioux were content to watch the fire from the bottom. Little did they know that the Crow were busy tying materials together end-to-end—and lowering themselves down the far side of the butte. All escaped.

"Among the Sioux, was there hell to pay the next day for letting the Crow escape?" I wonder aloud. "Or did the Sioux consider it a lesson learned, to be passed down through generations?" I wish I could've heard the thrilling story the Crow told their community once they arrived home safe and sound. What they said is likely why this bit of history has passed down to their descendants in the 21st century— and to people like you and me.

• • •

Now it's 7 a.m. I'm on the barracks porch, waiting for the morning cool to wear off. I'll walk 100 yards to the spot where Crazy Horse was killed and then ride away from the sunrise to old Fort Laramie in Wyoming. For decades, the fort was the main military outpost on the Northern Plains and the primary transportation and communication hub in the region. Travelers on the Oregon, Mormon, California, and Bozeman trails found Fort Laramie to be a welcome stopover point, as did Pony Express riders and Transcontinental Telegraph workers. Covered wagons apparently managed to advance just eight to 20 miles a day.

From Fort Laramie, I'll explore the hip city of Laramie, as well as Cheyenne and its wondrous 24-hour-a-day freight traffic Union Pacific Depot. It's a stone's throw from the Plains Hotel, a 1911 treasure built to host visiting dignitaries, celebrities, and business titans. The hotel now extends a warm welcome to Old West fans from around the globe, who arrive by the busload—or, in my case, on a Harley Road King.

Hour by hour, I'll ride south, the Rocky Mountains looming to my right. It will then be up and over a mass of mountains, stopping at 12,200 feet to walk the Tundra Trail in Rocky Mountain National Park.

In the following days, I'll pull up here and there and spend a whole night at the 1886 Delaware Hotel in Leadville, Colorado, one of the world's historic mining centers—think molybdenum, silver, gold, zinc, and copper, not to mention the sometimes-deadly lead. I will learn all about it at the National Mining Hall of Fame and Museum.

The Cliff-Dwelling Peoples Who "Mysteriously Vanished"
SEPTEMBER 6, 2015

At 6 a.m., I wake up in a lodging atop a mesa in Mesa Verde National Park in Southwest Colorado. I soon find myself in dwelling-rich alcoves, carved by nature into the faces of cliffs. Some 100 feet below the mesa top and 600 to 800 feet above the canyon floor, the alcoves are sheltered from severe weather. Like the residents of yesteryear, visitors climb down a ladder or a steep trail from the mesa top to reach the dwellings.

Built in the late 1100s and the 1200s, some structures resemble three-story apartment buildings. Over 100 people resided in one such dwelling now called Cliff Palace, the largest cliff structure in North America. Mesa Verde—which consists of several adjoining mesas—is blessed with about 600 sites that were built into cliff sides, most small and unexplored even today. Many were single-room food storage units.

Small villages, gardens, and farms dotted the nearly flat top of the 7,000-foot-high mesa as early as 600 AD, although these spaces were used seasonally as early as 7,500 BC. By 1200 AD, Mesa Verde's population was about 20,000 strong—greater than the number of people who live in the region today. Mesa Verde was abandoned by 1300, perhaps due to a multidecade dry spell and factors such as soil depletion, deforestation, overhunting, and civic unrest.

To the southeast, just a few days' travel by foot (a millennium ago) lies northern New Mexico's Chaco Canyon, built centuries before Mesa Verde. Here, one finds the most sweeping array of ancient ruins north of Mexico. Its urban ceremonial center is unlike anything constructed before or since. The Chacoan culture peaked between about 1020 and 1110.

Over the last few generations, some non-Natives have assumed that the people of Chaco Canyon and Mesa Verde, as well as nearby communities, *mysteriously vanished*. But in truth, they didn't. And who might explain to us what truly happened? Their *descendants*!

Today, many descendants of the people who once lived in Chaco Canyon and Mesa Verde can be found in 19 New Mexico pueblos— each a sovereign nation—and the Hopi Reservation in Arizona. But others born in today's pueblos live and work in Albuquerque, Santa Fe, Grants, Gallup, and further afield. As I learned, a Zuni Pueblo-born woman works at the headquarters of a supermarket chain in Phoenix. Her cousin lives with his wife and five children in Oahu, Hawaii. He is a United States Navy nuclear reactor mechanic, who every year spends months at sea on a submarine in the far reaches of the Pacific Ocean.

I'll learn more about these descendants soon. But first, I ride from the Mesa Verde region to Arizona—and into the Navaho Nation.

From Navaho Lands to Hiroshima
SEPTEMBER 10–16, 2015

The sun sets over the Navaho Nation as I ride into Window Rock, the nation's capital. This 27,000-square-mile nation extends from northeastern Arizona into New Mexico and Utah. Its citizens are the Diné, the largest indigenous tribe in the United States. I've come for a reason. I add my motorcycle to a couple hundred other machines of transportation parked in a field; it seems that a significant portion of the Diné people have already arrived. I stroll to where the action is.

A powwow starts at 7 p.m., but so does the rodeo. I saunter from one to the other through a brightly lit midway, like a big county fair —all part of the 59th annual Navajo Nation Fair. Thrilling all of us are galloping horses and Navajo cowboys and cowgirls roping calves, some riding bucking broncos and bulls. It looks like I'm the only nontribal visitor, but all are welcome.

From my new base in nearby Gallup, New Mexico, I'll return to Window Rock tomorrow. The fair lasts more than a day—eight, in fact! Take your pick: horticulture, wellness, Native arts, Miss Navaho, science competition, livestock, and song and dance, to name a few of what's on offer. And more cowboys, cowgirls, calves, broncos, and bulls.

• • •

Following my eye-opening Navaho side trip, I follow the trail of Mesa Verde's Ancestral Puebloans by visiting a few of the 19 New Mexico pueblos where their descendants live today. The people of these Native American communities speak several different languages. Zuni, south of Gallup and close to Arizona, is the largest pueblo, with 12,000 people and 450,000 acres of surrounding land. The history of Zuni, although going by other names, goes back to perhaps 40 centuries before the Spanish arrived. Coronado appeared in 1540, looking for gold, believing Zuni was one of the Seven Cities of Cibola, the mythical empire.

In 1630, the Franciscans arrived and began to erect a church and convent. Forty years ago, a Zuni artist painted sacred Zuni figures wearing colorful costumes on the walls inside the church. They illustrate beliefs that are not, of course, Christian. Catholic priests were uncomfortable saying mass with these figures dominating the service, and the church was deconsecrated. Yes, my guide repeats in a hushed tone, "deconsecrated." (If accompanied by a guide, one may visit the church and the old neighborhood surrounding it.)

Zuni's history continues in the 21st century. Visiting the museum, I chat with a worker who explains that he's a member of the Eagle Clan through his father and also of the Sun Clan through his mother. Since Zuni has a matrilineal society, the Sun Clan is predominant in his life.

"What is an important issue the community faces now?" I ask.

"It is one of communication," he explains. "The many distractions, such as the cell phone, car, TV, and computer, hinder communication about important issues."

I'd like to visit Zuni again, I tell him, but may have to fly from Minnesota to Albuquerque next time. He suggests that I leave my motorcycle in Zuni: the museum will take care of it for me. I'm very tempted, but I live a long way away, and I'll keep riding.

Leaving Zuni, I turn onto a dirt road just outside town. I stop at a private home—it doubles as the Paywa Bakery. I buy a loaf of fresh sourdough bread from the women inside. Out back, bakery co-owner Jerry tends a large brick oven all fired up and pouring out heat. I'm not sure if today's the day he'll bake 90 loaves, but two women inside are working real hard with fresh dough.

• • •

Days later, north of Santa Fe, I stop at the government offices in Santa Clara, another of the 19 pueblos. I hand 20 photos to the office secretary —photos I snapped at the National Museum of the American Indian in Washington, DC, in July. The pictures show the museum's Santa Clara Pueblo exhibit, one of many that tell us about native cultures from Alaska deep into South America.

The secretary and I converse about a burning topic in the community—fires that swept through the nearby canyon, destroying the pueblo's cabins and picnic facilities. Overhearing our conversation, a Santa Clara official comes out of his office. He introduces himself as Governor Chavarria and hands me a beautiful tribal lapel pin. He wants me to know that the fire-ravaged canyon they are working to restore is part of the people's natural world; it is their spiritual sanctuary.

As I leave the office, secretary Jessica, like so many people I meet on this trip, wishes me a safe journey. It was a couple weeks earlier— in Aspen, Colorado—that I ran into a couple from Tulsa, Oklahoma. Both 75 years old, they were interested in what quest I'm on with a bag-loaded motorcycle. The man suggested the three of us join hands in a circle on the street and, after asking me if I have Jesus in my heart, proceeded to say a touching prayer. He wished me divine protection on my journey. "Yes," he repeated for emphasis, "divine protection." The gentleman returned a minute later, wishing to take a photo of (helmet-protected) me.

You can also visit Taos Pueblo, another of New Mexico's 19 pueblos that was very likely founded in large part by the Ancestral Puebloans who left the Mesa Verde area in today's Four Corners region. Taos has been continuously inhabited for over 1,000 years. Early on, it became a key center of trade and communications between American Indian tribes, and later, between the Indians and the Spanish.

Today, you may ask a young Taos native to guide you or wander around on your own. Do both, I suggest, since you will make the time! You'll find multilevel houses and thick adobe walls. The warrior council takes responsibility for the environment, and a pure water stream runs through the pueblo from the nearby mountains.

• • •

Ghost Ranch, hours to the west, is where Georgia O'Keefe painted her desert and mountain environs. A minibus takes a group of us through the ranch lands to view many of the backdrops for O'Keefe's paintings. We learn what she saw through her eyes—because we now see the very same natural world through ours. At the ranch, I find myself sitting in what was once an airplane hangar for ranch visitor Charles Lindbergh. It's now a dining hall for visitors.

• • •

A journey through northern New Mexico would not be complete, for me, without stopping at "a town that never was." Upon arriving, I rush to see the documentary film shown thousands of times a year, aptly titled "The Town that Never Was." Young workers of yesteryear may have found "some things to their liking: an average age of coworkers of 25, no unemployment, no in-laws, and no idle rich," according to the video in the popular Bradbury Science Museum. As a beehive of top-secret activity, the town did not officially exist.

The crown jewel is the Los Alamos National Laboratory. The film describes the building of the atomic bombs dropped on Hiroshima and

Nagasaki on August 6 and 9, 1945. Los Alamos was a secret boomtown from 1943 until the bombs were built. At the next stop, the Los Alamos Historical Museum, I discover details about the July 1945 atmospheric test in southern New Mexico, the loading of the Hiroshima bomb into the B-29 Enola Gay at a World War II airport on Tinian Island in the Western Pacific's Northern Mariana Islands, and the bomb's detonation over Hiroshima at 1,870 feet. The Nagasaki bomb, also loaded on a Boeing B-29 Super Fortress on Tinian Island, detonated at 1,540 feet. Both altitudes were set for "maximum effect." The two atomic bombs, the only ones to date used in warfare, killed between 130,000 and 226,000 people, half the deaths occurring on the day of each bombing—many within one minute. More died in later years.

Museum official Emma may explain that her husband's grandfather, Dr. Darol Froman, worked with the original team developing the bomb's technology in Chicago starting in 1941 and moved to Los Alamos to help build the bombs. She'll confide that relatives in her family who were archaeologists and geologists were far more interesting than those who were nuclear scientists. Today's biographical sketch of the late Dr. Froman, though, reveals that he would've had immensely interesting stories to tell his family, assuming secrets had not been kept under wraps for decades after the war ended.

Emma's heritage is Pueblo Indian, Apache, Navaho, Spanish, and Mexican. When she visited Hawaii, she says, she received store discounts for local people because they thought she was Hawaiian. I know the feeling. "What tribe are you?" an Indian woman in northern New Mexico asked me, saying I look Native American. I answered that, although I was born in a town with the Ojibwe name of Biwabik, all my grandparents were natives of Finland.

The Los Alamos National Laboratory is still going great guns on scientific work, but today it focuses on nanotechnology, supercomputing, and space exploration. This research must be supersecret too, like that in the 1940s. But, just for kicks, why not drive a mile to the newer lab property?

I show my driver's license at the gate. I accidentally proceed into the area warning that one must possess a badge to enter. Before I find my way out, one or two of my cameras become hyperactive. I now drive to the exit, a big SUV alongside me. The emblem on its door signifies it is property of the National Nuclear Security Agency. ("You came in close contact with one of the top guards," a museum worker will later say.)

I soon sit alone at a long wooden table, sipping coffee in the middle of Los Alamos town. Between 1943 and 1945, one could have walked in a minute from this very spot to all of the 20 or so buildings, now dismantled, that were part of the Manhattan Project that built the bombs.

I find myself reminiscing that I've now been at the spot on Tinian Island where the Hiroshima bomb was loaded into the Enola Gay, in Hiroshima at the hypocenter below the precise detonation point, and now where, with the right badges, one could once have accessed all the Manhattan Project buildings.

The century-old wooden table on which I rest my coffee cup and idle thoughts is now inside a busy Starbucks—a sure sign that the town that "never was" in the 1940s now definitely *is*.

• • •

In the 4,587th mile on the 32nd day of my motorcycle adventures of 2015, I roll into my Northern Minnesota driveway. My Moleskin notebook's last entry reads "ARR 5:30 p.m. Grass grew! 4" of water in rain gauge. Boat still chained to dock. Birch clump near bedroom window fell down. Phoned Marvin and Irene, Leah, Mary (James on the way home from Europe). Plan Sunday's Generic Party for friends here. *Loved the trip!*"

MOTORCYCLE ADVENTURES OF 2016

Eagle Butte, Where a Book Isn't Judged by Its Cover

AUGUST 21, 2016

I'm just a day and a half into my motorcycle adventures of 2016, but I feel my favorite town will be Eagle Butte, South Dakota.

Let me tell you a bit. I walk into the service station to pay for gas —leaving my motorcycle parked by the gas pump for half an hour. In the adjacent Dairy Queen, I buy a dipped cone from the young woman a few years out of high school who trains the other workers. They all live in Eagle Butte or in neighboring rural areas.

Back in the gas station with the cone, I buy two days of the *Rapid City Journal* (Headlines: "Bikers for Trump, or Bikers for Profit?"). The café cashier tells me which coffee is his favorite, and I select that one. Outside, a construction worker tells me he is home in Eagle Butte for just a few days before he goes back to work in Rapid City.

I now ride up Main Street. It's a side street off of US Route 212, a highway that begins in Minneapolis and dissolves on a map near Yellowstone National Park in Wyoming.

Why is it, I wonder, that every car and truck on Main Street travels very, very slowly, stops completely at each stop sign, and waits a few seconds before moving on?

Minutes later, a tall young man walks down Main Street. His name, I find out, is Fritz Frost.

"Fritz," I say just a couple minutes into our conversation, "how would you describe your hometown to someone your age in Minnesota, Michigan, or California?"

"It is very peaceful," he says. "The young people are laid-back; they have it easy. In a city, they have drama, they have crazies. People here are nonjudgmental. In a city, they judge a book by its cover."

I'm about to ask Fritz if any white people live in town but skip it. Instead, I find out he is a senior in high school. And football season is just starting.

"I size you up to be a tight end, quarterback, or running back, and any position on defense," I tell him.

"I'm a running back," he answers, "and I play safety on defense."

"Fritz, I see you breaking a couple of tackles and going for a 46-yard gain."

His smile and nod tells me he could say, "Yes, I could do that—have done that—and you could add some yards to that number, if you wish."

"I haven't seen a town for the last 40 miles," I say. "Do you travel far to your away games?"

"Yes. Sometimes it's a five-hour trip each way," the breakaway running back tells me.

I show Fritz the photo I have just snapped of a mural on the side wall of a vacant building on Main Street, offering my opinion that it is the best mural anywhere. It's set on a gray wall. It shows a hand peeling back the gray "paper" to discover what is behind this "curtain." Native American designs, horses, and the colorful life of the community and its heritage are revealed, although some never observe it in the real world around them—unless they make an effort to see behind the curtains shading our various cultures.

Fritz and I bid goodbye to each other. I continue my travels across his Cheyenne River Sioux Reservation in west central South Dakota, a land first occupied by the Lakota Sioux in 1775.

The Motorcyclist and the Tree
SEPTEMBER 3, 2016

Although fraying at the edges with gnarled and exposed roots, he was inspired to learn to ride a motorcycle. It wasn't a snap at his age. Soon, though, he's gliding among trees on glorious forest roads. He's felt for decades that he was a tree in a prior life, or something living very close by. So he knows whereof he now speaks.

The tree that fills his vision may or may not talk to itself, but it is aware of its surroundings, he feels. It may be aware that a motorcyclist has dismounted and approached it.

"Is the motorcyclist taking a photograph because he weeps over my exposed roots?" this tree could wonder. "Or because he sees me splendidly looking west toward the sunset? It is both, I conclude, as I absorb the motorcyclist's feelings about me.

For decades, the tree has persevered and thrived on Inspiration Point, Bryce Canyon National Park, Utah. The tree inspired a storyteller in 2016!

"The motorcyclist walks around me on my forever nourishing southern side. He takes a second photograph. It shows what I face to the east over the cliff every sunlit moment of my long and proud life. Is he taking the photograph because of the shapes of the canyons, fins, and spires he sees—or their colors? Or the fact that 85 billion cubic feet of sedimentary rock layers created in half a billion years have, to date, eroded from the geologically uplifted Paunsaugunt Plateau rim I thrive on?

"If the motorcyclist-photographer returns in his current lifetime, or as a young tree near me while I am still alive, we may commune about the questions we have and what we see on this exquisite planet."

Utah's Cliff Spendlove and Arizona's Ron Wadsworth
SEPTEMBER 11, 2016

"I come here to the Grand Canyon's North Rim. It's not commercialized like the South Rim," a man older than me comments.

"Where do you live?" I inquire.

"The other side of Zion National Park in Utah. I drove a snowplow in Zion. That was the 1930s."

"The 19-*thirties?*" I blurt out incredulously.

"How old do you think I am?" he counters.

"Hmm. That's a good one, but not old enough to have driven a snowplow in the 1930s, I'd say."

"I am 99 years old."

"Wow! What advice for longevity can you give me?"

"Well, the Good Lord is giving *me* many years so that I have enough time to *repent*."

Thrown off balance, I simply ask, "When is your birthday?"

"In March. I want to reach 100. There is just one reason I may not live to 100."

"Oh, what is that reason?" I inquire carefully, still off balance.

Cliff Spendlove, at 99 years of age, enjoys the North Rim of Grand Canyon National Park in Arizona.

"I could get shot by a jealous husband!" he declares.

"Be careful, sir! And have a happy birthday."

We go off in different directions. If, perchance, I ever have the opportunity to meet this man again, I hope I will hear more stories of his 99-plus years. By luck, just a few minutes later, he walks by me as I take a picture of a pinyon pine tree. (Seeing —and even visiting—trees of any shape, color, and heritage thrill me.) I learn that the name of the other wanderer is Cliff Spendlove—I wonder if a friend once warned Cliff that he should never spend his love carelessly or he might get shot by a jealous husband.

Cliff, a World War II vet, explains that when he was young, they used the sap (or pitch) that oozes out of the pinyon pine to make a salve. He rubbed the salve on infected scratches and cuts. The salve killed the infections, Cliff tells me. Soon, in the parking lot, a car pulls up. Cliff gets in, and he's gone.

I stand there wondering whether Cliff's family, or its Anglo-Saxon immigrant ancestors, was the first to discover the sap remedy when they moved to the American Southwest. I find out the answer a week later. It is 79 miles, as a hawk would fly, over the Grand Canyon, above part of the Navaho Nation and into the center of the Hopi Indian Reservation at Second Mesa, all in Arizona.

In a rush to tell you this story, I skip right over the otherworldly South Rim, Flagstaff's Museum of Northern Arizona, and Lowell

A tilted view of the South Rim of the magnificent Grand Canyon.

Observatory, and, in Phoenix, two of the planet's top museums, the Heard and the Musical Instrument Museum. In themselves, they are worth a trip to Phoenix, but several more could extend a visit several days. And I just mention in passing, "standin' on a corner in Winslow, Arizona . . . such a fine sight to see."[24]

I didn't travel from the North Rim to Second Mesa in 79 miles, as a hawk might fly. I did, nevertheless, arrive. At Second Mesa, I meet Ron Wadsworth, a Hopi Indian guide. I jump into his pickup truck. We drive from the mesa down to a remote horseshoe-shaped canyon at the end of a dusty road. Ron explains many picture-perfect petroglyphs carved over several centuries into the rock walls. Each one of the hundred or so has a specific meaning, most of which Ron knows.

[24] The irresistible song "Take It Easy" was recorded by the Eagles in 1972. Jackson Browne and Glenn Frey wrote it. It's pretty easy finding Winslow's Main Street from Interstate 40. Right away, you'll notice some of the 100,000 annual visitors from around the world "a-standin' on a corner," smack on Route 66, of course.

Guide Ron Wadsworth of the Hopi Reservation explains the deep meanings of petroglyphs carved over centuries into rock walls of a remote canyon.

Ron is excited upon seeing two hawks circling overhead. This is a positive sign, he informs me. His pickup then climbs to the top of Third Mesa, moving through the villages of Bacavi and Hotevilla, each having its own special history.

At noon, we walk in the village of Old Oraibi, at the tip of Third Mesa, overlooking a vast stretch of central Arizona. Ron points at the stone Catholic church, still half destroyed from the day in 1680 when the people of this town revolted. Together with Native American pueblos in present-day New Mexico, they had secretly coordinated a revolution against Spanish officials and priests, as well as their cruel and ruthless military enforcers. Old Oraibi is more ancient than just the 336 years since the revolt. Its history goes all the way back to its founding in 1150 AD. It's sometimes called the oldest continuously inhabited town in North America.

I must ask Ron a question before I hop out of his truck and onto my motorcycle: "Ron, do people use the sap of a pinyon tree to—"

Ron interrupts me with his answer: "Yes, we heat the sap and skim off the impurities that rise to the surface. We make salve. It's called *saana*. We apply it to infections from cuts and scrapes on the skin. Some older people also ingest the medicine—it cleanses the digestive system. People have been using the saana remedy for centuries," Ron adds. "Our ancestors also shined their arrows with saana to reduce drag in flight."

I spent only half a day with Ron Wadsworth. Still, he gave me years' worth of information and insights. I tell Ron I hope I have the chance to go on a pickup ride with him again. In the meantime, he'll continue advising on archaeological excavations near Flagstaff; visiting Houston, Texas, each year to address spiritual groups and speak to college students in world religion classes; traveling to Chiapas in Southern Mexico for discussions about traditional medical treatments with Maya people, whose culture is related to the Hopi's; and being the spokesperson for his chief.

As for the Minnesotan, he's now traveling northeast. May the hawks fly with him.

Bingo! Zip 81149
SEPTEMBER 13, 2016

Keep an eye out for a place to settle down and chill out, I say. Somewhere small enough so the zip code belongs to just a few of you—493 is the perfect population. It needs a proper elevation—7,707 feet is neither a meter too high nor a meter too low. A nearby river from epic mountains would give it a leg up on any run-of-the-mill place.

Icing on the cake, if any is needed, would be an iconic café, especially one you can hang out in from 7 a.m. to 3 p.m. The kind of place where, if you show up at 3 p.m., and both signs in the windows read "Closed," you can just push the door, walk in, sit down, and order a quick piece of peanut butter pie and a cup of coffee—with a refill, please.

Remember to locate a home with a roof over your head that doesn't leak. Neighboring homes should be almost as appealing as yours.

Pay no heed to a bank inscribed with the numbers "1880 1913." It's an institution that didn't die off in 1913. The door is wide open as of 3:30 p.m. today, letting in the mountain breeze flowing down the main street.

Finally, you should find a town whose name has a secret local pronunciation. "Sa-watch" seals the deal!

I present to you Saguache, Colorado, 81149. Perhaps you'll send me letters soon.

• • •

Torn between affection for two communities, though, I return to my Minnesota abode a few days later. I reach my final destination on the 30th day, at the end of the 4,912th mile.

MOTORCYCLE ADVENTURES OF 2017

The Land Due South

AUGUST 21, 2017

"I want to stand across a barbed-wire fence from a herd of cattle," I tell lifelong dairy farmer Craig Trytten. Since he knows more about how cattle behave than anyone but the one in a million who does know all, I ask, "What will cows do, Craig, during a total eclipse of the sun?"

"They won't notice. They'll keep eating, or lie down. They'll be happy for some shade," he tells me.

I am surprised but undeterred. "I'd still rather be near a herd of cows during an eclipse than with 20,000 people in a stadium, which is all the rage with some humans," I conclude.

Days later, I begin a motorcycle journey that takes me due south to Duluth-Superior at the tip of awesome Lake Superior. I slice through parts of Wisconsin and Minnesota (again), sleep a night in Ottumwa as I cut Iowa in half from north to south, and finally, I pierce Missouri, aiming for its geographical heart.

• • •

As I look skyward, lying on my back in lush, green grass, I see nothing. Nothing, astrophysicists might say, except for an object insignificant to an infinitesimal degree. For its kind, it's just average in size. It's also one of 100 billion or more others in our galaxy, and there might be one trillion or more other galaxies.

I stare at this star without retinal damage, since plopped over my eyes are filters meeting the ISO 12312-2:2015 requirements. The green, green grass is not of home, but of Central Missouri. The day is August 21, 2017. Thanks to the exquisite timing of our planet rotating and our moon revolving, our sun is about to disappear behind the moon. As the sun vanishes from view, except for its outlying corona, the early afternoon turns, to my eyes freed of protection for two minutes and 41 seconds, an ominous purple color. As the couple dozen people near me stargaze, they burst with delight. Some take the opportunity to look at Venus.

For all the grass, this is no cow pasture: I am on the outskirts of Colombia, Missouri. So I don't know if cows kept eating, lay down, or mooed like crazy during their once-in-a-lifetime experience. On that point, I am still in the dark.

Heart, Mind, and Soul
AUGUST 21–SEPTEMBER 6, 2017

Once all is said and done, eclipse-wise, I hop on my motorcycle. I ride US 63, then 54, south. It's stop and go for a hundred hot miles in the choked-up post-eclipse traffic. It seems to me that a big portion of the seven million or more Americans who traveled today to get into the path of the coast-to-coast eclipse are right here, heading south with me!

I turn onto a bucolic side road, seeking to semicircle around the traffic, but discover that Lake Ozark is an unyielding obstacle. I feel certain that the convenience store on the looming hill can help me with my route, though.

"No, you must go back and get on 54 again!" the attendant informs me. "A biker couple dressed head to toe in the newest motorcycle gear just left; they'd been thinking like you," he tells me. "They were so hot, I had them sit down inside the beer cooler," he adds.

Back to 54 it was for them and—without a beer cooler break—for me.

• • •

Over a two-week period, I am planning to hit Fayetteville in Arkansas, Oklahoma's Tahlequah, Muskogee, and Tulsa, then head over Route 66 to Oklahoma City, and onward to Amarillo in the Texas panhandle, New Mexico's cities of Tucumcari, Las Vegas, and Albuquerque, and ancient and thriving Native American Acoma Pueblo and Zuni Pueblo. Thence turning north, I expect to find the Navaho Nation in Arizona and Utah.

• • •

Let's not get ahead of ourselves. Let's travel slowly enough to ponder whether there is heart, mind, and soul in what some say is our divided society. Will we escape the gloom of television and radio commentary and discover for ourselves what the lives of others along our way behold?

Let's move along to far-flung places that appear in the aftermath of the total solar eclipse.

Lilly introduces herself. She teaches about a way of life forgotten in most of our own family lineages for perhaps two, three, or five centuries. Raising a blowgun, she places a dart in the end. She fires it at an imaginary rabbit, explaining that dart tips are poisoned.

Lilly introduces Neal who, right before our eyes, chips and flakes stones into spear points and arrowheads. His skill seems magical—and quick magic at that. Neal makes an arrowhead in 10 minutes flat!

"Our forefathers spent a great deal of time making arrowheads and spear points. They needed *many* for hunting expeditions," Neal explains.

Lilly next leads us to archers practicing with bows and arrows made in the ancient tradition.

"What is the most important thing when making an arrow to be sure it works?" I ask.

"The feathers," an archer answers. "If we don't design the feathers just right, they can whistle—and alert the target animal."

Lilly now guides us past players competing in a fascinating game of poleball. In the original stickball version, it was sometimes used to settle disputes, "even between tribes," Lilly says. (The game of lacrosse may have been derived from stickball.)

Lilly, Neal, the archers, and players welcome travelers to the Cherokee Heritage Center in Tahlequah, Oklahoma. Lilly works here as a guide—whenever she's not in a college classroom, working on her major in Indian Studies.

• • •

Move just 69 miles up the road to Muskogee, Oklahoma, walk into an old brick building, and get blown away by the works of an artist most have never heard of: Jerome Tiger. In 1967, Tiger, a Creek-Seminole, died in 1967 in a handgun accident. He was 26. "He lit up the art world for just five short years [but] his work has left a masterful impression," I'd read in a *Cowboys & Indians* magazine review this year.

In the same building, high on a hill, are stories of the Seminole, Muskogee (Creek), Cherokee, Chickasaw, and Choctaw. These "Five Tribes" were among those forced to resettle here by the Indian Removal Act of 1830. From their ancestral homes in the Southeastern United States, they were driven on deadly journeys over the Trail of Tears. The Five Civilized Tribes Museum is not large, but it is another key to my education on this journey.

Traveling northwest just 50 miles takes me to some of many highlights Oklahoma has to offer. Tulsa's fabulous Gilcrease Museum showcases the world's largest collection of art of the American West— from modern Native American and historical Native art to leather clothing of the Plains Indians, drawers filled with moccasins and jewelry, and so much more.

The Philbrook Museum of Art, housed in an Italian-style villa, features art from renaissance to medieval, sculptures to paintings, and Native American to modern abstract. One might even find a special exhibit—perhaps Cheech Marin's collection of Chicano art.

Discover a nearly hidden gem, too—the Sand Springs Cultural and Historical Museum. It jumps out at visitors in this cool town set just a bit toward Oklahoma City. Built as a library in 1930 by a philanthropic oil man, the art deco exterior and interior stand out in the middle of a most pleasant community.

I marvel at how these wonderful museums connect us to the lives of hearts, minds, and souls past.

• • •

Are people who travel Route 66 today—or live on it—still like some of those who used to live on it or famously traveled it decades ago?

Meet Chris, age 18 or so, a waiter in an iconic Route 66 café between Sand Springs and Oklahoma City. What does Chris's life look like? He's on his high school's football, wrestling, and weightlifting teams. With a passion for cinematography and sound, he wants to be a radio disc jockey. Right now, he's making a documentary film about an athlete from another town. If he were to attend his dream university, where might he go? Oxford University, he answers. Although Oklahoma or Oklahoma State may be more realistic, he allows.

Chris has probably watched hundreds of movies. Perhaps because of the movie *Fargo*, I later guess, Chris asks me to "please say, 'Eh,'" after I tell him I'm from Minnesota. Reluctantly, I oblige. I dream I'm auditioning for a role in one of his future movies or radio stories. No one on this trip has gotten a bigger kick out of anything I've said than Chris hearing my on-demand "eh." First time in my life I've said that, I swear.

Adiós, Chris of Route 66. And adiós to the café made of local rock in Stroud, Oklahoma. Built in 1936, the Rock Café may still be serving Route 66 wayfarers a hundred years from now.

• • •

Since we are all about Route 66, let's say howdy to Allan Karl. This year, he's riding his BMW motorcycle from Los Angeles to Toronto. His journey didn't start out in Los Angeles, though, and it didn't start out this year. This is his eighth year riding his BMW around the world— three weeks each year. He stores his motorcycle in whatever country he's in after three weeks of travel. He left it in Iran for 50 weeks and then paid a $1,000 fine. His journey has included the Silk Road across part of Asia.

This year's trip, part of it on Route 66, concludes Allan's motorcycle odyssey. He'll soon be back in his native Austria. I should search for him on the internet to see if he has written that book he planned—the one to be filled with photos!

After zipping through the Texas Panhandle and well into New Mexico, I'm off the interstate, which death-knelled most of old 66. I ride back and forth in Tucumcari, past abandoned buildings and motels with names like Buckaroo, Safari, Pony Soldier, and Blue Swallow.

Tucumcari's Main Street, found a few blocks north of 66, is even quieter—but a delicious quiet. In a curio shop, lyrics flowing from a small $1 battery-powered radio drift over artifacts like the Bee Gees wanting help mending their broken heart, and John Stewart turning music into gold.

The next song, I didn't hear. All because, as I moseyed among antiques, I couldn't get the lyrics of the first two out of my head. I was itching to pay a dollar for that radio, but I had no space in my saddlebags. This brought me back to when I was about nine. A boy in a mining town was moving away and selling his rubber baseball.

"Why can't you take it with you?" I asked, feeling sorry for him.

"We don't have room," he answered quietly.

I wondered why he couldn't just hold the ball on his lap as their old car carried them hours or days to their next home.

But once I'd given the boy a coin, the ball was mine! I remember it to this day. In the year that followed, I threw that ball a thousand times against rock and brick walls, most times pitching a strike against an imaginary, two-dimensional batter.

If I go back to Tucumcari, I'll make sure to keep a little spare space in a saddlebag for that radio. And for the next hundred miles, I'll hear about a guy jumping in his car and throwing in his guitar.

• • •

It's late Saturday afternoon. Eighty miles to the northwest of Tucumcari on Route 104 sits one of very few ranch houses in the wide-open high plains. I pull to a stop on the highway, hoping to do some kind of fix on my deflating rear tire at this ranch.

The heavy-duty steel gate across the driveway is shut tight. The dogs bark. The wife tells the husband he'd better go out and look. Soon, I sit inside, chatting with LeRoy and his wife. The couple, I learn, owns this 160-acre ranch, with cattle and horses. As we talk, I gaze at the mounted heads of an elk, deer, and oryx that LeRoy bagged here in New Mexico. The oryx is especially beautiful, looking right at me like it does.

I'm not the first stranger who's found himself in the couple's home. One day, LeRoy says, he observed a man wandering on the highway near his ranch. The man mumbled that his car broke down—but what he needed most was a drink of water. He came in, sipped water, and waited as LeRoy made phone calls to get his car running again. That was years ago, and the man was in his 80s. To this day, the motorist's children send LeRoy and his wife cards, thanks, and a gift or two.

Just a couple years ago, a New Yorker stopped by, LeRoy tells me. He wanted to buy the place—lock, stock, and barrel. The gentleman left his card. LeRoy's wife urged him to "throw that card away!" The New Yorker phones up occasionally. I don't think the couple will be budging off their high plains ranch—one without neighbors, it seems to me, within a two-day horseback ride.

Like that elderly man's family, I owe LeRoy thanks too—he trucked my motorcycle quite a distance to a shop in exquisite Las Vegas, New Mexico, one of my favorite cities in the West. I settled in at the Plaza Hotel for the weekend, soaking up its history since it opened in 1882. The city, a few decades older than the hotel, is filled with landmarks, legends, and lore; five Main Street historic districts; and 900 buildings on the National Registry of Historic Places.

As I wander the streets on foot while my motorcycle sits in a repair shop, I imagine stories that LeRoy will tell a stranger who might stop at his ranch in a few years, searching for help. He'll describe the elderly man desperate for a drink of water; the New Yorker who calls him now and then wanting to buy his place lock, stock, and barrel; and perhaps the Minnesotan whose motorcycle tire went flat right by his ranch gate. I hope to ride by again in two or three years and get updated on LeRoy's stories. And I hope to pull out an old transistor radio I found that day in a Tucumcari curio shop and tune in songs out of the past.

• • •

Please don't ask me if my rear tire went flat again, and how many more flats I had, or whether my gear linkage rod broke. I'm focusing, instead, on where the highway takes me now. Over the following week, I stop and sleep in Albuquerque and Zuni Pueblo, cruise due north through the Navaho Nation in eastern Arizona, overnight in a Monument Valley lodge, and, after a visit to Bears Ears National Monument, bed down in Bluff, Utah. The next morning, the road carries my motorcycle to a fortuitous spot in southeastern Utah where two biozones meet—the Pinyon-Juniper Uplands and the Sage Grasslands. It is, therefore, doubly rich in plants and animals essential for food, fiber, hides, and building materials. In short, *a good place to call home.*

And home they called it! First came hunters and gatherers 11,000 years ago. In a more recent era, the Ancestral Puebloans (once called Anasazi) created a good life for many generations from the 700s to early 1200s.

The ancient sun marker, as reimagined by a 21st-century artist, at the wonderful Edge of the Cedars State Park and Museum, Blanding, Utah.

In the year 2017, on a day called "today," I find myself circling a rebuilt one-thousand-year-old home. It was masterfully constructed with stones, mortar, and chink pieces. I grab onto a ladder that seems as old as the home and descend step-by-step to an underground kiva ceremonial room next to the house. The kiva is also one thousand years old—or more.

These homes and kivas were the heart of hundreds of activities common in Ancestral Puebloan communities on the Colorado Plateau that rose millions of years earlier. One might dream about what life was like when traders from near and far visited with exotic goods and strange stories. Today, as recounted earlier in this book, descendants of the Ancestral Puebloans live in 19 New Mexico pueblos such as Acoma, Zuni, and Taos, and in the Hopi lands of Arizona. The old values are guarded, nurtured, cherished, and passed on to each new generation.

Although my well-oiled riding machine is ready and rarin' to go, it must cool its heels—for I spy a mysterious structure just downhill from the house and kiva. The object is a sun marker—the most remarkable thing I've seen in many a moon, and perhaps in my entire life.

Sun markers are ancient instruments timed to the solstices and equinoxes. They likely guided farmers on when to plant and harvest crops—a life-and-death decision. For generations of indigenous people, a local sun marker was their grandfather's clock! These instruments must have been enthralling works of art to those people, besides being vital for community survival. The sun marker I see today has been reimagined by a 21st-century artist, Joe Pachak. It's a hybrid of ancient wisdom and today's artistic inspiration.

Just where does one discover this biozone and the stone house, underground kiva, and one-of-a-kind sun marker? At the Edge of the Cedars State Park and (incredible!) Museum in Blanding, Utah.

• • •

Now is the time to head east to the Hovenweep ruins on the Utah-Colorado border. From 700 to 1270 AD, Ancestral Puebloan communities thrived here, where the living could be good above, and on the slopes of, water-fed canyons. As far back as 10,000 years ago, though, Paleo Indians visited this area to hunt game and gather food, following seasonal weather patterns.

The Hovenweep people of a thousand years ago terraced the hillsides, formed catch basins to collect stormwater, and built check dams to prevent soil erosion. The stone workmanship was magnificent, and some buildings are still intact after 700 years. In the late 1200s, the inhabitants left, perhaps due to drought, depletion of resources, conflict, or warfare.

Mancos, Colorado, I've discovered, is my ideal base for exploring the many stunning historical sites of the Four Corners region, including Mesa Verde, Chaco Canyon, and Canyon de Chelley, home to ancestral communities of tens of thousands of people today. And in Mancos, I can enjoy the Mesa Verde Motel and the ever-popular Absolute Bakery & Cafe.

Unfortunately, it's time to leave. I jump out of my motel bed as the Mancos towing truck arrives, cables my motorcycle onto the down-tilted bed of the truck, and hauls it, my bags, and me 30 miles to Durango's Harley dealer, where the tire repairman finds a screw that deflated my rear tire as I rode into Mancos a couple days earlier. (Ten days ago, in Tucumcari, it wasn't just a screw that deflated my rear tire: it was a nail, too.)

At the Durango dealer, I have time to buy a new helmet, since mine crashed onto the pavement—luckily, without my head in it—while I was riding at 50 miles an hour up near Hovenweep. The helmet was poorly strapped to the top of my saddlebag while I wore a cooler, less-protective half-helmet prized by motorcycle cops.

A new helmet, new rear tire, and new boots send me on, clear sailing to San Luis, Colorado, enjoying the greatest flatland ride of my life—the land sloping gently up on both sides of Highway 142, with sage of different colors resplendent as far as the eye can see. Even in the 21st century, we can be riders of the purple sage!

In San Luis, the oldest town in Colorado, it's time for a vanilla ice cream cone at the oldest business in the state, the R&R Market, owned by the same family since 1857. The town was settled in 1851 by Hispano farmers—descendants of Spaniards who lived in the Southwest at the time it was annexed to the US. At 7,979 feet, one end of the gently curving Main Street seems to float off into the sunset, and the other into the sky.

The next highlight to blow away many other highlights is the Great Sand Dunes National Park. The dunes, some 700 feet high, run as far as the eye can see. Streams of warm water flow through the dunes, filling a boot bottom of mine with the planet's finest particles of sand. The sand did not appear out of thin air. Instead, over thousands of years, it's been deposited by mountain streams and blown up from dried, ancient lakes. The shape of the dunes is, of course, entirely at the mercy of the winds.

In the city of Del Norte, my head gets bedded down after an elk dinner with mole sauce—made of chocolate, peanut butter, and other flavors. My pillow and bed are upstairs from The Dining Room in the Hotel Windsor. It's straight out of 1874, rejuvenated through a strong Del Norte community push.

• • •

A day later, I'm back in my favorite town: Saguache, Colorado (the subject of "Bingo! Zip 81149" in my motorcycle adventures of 2016). It's nine o'clock at night. I sit on a sturdy old wood chair that rests on the main street's sidewalk. I fall into a deep relaxation—no voices, no television, no radio, nary a sound. A full moon shines; a southerly breeze flows past my face. The Rocky Mountains jut upward outside of town.

Four other mismatched and untethered chairs sit in the positions they were in back at 4 p.m., when hardcore Saguachans finally rose, having eaten a late lunch or a slice of homemade pie from the 4th Street Diner and Bakery located just behind the chairs.

A car or two pass—slowly. A bicyclist slips through the dark intersection a block away. No one mills about at the Ute Theatre across the street, which, according to the sign, is "For Sale."

My Big Valley Motel room waits for me, five minutes away by foot. The public library is likewise minutes away. A small general store, just down the block, is run by Saguache Works, a nonprofit organization dedicated to making the town work better in today's world. The *Saguache Crescent* newspaper office is a block from my desolate chair.

Finally, I rise, though I doubt I would've ever had reason to. I walk down the center of the main street toward the motel. Another person, strangely enough, is out walking. We cross paths.

He takes a walk every night, he stops and tells me. He's a senior in the school at the end of the four-block-long main street. He loves mechanical work—he was just now working on his Bronco. He's learned much from his father, an expert mechanic. He's also fascinated by marine biology. He and his friends chill out in the park, cruise around town in a car, or go four-wheeling in the hills. He'll take my advice to sit in a chair in front of the diner some evening and sink into deep relaxation. One place he won't walk at night is the side of town nestling up against the Rockies, just four blocks away. "Coyotes may be on the prowl!" he warns.

Early the next morning, outside the 4th Street Diner, I meet a woman named Sky and a man named Dave, who I learn is a native of Northern Minnesota like me. They sit in the mismatched chairs still askew from yesterday.

"Did you see the deer and elk in town last night?" Sky asks.

"No," I answer. The animals didn't walk down the main street, I figure, or else arrived after my mechanic friend and I left.

Sky advises me that "mountain lions come into town too, and coyotes. And bears, lots of bears." Last night's streetwalking student, I figure, has a compelling reason to avoid the edge of town facing the mountains.

Inside the diner, I eye the display of homemade cream pies. I query the man sitting on one of the four stools whether the chocolate cream pie would be a good choice.

"Let's put it this way, son," the man wearing a sharp Western hat and boots answers. "I've walked seven and a half miles to town when it snows. I shovel the diner's sidewalk. And they give me a piece of chocolate cream pie and cowboy coffee."

"Ken [I've learned his name: Ken Minor], what was your job most of your life?" (a rancher, surely).

"Let's put it this way. I was born a Comanche Indian and Welsh." Ken seems satisfied that this adequately answers my question. I never find out if he was a rancher, for our conversation moves forward at breakneck speed.

"I've moved into an apartment in town," Ken relates. "I fell and broke open my jaw. The manager saw me and said, 'You're bleeding like a stuck pig.' Three women helped me. This morning, I bought this new hat and these boots. I walk hundreds of miles."

I admire out loud his sleek black hat—completely devoid of extravaganza—similar to the black lenses of his eyeglasses.

Ken then tells me about a woman he knew—how this came up, I don't remember. He says she inquired if he knew Elvis's "In the Ghetto." "I answered her like *this*," Ken tells me, and then sings the first two or three verses of the song for me.

"Ken, you sing as great as Elvis," I blurt out.

"That's the first time anyone ever told me that," he says.

Ken leaves to put a mile or two on his handsome new boots. I mention Ken to Chuck, a summer waiter who makes money at the diner to fund his passion: *shooting*.

"Ammunition is not cheap. Targets aren't either," Chuck tells me. Chuck lets me know that Ken comes in every day—he's "a pie fanatic." I leave an extra $4.75 with Chuck so he can serve Ken his next piece of pie and strong black cowboy coffee. I'll be a bit north of Saguache when Ken, who makes Elvis come alive, walks into the diner and sits on his stool tomorrow.

• • •

Over the next eight days, I spend nights in Colorado's Buena Vista, Aspen, and Georgetown; in Cheyenne at the Plains Hotel from 1911; in Kadoka, South Dakota (that's past Wounded Knee, on the edge of the Badlands); and in Wahpeton, North Dakota. The next day takes me home, after 4,485 miles, 29 days, 37 fills of my gas tank, and four flat tires—the first ones I've ever had on a motorcycle.[25]

The next day, I study the motorcycle parked in my garage. I'm surprised by how large and heavy it looks now. Although it was probably as charmed as I was by many locales, only I experienced the hearts, minds, and souls of the many people along the way: Lilly, the Cherokee guide; Chris, the Route 66 café waiter; LeRoy, the New Mexico rancher who's a godsend to travelers in a pinch; Ken, a diner's Elvis singer; and many more.

Journeys reveal what the lives of others behold. I believe we can answer with a powerful *yes* the question of whether we find beautiful hearts, minds, and souls in what some say is our divided society.

Her Name, I Forgot

Three days after completing my motorcycle adventure through 15 states, I see a certain someone in the pool at the Mesabi Family YMCA.

---

[25] To see the map of where the 37 fills of the gas tank led, check out the 2017 route on pages 142-43. The same map is posted, in spectacular color, on the maps pages of TomsGlobe.com.

"You changed my life!" I tell her. She is surprised. She doesn't know what I mean.

"Five years ago in the whirlpool," I explain, "when we talked about the potato crop in your garden, you told me you and your husband used to go on motorcycle trips. I asked where you liked to go. You said you loved South Dakota and Wyoming. I absorbed the beauty of your memories at that moment.

"It had never occurred to me that I could go on a long motorcycle trip," I explain. "I assumed I couldn't. But that time five years ago in the whirlpool, I thought 'I can do that. I *can* do it.' Thinking that 'I can' was a revelation to me. I've been doing it for five years now. I came back Saturday from a month in the American West."

I say all this to a woman whose name I'd forgotten. I now ask her to remind me. She is Pearl Hawkings.

"Pearl, if you and your husband had not been motorcycle adventurers, and if you hadn't told me this in the whirlpool, I might never have tried it. *You changed my life.*"

Pearl and her late husband started their adventures in 1948, when she was 21. They did it for years, but exactly for how many years, she doesn't remember right now. "I'm almost 91 years old," she tells me.

My five western trips have put 20,456 miles—traveled over 134 days—on my 2003 Harley Road King, each and every mile and day experienced thanks to Pearl.

Thank you, Pearl Hawkings. Thank you.

MOTORCYCLE ADVENTURES OF 2018

The Presidents

AUGUST 25, 2018

I'd read with a thrill what someone had written—"In a stunning American setting, you can see four Presidents *all* together."

A thousand people from dozens of countries have beaten me there the day I ride up. I nudge and elbow my way through the throng to be as close to the presidents as I can. I raise my camera. I blame my eyesight for not getting all four in the photo on first try.

Second try, a boy and I are in the same boat. He tells me his name is spelled like this: "d-a-n-i-e-l." He's five years old and from Wisconsin. I hear him say, "There's George Washington. And the other one. Mommy! There's George Washington! And the other one."

Third try, I am on my own again. I botch it—again. You might too, if you got wedged between a rock and a hard place and couldn't wiggle free anytime soon.

I know what you're thinking: *Next time, buy a postcard.*

Proof of a photographer's troubles in capturing all four presidents together!

A Glimpse through the Window
SEPTEMBER 1, 2018

A solitary figure—he says his name is Jasper—walks down the main street, glances through a window of 1880s vintage, and looks over the shoulder of a man seated inside. Nowhere else in the world does anyone get a glimpse such as this today, Jasper believes. And once a handful of years goes by, it is likely that no one will ever catch this glimpse again.

Jasper doesn't know if the man inside is aware someone is peering through the window behind him. The man certainly doesn't let it distract him from his job, a demanding one that no one else on our planet has. And once he lets go, no one will ever have this position again.

That's why Jasper lingers long enough to remember this moment deep into the future. If you walk by and see what Jasper sees, you may not know what the man is doing, unless you're steeped in glimpses of a particular history yourself.

The man is setting lines of type—one line at a time—for this week's newspaper. He doesn't use a computer, for he's not steeped in that history. Instead, he's using a machine invented by German immigrant Ottmar Mergenthaler in the 1880s. It's called the linotype machine. The machine heats metal bars of a lead alloy into a molten state while the operator types out lines for the next newspaper edition—perhaps: *Practice up your hog-callin' and chicken-cluckin' because the 6th Annual LOCAL! Harvest Festival is right around the corner!*

Jasper knows the molten metal is channeled into a small chamber and hardens around the letter molds the operator has typed on the 90-character keyboard. The metal line of type (the "slug") hardens quickly, although still burning hot to the touch. The antique machine stacks up the slugs one atop another until it jams.

Dozens of metal slugs make each column of a newspaper page. The page is clamped up tight. Soon thereafter, a mechanical roller

The "last in the world" Linotype machine at the weekly *Saguache Crescent* paper in Saguache, Colorado. The typesetting machine has a 90-character keyboard.

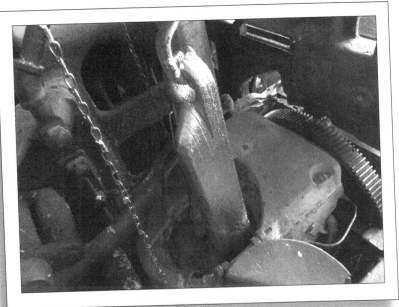

The lead bar drops slowly into the Linotype's heating chamber, becoming scorching hot liquid that forms lines of type.

coats the face of the type with black ink, and the operator then feeds a blank sheet of paper into the rotary press, printing a page. To print a hundred copies, the inking and feeding is repeated a hundred times, in as few as 120 seconds.

In a couple of days, the now useless metal slugs will be dumped, dozens at a time, into a stove superheated enough to melt lead. The molten lead will then be ladled into bar molds that the linotype operator will use for next week's paper.

Jasper recalls that at age 18, he thought about forsaking college and instead undergoing the training and apprenticeship to become a linotype operator—with union wages and job security for life. Instead, he earned money for college running the rotary press and all the machines, except the linotype, at the *Biwabik Times* in another state.

The *Saguache Crescent* weekly newspaper is described as "the only Linotype newspaper in the country, and maybe even the world" that has survived.[26] Jasper, who's traveled to several dozen countries with eyes wide open, believes that no other newspaper in the world is still set by linotype machine. In fact, Newspapers in Education, a program designed to help teachers teach children about newspapers, flatly declares that the linotype machine "is no longer in use."

Not a soul has yet suggested to Jasper—who rolled into town an hour ago on his Harley—to stroll the four-block length of the main street and discover the iconic 4th Street Diner & Bakery, the Saguache Works nonprofit thrift and local foods stores, and the Saguache County Courthouse, where one might catch the tail end of a criminal trial, the whole works happening in both English and Spanish. And then to wander off the main drag to check out some log buildings, an abandoned adobe hut, the public library, and the exquisite Wapiti Coffee House.

Jasper does not know that his acquaintance and alter ego, Thomas, visited the interior of the *Saguache Crescent* shop a year ago during

---

[26] Shelley Goldstein, "Between the Lines," *American Lifestyle* magazine, Issue 105, http://www.americanlifestylemag.com.

his last visit to his favorite town. Thomas, aka Tom, had forthrightly walked inside, taken photos, and chatted with the publisher. It never occurred to Thomas, however, to peer through the window of Publisher-Editor-Linotype Operator Dean Coombs while he's concentrating on his job, now one of a kind in the world.

A Glimpse Above
SEPTEMBER 13, 2018

Sitting by himself with no one else in sight, the solitary figure—now popularly known as Jasper—casts a glimpse straight up above his head. High above, he observes log after log after log, parallel to the ground and to each other—beams holding up the roof! Those with a vocabulary better than Jasper's, or reared in Mexico or New Mexico, would later tell him "those beams" and "those logs" are called *vigas*.

"When was this place built?" becomes of secondary order, for now that Jasper has his head turned upward, he must count those beams. "1, 2, 3, 4 [all silently to himself] 10, 11, 12 . . . 17, 18, 19 [and as his head rotates to the rear] 30, 31, 32 . . ." and finally, "43, 44."

"Does anyone in town know that 44 beams hold up this roof?" is another premature question, since Jasper is still alone in this soothing, meditation-inducing sanctum. He now lapses into a long gaze at the foot-tall white cross up front—surrounded by four flickering candles—and at the trophy-sized deer heads mounted on the side walls, two on the left and two on the right. But, for all Jasper knows, they might be elk heads.

Now entering the rear by means of the one and only door (under beam 44) are a youthful couple and five children. All that is said is respectfully quiet, even somber, including Jasper's first question. The husband answers that this structure is "very old," suggesting he introduce Jasper to his much more knowledgeable uncle, who, he says, lives a stone's throw away.

Once outside and a stone's throw away, Jasper is introduced to the uncle. As always, Jasper is wont to inquire about what he does not know.

"That incredible place was built under Spanish orders by the people of this community," the uncle informs Jasper. "They did the work between 1629 and 1641."

"Yes, the roof has 44 vigas, or is it 48, I forget now," the uncle continues.

Jasper doesn't need to inquire how long the vigas are, since he'd measured the length by walking step-by-step in his 12-inch-long shoes. The vigas are 32 feet long, Jasper had concluded.

"The vigas are of ponderosa pine, but these trees are not found anywhere near the pueblo," the uncle explains. "They were cut on the mountain 40 miles away. Rotating groups of men carried each log all the way to the pueblo, never resting them on the ground. The only time they touched the ground was when they were felled."

"The family across the street makes the best tamales—you might want to have one for lunch," the uncle now tells Jasper.

"A little later I will," Jasper answers. Right now, Jasper is drawn toward the sounds of drums, bells, and song that resonate throughout the pueblo.

Jasper makes his way left and right on the mesa top's jerky streets. In a couple minutes, he stands in a single spot for one hour, mesmerized by Native American chants and the dancers' dress, jewelry, sandals, headwear, body painting, and ornamentation.

Standing behind Jasper are two local men appreciating the tradition in silence. Like the majority of the tribal members, the two live short miles away in one of three communities in the valley, they say. Some, however, have moved to Grants, Albuquerque, Baltimore, or elsewhere. Nearly all, though, have come home for this annual feast day honoring the pueblo's patron saint, San Esteban. Feast one may, for all manner of foods are sold at tables near peoples' adobe and sandstone homes.

Jasper splits from the two local men, thinking their paths might cross again—though with thousands now flooding the crooked streets, it's likely not meant to be.

A half hour later, Jasper, back near that uncle's house, sits alone at a table in the cool shade. He's enjoying a green tamale. He then spots the two local acquaintances and calls them over, offering to treat them to tamales. That sounds like a good idea to all concerned. The three agree that whether the tamales are green or red, they are really hot!

Jasper's newfound friends now suggest they go to their family home together. That's why people from far and wide return to their native land: family and community.

"How far is your family home?" Jasper inquires.

"A minute, a minute and a half," the younger one says. It's agreed they'll head that way, their three mouths still fired up from the hot tamales.

Aerial view of Acoma Pueblo in Arizona—from a photo displayed below the mesa in Haak'u Museum.

Twenty or thirty minutes later, they aren't quite at the family home yet—not because the distance is long, but because the three are striding every hard-packed dirt street in town, admiring the jewelry, pottery, and art for sale—products of centuries of experience and tinkering.

Almost home, the younger of Jasper's acquaintances stops to examine and buy a pendant. "It is an eagle" he says. "I am in the eagle clan."

The older acquaintance opens the door, and the three walk into the family home. The friend wearing an eagle pendant approaches the traditional offering altar and says a short, silent prayer.

Ten other family members are eating, have eaten, or are too busy visiting. Two tables placed end-to-end overflow with dishes of—well, don't ask Jasper because he's not too sure, but he sees fruit after fruit, and one dish bears a striking resemblance to lasagna. He learns others are a stew, a chicken dish, oven bread, sweet rice, and chocolate cake topped with pineapple slices. And there are more. The family insists Jasper enjoy as many as he can. He does.

The family members, which include the older acquaintance's wife and children and the younger one's grandmother and her sister, are surprised that Jasper has come from a faraway state. They suggest he visit them again. Later, as Jasper is saying his thanks and goodbyes to the women sitting at the far end of the tables, someone at the other end has packed a bag for him. Out on the street a few minutes later, Jasper peeks into the bag. He finds a loaf of brick-oven bread, oranges, apple tarts, and beverages.

This is Acoma Pueblo, in New Mexico. (A stickler for pronunciation, if not vocabulary, Jasper learns that in pronouncing "Acoma," the "a" is like the a in cat, with a slight emphasis on that first syllable). Resting atop its own, quite circular private mesa 370 feet above the desert floor, it has been lived in for about 920 years now.

Before descending to the desert and visiting the pueblo's Sky City Cultural Center and Haak'u Museum, Jasper passes the house of the uncle once more. It's a stone's throw from the San Esteban del Rey Mission Church. The uncle listens intently as Jasper recounts that they met only because he'd talked to the man's nephew in the church—whose roof has at least 44 timbers that were carried from a mountain in the 1630s without touching the ground.

And because Jasper had lunch at the uncle-recommended tamale house, he met his two acquaintances from the dancing grounds. The two then showed Jasper how the feast of the year is celebrated inside family homes on the mesa top.

"What a privilege it's been to experience a family celebration!" Jasper tells the uncle.

The uncle absorbs this trail of interconnected events for a few moments.

"It was meant," he concludes.

Indeed, it seems as if all that Jasper has experienced throughout this day "was meant."

• • •

Books have been written about Acoma Pueblo's incredible history, people, and culture. In the year 1599, January 22, 23, and 24 were three deadly days, one learns. Armed with a cannon and other weapons, 70 Spanish soldiers burned most of the village, killing 800. They cut off the right feet of surviving men over age 25 and enslaved them for 20 years. They enslaved girls and boys over 12 for two decades, too.

The youths and their families did not succumb to these atrocities —but their descendants did not have it much easier come the US Bureau of Indian Affairs in the 90 years after 1869. Acoma children were forced out of their communities and into English-only boarding schools.

Wave after wave of forced removals occurred across the United States. "Kill the Indian in him and save the man" was the government's mindset. In all, hundreds of thousands of Native American children were placed in 357 boarding schools across 30 states.[27]

• • •

When departing Acoma Pueblo today, a visitor cannot escape the profound recognition that this may be the oldest town in North America —and among the most resilient.

---

[27] The National Native American Boarding School Healing Coalition, Minneapolis, MN (www.boardingschoolhealing.org). Likewise, in Canada, nearly 150,000 Indigenous and mixed-ancestry children (European and Indigenous) were forcibly separated from their families and confined to government-funded, church-run residential schools in an attempt to assimilate them. After marginalizing these peoples for most of its history, Canada enshrined the Charter of Rights and Freedoms in the Constitution, including the rights of Aboriginal peoples, in 1982, though it left the particulars for the Supreme Court to define, reports *The Canadian Encyclopedia*.

MOTORCYCLE ADVENTURES OF 2019

For the First Time
JUNE 13–27, 2019

This is the first time I'm riding a motorcycle into the American West for such a short time. Why just 15 days?

Never before have I stuffed a sheaf of papers into my saddlebags that tell original stories set in China, Laos, Vietnam, and Japan; at the tip of South America among penguins; on top of a thunderous Argentinian glacier among crevasses, sinkholes, streams, and glacierologists; and deep in an underground Bolivian mine among silver, zinc, lead—and miners who may die before they're 50.

For the last three years of motorcycle travels, I did carry a small packet of stories, about Cuba or the Guatemala town in the mountains where I hang out or about meeting a fellow Minnesota Iron Ranger named Bob Dylan in New York City.

But this year, I pack a sheaf of 150 pages—single-spaced. This summer, I have a novel job to do—and do it, I will.

For three days, I plunge into my work at my favorite coffeehouse in the American West, the Bean Broker, and at the nearby public library, both in Chadron, Nebraska. Checking out of the Westerner Motel, I continue moving westerly toward Lusk, Shawnee, and Casper, Wyoming. Riding through the reemergent 21st-century downtown of Casper, I discover The Metro, another cool coffeehouse. I do my job at a relaxing table there too.

Moving north, now, and about to pass right through Buffalo, I decide on the spur of the moment to spend a night in my favorite hotel from my ride in 2013, the Occidental. The hotel and cowboy bar were also favorites, more than a century earlier, of Theodore Roosevelt's, Butch Cassidy's, Calamity Jane's—wait! I've already told you this and much more just an hour ago, in "The Cowboy You Meet on the Next Stool."[28]

The incredible Johnson County Library is just a four-minute walk in the rain from the Occidental and worth every soaking drop. So, I work on my sheaf of papers there too.

Northerly toward Sheridan, the Bighorn Mountains rise to 13,000 feet on my left. Downtown, a joyful parade of Wyomingites course over the sidewalks carrying rainbow flags. This is the very first Gay Pride Parade in Sheridan's history, I'm told, and many hundreds joined. Next year, they'll apply for a permit to parade down Main Street—with a few horses, I'm guessing.

Reading the *Sheridan Press* newspaper, I find out that the annual reenactment of the Battle of Little Bighorn in Montana is tomorrow! Getting there is lightning fast, for you know I'm on a motorcycle or, you and I might imagine, a horse *a la* Butch Cassidy and the Sundance Kid.

The battle's reenactment is told largely from the victors' point of view—not many on Custer's side survived to tell the tale.

I go for the history but stay for the aftermath. If you go, don't miss the opportunity to wander about on the battlefield, as the bareback warriors mix peacefully with the saddled soldiers. Look up to a warrior —and his boys, who sit bareback behind their dad. Exchange greetings. Enjoy each other's company and learn that the 101st annual Crow Fair Celebration Powwow and Rodeo will be celebrated in August. "Bring

---

[28] Recall pages 145-49, and Ernest Hemingway, Dean Koontz, and 21st-century cowboy Kerry.

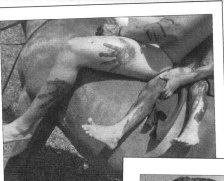

Bareback warrior Faron and sons relax after the reenactment of the Battle of the Little Bighorn of 1876.

A warrior and soldier meet after the reenactment near the Little Bighorn Battlefield National Monument in Montana.

your tent, stay four days, and enjoy the biggest Native American event in Montana," the warrior suggests.[29]

Heading back east, I check out some of my favorite places in Miles City, Montana, in rapid-fire order: the bullet-riddled Montana Bar, the don't-miss Range Rider's Museum, the Girl-Ran-Away eclectic shop, and the Olive Hotel, right out of 1889.

A day later, at high noon, I cannot resist an exit from Interstate 94 in North Dakota—hoping for any little surprise in downtown Jamestown. I'm rewarded! At Babb's Coffee House, I discover the best coffee in hundreds of miles, with lunches and desserts that satisfy every single taste bud.

[29] A racehorse-fast four-minute YouTube video shows scenes from the author's motorcycle trips, including the reenactment of the Battle of Little Bighorn. Link to the video through the blog page of TomsGlobe.com. This video is Episode 6 of the initial episodes of Tom Mattson's Virtual World Tour. Check the website to catch future videos to be added.

Still at Babb's, I do the last whit of work on my stack of papers. I make the deadline! It's a one-of-kind-job for me: finalizing my manuscript for the first book I've ever written. But the price is that I must be satisfied with a much-shortened trip in the West, since marching a book like this along involves many more tasks than just writing, such as working with my graphic artist to create and fine-tune maps, assembling dozens of photos, drafting catchy captions, and beginning to set up a website. Once my editor works her magic on my manuscript—and I "approve," "disapprove," or build on her suggestions—and my team jumps the other publishing hurdles, it will be released as *The Other Worlds: Offbeat Adventures of a Curious Traveler*.

Fast forward: Yep, my first book went to market on time in 2020.[30] The production of the book you're reading right now involved most of the same array of challenging but joyful tasks.

---

[30] *The Other Worlds* is available online at Amazon and Barnes & Noble, and at locations named at www.TomsGlobe.com.

ASIA

CAMBODIA

The Killing Fields
MARCH 5, 2017

three summer days in 1971

On a 19-month hiatus between finishing my schooling in Minneapolis and buckling down just across the Mississippi River in St. Paul, I landed in Phnom Penh from Saigon. It was June 1971. I started searching the capital for a place to sleep. A small hotel owner refused my request for a room. My presence seemed to make him nervous, and he wanted me and my backpack out as fast as possible. Was I CIA? Or KGB? Or just an all-purpose risk that could get his hotel bombed? I'd like to get that answered sometime.

I *was* accepted at an elegant, walled-in French-era hotel. It wasn't expensive, since few innocent outsiders ventured into Cambodia back then. The front desk soon handed me precise directions to the Cambodian National Tourist Office, where tourists like me could get information about the city's highlights.

A military barricade wound with barbed wire blocked the downtown street that held the tourist office. The far corner past the office, I could see, was also barricaded and topped with barbed wire. As I climbed over the barricade in front of me, a shot rang out. Startled, I jumped down, ripping my pants. A soldier armed with a rifle burst out of his guard shack, yelling at me. After some minutes of explaining, he let me go through. Just a year earlier, the Lon Nol regime had ousted Prince Norodom Sihanouk in a coup. Perhaps the new regime was skittish.

The four tourist office employees, all standing around with nothing to do, were very pleased to see a visitor. They urged me to sign the guest register. I noticed the last tourists to sign had visited Phnom Penh two months earlier.

I hoped to visit the 12th-century Angkor ruins of the Khmer Empire, just a short plane ride away. I couldn't; the ruins were closed. The country, after all, was at war, and peace nowhere in sight. Pol Pot's Khmer Rouge were advancing into government-held territory. The war in neighboring Vietnam had spilled over the border into Cambodia, too.[31]

I could travel, but only to a nearby village in a bicycle rickshaw. At the end of my visit to the village, a soldier asked if he could hitch a ride back to the city with me. Within a couple of minutes, though, the soldier implored the driver to turn around: he'd forgotten the rifle he'd hidden under a house. Once in Phnom Penh, the soldier asked to see my charming hotel. The hotel guard refused. After some tripartite negotiations, we got to a reluctant, "Yes, for five minutes."

Once in my room, the soldier spotted my transistor radio and politely inquired whether I could give it to him. I thought I loved that radio more than he did, so I said no. But over the years, I've kept wondering whether the soldier might have enjoyed the radio twice or maybe ten times more than I did. He probably died by way of execution, torture, starvation, or battle—while the radio would have probably kept on living a useful life. Instead, I kept the radio, listened to music and news while in Asia, and years later couldn't remember what happened to it.

What happened to the soldier, or any other person living in Phnom Penh when I was there in 1971, I could never be sure—until another visit some 46 years later.

---

[31] The author's 1970–71 travels through Asia are described in his first book, *The Other Worlds: Offbeat Adventures of a Curious Traveler* (Dudley Court Press, 2020). See "Around the World in 400 Days," pp. 57–73.

mr. phi lay ob

In 2017, I traveled back to Cambodia for a week. Since I'd be visiting Battambang—a few hours northwest of Phnom Penh—my cousin Jeff Lippincott, who lives in Bangkok, suggested a father and son motorbike tuk-tuk driving pair to show me the Battambang environs. I engaged the 61-year-old father, Phi.

Together, Mr. Phi and I bumped over dirt roads and a six-foot-wide bridge, explored a thousand-year-old temple up 358 stone steps, and hiked down into a killing cave where body after body had once piled up, pushed by the Khmer Rouge through an opening in the ground high above. Now, down in the cave, bones of the murdered are displayed. It is a memorial to victims who were never identified, perhaps because they had no recognizable clothing when found.

Mr. Phi turned out to be much more than a driver and guide. He told me what happened to him as a teenager and young man. For him, like for almost every other Cambodian, life changed irrevocably on April 17, 1975. On that day, Pol Pot's victorious Khmer Rouge marched into the capital city. They ordered every man, woman, and child into the countryside.[32]

"I was a high school student when you visited Phnom Penh in 1971, Mr. Tom," he tells me. "On April 17, 1975, I rushed home from school and beseeched my father to go hide in an elementary school. I brought food to him that night. I told him everyone had to leave Phnom Penh. The Khmer Rouge were breaking into homes and killing anyone they found hiding.

"Ten days later, I met my family some distance away. My mother had been a schoolteacher, my father a colonel in Lon Nol's army, and my uncle an air force pilot. I didn't see them anymore after that. They were all killed, or they starved to death—my father, my mother, my brother, my uncle, and other family members.

---

[32] For readers curious about the complex history of Pol Pot, who was born Saloth Sar, or the roles other Cambodian leaders and foreign nations played in the conflict, a good place to start might be *Pol Pot: Anatomy of a Nightmare* by Philip Short (New York: Henry Holt & Co., 2007).

"I was 19 or 20 years old. I was always hungry and I couldn't sleep. My hair fell out. You could see my rib bones. I searched for crabs and snails. Once, I found a cucumber in a field. I ate food meant for pigs. I drank water from puddles, like an animal.

"We were forced to work in the fields every day. On nights with a full moon, we were ordered to work in the fields too. There was no Saturday, no Sunday, no holiday, no market, no school, no religion.

"One day, the Khmer Rouge called a meeting of workers and accused three of my friends of stealing food. In front of my eyes, my friends were beaten with a stick or board, and their skulls slashed with a farm hoe. They all died.

"In 1981, after Vietnamese soldiers invaded and overthrew the Khmer Rouge, I joined a sea of walking refugees. After a month, I made it to Thailand. I lived in a refugee camp for nine years. I married. We had four children in the camp and were then able to move back to Cambodia. We now have eight children. I drive a motorbike tuk-tuk to earn money. I take visitors like you around Battambang and out in the countryside, showing them my country of Cambodia."

Mr. Phi recounted his story in a soft, somber tone, looking down as if in prayer. It seemed to me that it was important to him to share his memories. So I wrote a few notes on a scrap of paper before getting out of his tuk-tuk in Battambang and waving goodbye.

the chao ponhea yap high school and its transformations
To my surprise, the school that Mr. Phi had attended in Phnom Penh was the Chao Ponhea Yap High School. I had not expected to meet anyone from that infamous establishment during my trip. The Chao Ponhea Yap High School, built in 1962, was once filled with promising Cambodian students like Mr. Phi—until April 17, 1975. No student has ever attended class there again, and I wonder how many of the former pupils are still alive today. After Khmer Rouge soldiers—some of high school age or younger—marched into Phnom Penh, Pol Pot's

security forces turned the school into Security Prison 21—or S-21. Classrooms soon held rows of prisoners bound together with ankle shackles.

Between 12,000 and 18,000 people suspected of undesirable convictions passed through S-21. Fewer than 200 were ever released. Some were tortured and killed in the classrooms, the others trucked blindfolded to a killing field. The Khmer Rouge kept meticulous records, each prisoner photographed upon arrival at S-21, and sometimes again after torture.

Today, S-21 is now the Tuol Sleng Genocide Museum. The former prison is in almost the same condition as when Vietnamese-led forces invaded in 1979, forcing the Khmer Rouge to flee toward Thailand. One finds tools of torture, classrooms subdivided into tiny cells, and uncleansed blood stains on walls and floors. Photographs taken by the Khmer Rouge are displayed: faces of hundreds of doctors, teachers, monks, students, lawyers, railway engineers, and peasants; faces of prisoners' families who were imprisoned with them; and faces of youthful Khmer Rouge soldiers who came under suspicion and were thus imprisoned.

"You, the contemptible, do not have to ask why you are here," some prisoners were told. "While getting lashes or electrification, you must not cry at all," an order posted in the classrooms warned. "Better we have made a wrongful arrest than let the enemy eat us away from within," commanders told guards. "Our mission is to sweep the country clean of traitors."

The tortured had to "confess" opposing the regime or being spies for the CIA, KGB, or Vietnam, and to accuse relatives and friends. A seafaring adventurer from New Zealand who had mistakenly drifted into Cambodian waters was captured, imprisoned, and tortured. In a forced confession, he identified his supposed CIA commanders as "Colonel Sanders" and "Major Ruse" and gave his home phone number as his spy operative number. He, like the others, was executed—in his case, tied into a tire and set on fire.

Streams of today's high school students visit the classrooms, most silently and some seemingly stunned. While I am there, three huddle, pointing to two photos. Perhaps they see a family resemblance. I learn

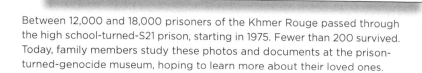

Between 12,000 and 18,000 prisoners of the Khmer Rouge passed through the high school-turned-S21 prison, starting in 1975. Fewer than 200 survived. Today, family members study these photos and documents at the prison-turned-genocide museum, hoping to learn more about their loved ones.

that one woman has discovered several people she knew. Thousands, in fact, have come searching for lost family members and friends, studying the photos and documents meticulously kept by the executioners.

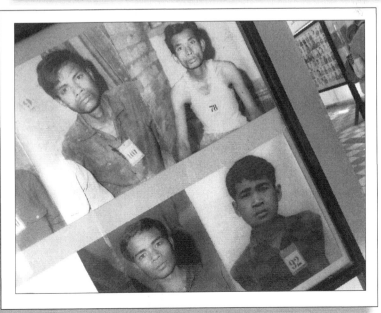

A genocide survivor painted this scene of an inmate shower—years after the Khmer Rouge and their leader Pol Pot were ousted from power. Painting shown at the Tuol Sleng Genocide Museum in Phnom Penh.

choeung ek, a killing field

Most of the 12,000 to 18,000 persons imprisoned at S-21 were executed 10 miles away in the Choeung Ek field, one of 347 killing fields in Cambodia. Their throats were sliced, or they were bludgeoned, beheaded, shot, or buried alive. Infants were hurled against a tree.

The bodies of nearly 9,000 victims have been exhumed from 86 mass graves at Choeung Ek. Another 43 graves have been left untouched. The Killing Tree, where the flesh of babies stuck to the bark, still stands. Thousands of skulls are displayed on a series of glass shelves in a tall stupa that commemorates the two million or so Cambodians—about a quarter of the population—who died from 1975–79 across Cambodia.

You may walk on trails between the mass graves that are now sunken and covered with undulating, fast-growing vegetation. During monsoon rains, bone fragments, clothing, and blindfolds bubble up from the fields. You may stand a foot from the Killing Tree, placing a hand or a commemorative item on it.

mother and father

At a Phnom Penh watering hole called the Foreign Correspondents Club, I chat with waiter Mr. Pov, who serves me a glass of dragon fruit juice:

"Pov, has your mother or father said anything to you about the war?"

"Thirty people, including my father, were marched to a killing field," Pov explains. "Twenty-nine were executed. The thirtieth—my father—was about to be executed, but the soldiers needed someone to dispose of the bodies. They asked him if he was willing. They ordered him to throw the dead in a boat, row to a certain place, and dump them out. He did it."

"Did the 30 people know what they had done wrong?" I ask Pov.

"Yes. They had eaten food. They were hungry. People ate the bark of trees if they had nothing else. That was against the law, too. They could eat only what the Khmer Rouge said they could eat.

"My mother told me the countryside's population exploded in just a few days because the city people were ordered out. If they didn't comply, the Khmer Rouge killed them. City people had soft hands. The Khmer Rouge sometimes killed people with soft hands first.

"My mother heard a commotion one day," Pov continued. "She saw a Khmer Rouge soldier split a woman's chest from top to bottom. The soldier pulled out organs and said how good they were to eat. That man is still alive. My mother knows him. She is afraid of him to this day."

"Do your parents ever visit Phnom Penh?" I inquire.

"My mother hopes I can afford to pay her bus fare. She wants to go to the genocide museum. She wants to look at the pictures and documents about those who died to find her lost brother. Her brother's wife and daughter are still waiting for him to come home."

Over the years, I've often wished I'd given Pov the money his mother needed to visit Phnom Penh.

child soldiers

As I visit the Cambodia Landmine Museum and Relief Facility, near Siem Reap, the site of the 12th-century Angkor ruins, I read these stories:

"When I was 14 years old, I worked alongside the Vietnamese army fighting the Khmer Rouge in Cambodia. One day we were out-numbered. Some of us were killed. Those of us running for our lives purposefully dropped certain AK-47 ammunition magazines onto the ground. The Khmer Rouge didn't realize we had added poison to the bullets so that when the gun is fired, it gives off poisonous fumes. Later, we returned to find the Khmer Rouge choking, which enabled us to kill them all."

"I fought for the Khmer Rouge starting when I was 10. In the early 1980s, when I was still a child, I defected to the Vietnamese army in Cambodia to fight the Khmer Rouge. I was required to go out at night and hunt for food with an AK-47 or M-16. Hunting in the jungle at night, I sometimes ran into my friends who were still in the Khmer Rouge who I had grown up with. They were also hunting for food. We hunted together. When we were through, we played together in the jungle. We were still children. The next day we would kill each other."

the old high school as a teacher of all

A Phnom Penh student asked me how I felt after visiting the genocide museum. Even though I spent four hours at that old school over two days, I could not put my feelings into words. I could only tell him, "It was important that I went. It was important."

Upon leaving the museum, a sign enjoins: *The archives here have been named a "Memory of the World." You, too, are a keeper of that memory. Tell others what happened so we may all strive for human dignity, compassion, and peace everywhere.*

As I read those words, I think of all that I've seen, all that I've read, all that I've heard, and all the people I've met. Most of all, I think of former student turned tuk-tuk driver Phi Lay Ob, who told me about some of his life and all the lives lost. It was important that he spoke, and it was important that I heard. It was important. I told him I'd be writing to you. So you, too, can be a keeper of memory.

THAILAND

Photographs That Should Never Be Published

MARCH 5, 2017

two years of longing for the idyllic village

The village pictured in *The New York Times* was idyllic. I wanted to go. I scissored out the image and its story. For two years, I looked at the photo, just in case I ventured to Northern Thailand. Take a look at the picture and long with me for a short time.

The New York Times published this photo of an idyllic scene in Ban Rak Thai, Thailand, causing a Minnesotan to long for the day when he might visit the remote village.

I did have two questions. Does a road even run to the village, nestled against the Burmese border? If so, is there any means of transportation?

I was well on my way to answering these questions as I sat in seat 8A on Bangkok Air out of Chiang Mai, bustling now as it bustled in 1450 AD as the center of the Lan Na civilization. How could I go wrong snapping up a one-way fare discounted to $25—because not too many wanted to fly?

a surprise awaits the longing traveler

The twin-prop plane takes me to the remote provincial capital of Mae Hong Son. After that, it is up to me. Renting a Honda 125 motorbike for $7 a day is a no-brainer, even with 50,000 miles of mountain roads showing up on its odometer. Satisfactory oral instructions from the rental agent trumps his poor map. I just have to remind myself to ride on the left side of the road the whole way.

Up and up I ride, around hairpin curves, past waterfalls, and through a giant bamboo forest and pleasant but non-idyllic villages. Next, I skirt the royal family's old vacation retreat, hillside tea tracts, and a strawberry field.

Finally, I get to Ban Rak Thai, also known as Mae Wa, the storied village in *The New York Times*. But the idyllic part is missing! I see no charming bungalows on rolling hills. Instead, I find a village that, while not unpleasant, looks like many other villages, with their corrugated tin roofs and cinder-block dwellings. Having checked into a guesthouse on the shore of the lake-like reservoir taking up the center of town, I attempt to find the view shown in the newspaper. Failing again in the morning, I sit down at a lakeside shop owned by two brothers, Avong and Jasada. While sipping my coffee, they bring me complimentary tea, as would a shop owner down the street, after she filled my Honda tank with gas from a soft-drink plastic bottle she grabbed from a shelf full of them.

Enjoying my coffee and tea, I pull the clipping from my knapsack. I didn't come here because of the history; in fact, I had forgotten all about it. The article, I see, describes Ban Rak Thai as a Chinese village, settled mostly by Kuomintang fighters from China who lost to Mao Tse Tung. These settlers never made it to Taiwan, like thousands of their compatriots did. Most of the fighters who came to Ban Rak Thai have now died, but their descendants live on, the newspaper tells me.

What would Avong, 28 years old, and Jasada, 24, have to say about this? Jasada speaks to me in English, but Thai is his best language, he tells me. He also handles Chinese and two languages from Burma, including Shan.

Jasada and Avong's late grandfather was a Kuomintang fighter. The Kuomintang in Southern China's Yunnan Province crossed the border into nearby Burma in their 1949 escape from Mao's forces. They made warring incursions into China for years—until China invaded Burma to end the war.

Brothers Jasada and Avong hold *The New York Times* clipping that details the history of their village, settled by defeated anti-Mao Tse Tung soldiers who fled China.

Meanwhile, their grandfather married a Burmese woman. Thailand allowed the old fighters and their families to move from Burma to Ban Rak Thai and other locales—if they agreed to fight the Thai Communists. Deal done. Peace has been at hand for decades now.

And what about my reason for *being* in Ban Rak Thai—the most idyllic village photo I'll ever see? It is *not* a photo of the village, as the newspaper caption said, but of corporate-built cottages dotting the hillside tea field that comes down just about to Avong and Jasada's place. The cottages are part of a high-end *resort*. And, as you might have guessed, they're hidden from view. Unless, like me, you walk up a steep pathway, stand on your tiptoes, and peer over a damned fence.

That photo should never have been published! I tell myself.

I return to Avong and Jasada's coffee shop (or tea house). I decide not to carry the newspaper clipping back across 11 time zones to Lost Lake to keep as a memento. I show it to the brothers. I ask Jasada if he'd be able to understand the big English words with help from his smartphone. And whether he could make a copy for a surviving 85-year-old Kuomintang warrior who lives a block away, since that man is pictured in a second *New York Times* photo.

"Yes, I can do all of this," Jasada tells me. He immediately becomes engrossed in the article, with his smartphone at hand.

I now tell myself that Jasada, Avong, and one of the last Kuomintang warriors in Ban Rak Thai have a memento of their history, published a world away in the planet's greatest newspaper—save for the occasional misguided photograph.

scouting and reconnoitering on the spur of the moment

It's time to ride my Honda back down the mountainside. But now that I'm here and none the worse for wear, why don't I just ride a short kilometer to the Burmese border and see if some sparks fly?

"No, you can't ride your Honda into Burma at this checkpoint, no, you can't! But I will take a photo of you with your camera, and you can climb the hill for a view." I understand this much from the 17-year-old Thai Patrol Platoon soldier through 12 words and hand signals, not these 34 words without signals.

At high noon, I trudge up the hill with a view. I find a Thai army camp looking down on a Burmese ethnic village a kilometer away—a village that does look idyllic. Two hammocks in the camp look like they're holding heavy men fast asleep, but since they don't move or make a sound, I assume the hammocks just hold bundled belongings.

I walk the length of a military trench that's been dug into the ridge of the hill facing Burma. Every 10 meters, I pass through a micro-shack covered with sandbags. I spy what appears to be a treehouse but discover it's a lookout tower with steps made of branches nailed into the tree trunk. I study a bamboo fence down the hill that runs parallel to the trench. "They sure know how to sharpen the bamboo ends into killer points," I mutter.

Sandbagged defensive bunkers on the Thai-Myanmar border—a photo that should never be published!

I'm all by myself. I'm the lone defender, except for the spiky bamboo fence. I've never felt so good about a wall in my life. If the other side invades, it'll be a fight to the last man standing—namely me. Meanwhile, taking photos and videos of all I see whiles away my time.

As I descend back toward the checkpoint manned by the patrol platoon, it occurs to me that a military edict may outlaw the photos and video clips I took, which reveal defenses at the border. *The photos showing the killer bamboo fence, the trench, the sandbagged shacks, and the lookout station SHOULD NEVER BE PUBLISHED*, I conclude.

Amplification: Once back in the provincial capital of Mae Hong Son, I search the online archives of *The New York Times* for the Ban Rak Thai story. The caption under the idyllic photo in the archives correctly describes it as a *resort*, not a village scene. *The Times* stands corrected and has been standing tall since it made its clarification hours after the story's publication.

In the future, I'll think twice about clutching an idyllic photo so dearly for two years—and 11 time zones. Yet something tells me I might do it anyway, since the first time turned out so well.

MYANMAR

Zoology 101 Final Exam
MARCH 26, 2017

online from yangon, myanmar

This exam has just three questions ("the professor is busy"), and getting one of three right earns an A- ("the professor loves happy people"). After you complete the exam in 60 seconds, you'll have unbridled discretion to give yourself an honest grade.

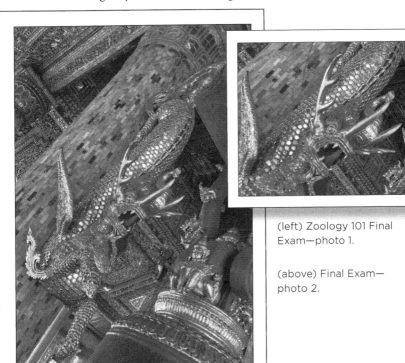

(left) Zoology 101 Final Exam—photo 1.

(above) Final Exam—photo 2.

Your professor's photo of the gold-covered Shwedagon Pagoda (on left).

Do not read Part A until you've taken a look at the photos that accompany this exam—the second a close-up of the first ("rules are rules"). The third photo shows a gold, diamond, and gem-laden pagoda on the left. It's not part of the exam but is for you to behold.[33]

Part A—Final Examination:
(Looking at the photos again is encouraged)

1. Does the creature climbing down the post represent a known animal? If so, what's the animal's name?

2. Is the figure, instead, an ancient mythological creature?

3. If it's a mythological creature, has its name and role in culture been lost in time?

---

[33] Remember to consult www.TomsGlobe.com on your smartphone or laptop as you read this book. All the photos and maps are posted in brilliant color.

Part B—Discussion:

Now that you've taken a fierce stab at the questions, let's discuss.

Toe-Nayar is one of many mythological creatures in Burmese folklore. This one has characteristics of a dragon (face, mouth, eyes), lion (legs), elephant (trunk and tusks), deer (antlers), and bird (wings).

Most Burmese mythological creatures are endowed with humanistic mentalities, an ability to converse with humans, and supernatural power. Today, in some regions such as Taunggyi, you'll see the Toe-Nayar appear each November on the first day of the 10-day Fire Balloon Festival.

Your professor, very truthful, admits that he never knew any of this until he visited the Shwedagon Pagoda, founded in 588 BC to enshrine four hairs of Gautama Buddha, the first Buddha. The famously tall pagoda was built in later millennia. It was covered, ounce by ounce, with 27 tons of gold leaf. Thousands of diamonds and gems were set on the exterior.

Bedazzled by the gold, diamonds, and gems within seconds of arriving, your professor sat on the floor in the shade—as the temperature hit 101—to figure out that the gold is worth $985 million today.

Fifteen sun-struck and heat-stroke minutes later, *befuddled* was the professor upon seeing a *thing* climbing down a post next to King Tharawaddy's 1842 bronze bell. He forgot about gold and dollars, diamonds and gems, and instead studied the four identical *things* climbing down four posts.

Bewitched is the only word to describe the professor as he sunk into the realm of these *somethings*. Never one hesitant to confess his ignorance, he beseeched women working at Shwedagon Pagoda and his hotel to tell him what it was he had seen. And that is how he learned of the Toe-Nayar, then fired up the internet to learn more.

Part C—Your Grade:

This is another fun part. You get to grade yourself. Just fill in the blank: *I give myself an ___-.*

Part D—Reckoning:

Your professor apologizes. He teaches both Zoology 101 and Mythology 101. He mistakenly gave you zoology students the mythology exam. Don't start complaining. He's hunkered down in Yangon, Myanmar (formerly Rangoon, Burma), studying a dozen other creatures. He's preparing to teach Mythology 102.

Althura, Belu, Magana, and Sarmaree are just a few of the other Burmese creatures. A pair of the folkloric beings may be a lover couple half bird and half human, and others a bird with a melodious cry, a benevolent guardian of treasures hidden in tree roots, and a man-eating humanoid capable of shapeshifting.

If you passed the Myth 101 exam above—or received a failing grade but tried hard—you may sign up for Myth 102. Just jet to Myanmar next month for some first-of-its-kind, hands-on field study.

We'll start Myth 102 attempting to validate some hearsay: Can our beloved Toe-Nayar breathe out flames, turn objects and creatures into ash just by looking at them, fly through the skies, and swim through the earth as if it were water? We may stay until November to meet the live one at the annual festival.

Those venturing to Myanmar who are also enrolled in the professor's Crime and Zoology course should first stop in Bangkok. You'll meet the reporter who wrote the jolting story in today's *Bangkok Post*: "Gang Is Stealing Elephants and Changing Their Identity." You'll then investigate elephant owners' complaints that a gang is stealing individuals from their herds, creating fake ID papers, and selling the elephants to a safari park hundreds of miles away.

If you're the one to discover information leading to an arrest, the professor is betting that the rightful elephant owner will take a viral-worthy picture of you riding his elephant back to the herd. Start thinking about a newspaper headline. You'll earn an A+ in the world's only Crime and Zoology course![34]

---

[34] Discover a hidden gem in Myanmar—Inle Lake, where villages are built on stilts over the water, and artisans and fishermen ply their trades—some in a way never seen in the outside world. See the Inle Lake photo blog on www.TomsGlobe.com, and the YouTube link to Tom Mattson's Virtual World Tour, at Myanmar's Inle Lake (Episode 3).

BHUTAN

A Road Trip through the Kingdom of Bhutan
APRIL 2017

from one farmhouse to another

At the beginning of this road trip, I write a brief note to Craig and Vicky Trytten, lifelong farmers who own a traditional dairy farm in Minnesota:

The last time I'd eaten a meal at a farmhouse, it was at yours —Thanksgiving week, five months ago. Tonight, though, sitting on Namgay Zam's wood plank floor, the first drink was tea the farm couple brewed from leaves and crushed stems of shrubs—they'd mixed in butter and milk, of course. The evening's last beverage was their warmed rice whiskey, with butter and eggs added.

I just might make these beverages after I sit on your tractor for a few hours this summer. I'll pick the stems and leaves near your back forty, add your hour-old milk and the butter you churn, and beat in eggs from your daughter Nicky's farm. Just before I head your way, though, I'll pick wild ferns that abound at Lost Lake and steam them just so in your kitchen.

How in the world would I know to steam ferns? Between the beverages, tonight's supper included curled but unwinding new-season fern tips. As is customary, much comes from the farmer's own land, like tonight's chicken and ginger soup, spinach, hard boiled eggs on rice, and ferns.

See you in a month or two, Craig and Vicky.

Tom

Taktsang Monastery (Tiger's Nest)

Yaks

Disputed Border

Tongshanjiabu 23,645 ft
Kangphu Kang 23,687 ft
Liang Kar 753

Jigme Dorji Nat'l Park

HIMALAYAS

Trashithang

TIBET

Namgay Zam's Farmhouse

Punakha

THIMPHU

Paro River

Drugyel Dzong

Paro

Haa

Me River

Wangdue

Dochula Pass

Journey Starts & Ends

Phobjikha Valley Trek

Haa River

Amo River

Tondu

INDIA

KEY

Route of the Roadtrippers

Tom with Author Kunzang Choden (Queen of Tang Valley)

Learn & Lend...

LEND the author a big hand by sharing a comment about my book on amazon.com (if you've purchased $50 or more in Amazon products in the last year).

An "Amazon review" may be as short as a sentence or two! If you haven't posted a review before, ask me for an easy step-by-step method. Just email: tomlostlake@yahoo.com.

LEARN much more at www.tomsglobe.com.

   Color photos
   High resolution custom maps
   More stories and videos on Blog page
   How to buy *The Other Worlds* and
          Meeting Strangers, Making Friends

LEARN about my newest explorations and where-abouts in my monthly Newsletter. Sign up on my website, www.tomsglobe.com, or email me at tomlostlake@yahoo.com. Your questions & comments are always welcome!

Thank you!

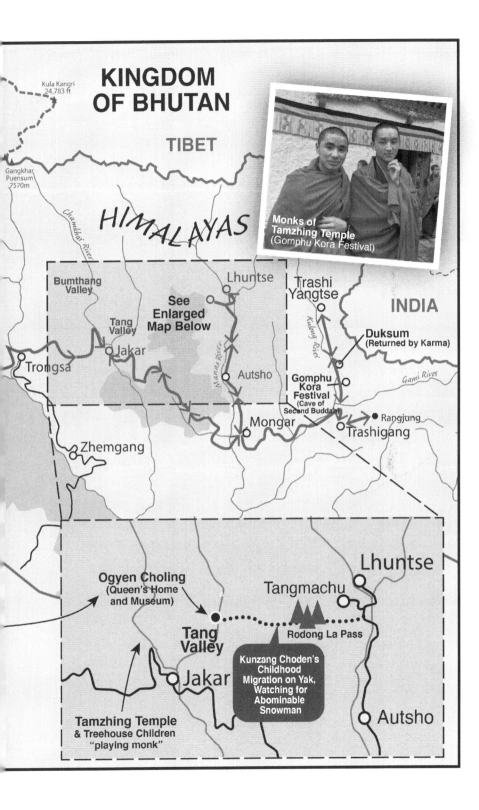

KINGDOM OF BHUTAN

TIBET

Kula Kangri
24,783 ft

Gangkhar
Puensum
7570m

HIMALAYAS

Monks of Tamzhing Temple
(Gomphu Kora Festival)

Chamkhar River

Bumthang Valley

Lhuntse

Trashi Yangtse

INDIA

See Enlarged Map Below

Tang Valley

Kulong River

Jakar

Duksum
(Returned by Karma)

Trongsa

Manas River

Autsho

Gomphu Kora Festival
(Cave of Second Buddah)

Gami River

Zhemgang

Mongar

Rangjung

Trashigang

Tang Valley (Enlarged Map)

Ogyen Choling
(Queen's Home and Museum)

Tangmachu

Lhuntse

Tang Valley

Rodong La Pass

Kunzang Choden's Childhood Migration on Yak, Watching for Abominable Snowman

Jakar

Tamzhing Temple
& Treehouse Children
"playing monk"

Autsho

• • •

Now I write for the world.

The farm mom, Namgay Zam, was born in the original house, a stone's throw from Namgay's, where I stay. Her mother prefers to keep living in the old house.

As the oldest daughter, Namgay Zam has taken ownership of the farm—that's the custom here in the country's west. Families in the east do it differently: the eldest son inherits the property. If a man from the west marries a woman from the east, the couple inherits no land; though today, some families custom-design the devolution of property.

This farm is up a steep and rough gravel road from the river valley town of Punakha. There was a time when the only way to haul anything up here, or get a load down, was by foot or on a horse. That time was the year 2000. Once the gravel road was built, families sold their horses to farmers not blessed with roads. In the last 20 years, hundreds of rural roads have been built. Now, many of the nation's people—about 80% of whom work in agriculture—no longer need a horse.

This farm is milking three cows; the others are pasturing. You don't drink a glass of milk in Bhutan, so I'll wait until I see Craig and Vicky to down glasses of raw milk. Here, all the milk goes to make butter, cheese, and the everyday "milk tea." The other kind of tea is "butter tea," which is, well, buttery! Still, I may lose weight since fresh vegetables dominate meals. Sugary and fatty deserts are not in vogue here.

• • •

From our road trip's starting point of Thimpu, we've traveled over the 10,301-foot-high Dochula Pass to get to Punakha today. Thimpu's the country's capital and largest city, with 80,000 people and growing.

Many visitors to Bhutan head out of Thimpu in the opposite direction, aiming to climb a two-mile-long trail that's centuries old. Some are not able to fulfill that dream once they start, while others behold a monastery called Paro Taksana, or Tiger's Nest, built high into the mountainside in 1692.

According to the legend, Guru Rinpoche flew on the back of a tigress from Tibet to that lofty spot in the eighth century. After arriving, he meditated in a cave for three years, which is how Buddhism was introduced in Bhutan. That spot is now one of Bhutan's most recognized and sacred places. I won't get there until the end of this adventure, in two weeks.[35]

• • •

My road-tripping car continues east, away from Thimpu and Namgay Zam's farmhouse. Not too many miles away is the country's tallest mountain, topping 24,783 feet. Bhutan owned an even higher mountain for years—until a pact with neighboring China moved the border.

"Are there any remote villages that take three or four days to walk to?" I ask Phuntsho, one of my two companions, since I see that these mountains are dotted with few farms and fewer towns.

"Even nine days," he answers. "Those people are nomads. Their lives revolve around the yak."

"Can people travel into Tibet?" I inquire, though I realize China governs Tibet.

"We have no border relations with China," Phuntsho (pronounced "foon-so") explains. "Soldiers are stationed on both sides. Travel there is illegal. Some do sneak across on trails to buy gems, though. They come back and sell the gems to traders from our southern neighbor, India."

Hour after hour, Phuntsho clues me in to life in Bhutan. "Because of earthquakes, no building in the entire country can be higher than six stories—it's the law," he explains.

---

[35] The author's photo of Tiger's Nest, taken after nearly two hours of climbing, is shown on the map of the kingdom on pp. 236-37. The road trippers' cross-country route through the Himalaya Mountains is traced on the map, too.

"Does a developer ever ignore the rules and build to seven stories?" I wonder.

"Yes," he answers, "but good luck on ever getting the government to install electricity or internet!"

A day later we journey to the Phobjikha Valley, distant from the outside world. In 2000, the government built a road here that connects to National Highway No. 1. No foreign visitors had ever come to this valley until then. We leave the car behind and hike down the middle of the valley, which stretches for miles. Most of this land is a communal cow pasture. All farmers are free to pasture cows here; fencing a part off is not allowed.[36]

"This valley is out of this world!" I tell Phuntsho. "If an entrepreneur proposed to pave a bicycle trail down the heart of the valley, thousands of tourists could enjoy a beautiful ride. And a hotel, restaurant, store, and bar would come next. Would they get permission to make these improvements, Phuntsho?"

"No, they most certainly would not!" he responds. "Bhutanese people value their way of life—and the environment." (So there goes the best profit-making idea I've had in Bhutan.)

Our hike takes us through a field near a village. Seed potatoes have just been planted. A stone fence surrounds a garden with beautiful soil. Three women wielding hammers are building the fence higher with old lumber. They greet us with broad smiles.

"You have to build a fence as strong as your neighbor's," Phuntsho explains. "Wild boars will eat up most seed potatoes in a night. The boars will look for the weakest fence. They can't do as much damage when the crop is mature, since they get stuffed fast with big potatoes.

"Tom, do you hunt wild boars where you live?" Phuntsho would like to know. "And do you have tigers or leopards?" I have to answer these questions in the negative.

---

[36] This diversion, like many stops and side trips, is illustrated on the map of the kingdom.

We find ourselves walking down a gentle slope. The dry-season grass is very short, the ground hard. Phuntsho describes what kids do during the rainy season, when the grass grows taller and the pasture surface feels lubricated: they slide down the hill on a short board as if on a toboggan. The activity is called *zhu-ta*. It's usually enjoyed by boys when they're pasturing cattle, Phuntsho explains. It whiles away the time.

To cross rivulets on the valley floor more easily, farmers have laid down what appear to be scraps of lumber. Phuntsho bends down to examine the tops and bottoms of a couple of boards. He discovers that they were *zhu-ta* boards. Adults have repurposed them. I'd like to know what a kid will say when he finds his favorite *zhu-ta* board being used as a "bridge." Will he be upset, proud, or simply amused?

Soon, it is time to continue our road trip, and our Hyundai Creta SUV climbs high out of the valley. Yaks graze on the mountainside.

"Yaks are not a wild animal, and a herd can number 80 or more," Phuntsho tells me. "Each herd is owned by a family. The families on neighboring mountain slopes stay in touch, advising about menacing predators, like wolves or possibly a tiger or leopard. The nomadic yak-herders sleep in tents, except when they live in a nomad village for short periods."

Phuntsho explains that yaks, being thick-furred, high-altitude animals, don't suffer heat well. As the season warms in March and April, nomads herd the yaks to higher elevations. The yaks may climb up for just a day and pasture for two or three weeks, finishing off the grass in that area. They're then herded higher and higher, and descend months later, when heavy snows begin.

Today, we see a tent, one yak-herding woman, and just a few yaks next to the road. We stop near the yaks, but under no circumstances do we get out of the car.

As you may have guessed, Phuntsho is my teacher, technically known as a guide. A government rule prohibits visitors from landing in Bhutan without prior travel arrangements through a travel agency —in my case, top-notch Access Bhutan.

Our driver is Dorji. He was once the foreign minister's chauffeur. He's the best driver I've seen anywhere in the world, expertly navigating the lightly traveled but most challenging roads I've ever seen ("most frightening roads of my life," a California visitor told me). Road improvements are under way, though, at the most furious pace in world history, I venture to say.

So that's the three of us new friends at the beginning of a road trip through the Kingdom of Bhutan. The trip could continue to wherever in the kingdom we choose to go.

north toward tibet

Dorji, Phuntsho, and I motor out of a city named Mongar on the east-west National Highway No. 1. We soon abandon the main highway and turn north toward Tibet. We thread the gorge created by the Kuru River over several million years.

Halfway to Lhuntse town—upriver 50 miles—a woman holding a child in her arms waves us to a stop. She asks for a ride to Lhuntse, saying her boy must go to the hospital. He's not quite one year old. The appointment is not until tomorrow, but if she waits until then, she may not find a timely ride. Her child is due to have several vaccinations. The two of them hop in, and we continue our journey.

Continuing into the nearly impassable north, we reach Lhuntse— 20 miles south of Tibet. For centuries, traders, yak-herders, Buddhist monks, and migrants have moved through the Himalayas between Tibet and this part of Bhutan. Folks on comparable missions, and perhaps abominable snowwomen and snowmen, have journeyed this way for thousands of years.

We drive up a wonderfully steep Lhuntse street. At the end, we find a 16th-century *dzong*—a combined monastery, temple, and government center. We stop and meander our way through the nooks and crannies of this *dzong*, just as we do in other provincial centers. Every *dzong* is unique, and to the nth degree, magnificent.

Returning south along the Kuru River, we veer off the highway. We motor up the mountainside on six miles of winding, largely one-lane road. On the way, we stop and chat with another wayfarer. His first language is Kurtoep, one of 21 less-spoken languages in Bhutan. Thus, he speaks the nation's main language of Dzong quite slowly and with an accent affected by the phonetic sounds of his primary language.

The local man reveals that a tigress was once seen drinking water at the river. The man's village took the name Tangmachu, meaning "the drinking water tigress." Since the account is recorded in an ancient Buddhist writing, this happened very long ago, Phuntsho tells me.

We drive thousands of feet higher, to "Drinking Water Tigress" town. We soon walk the grounds of a new temple, modern and sleek, unlike those from the 7th and 16th centuries that we're growing accustomed to. Inside, we see that 40 monks are commemorating a recently passed Buddhist Master. Upon paying our respects and making a prayer, each of us receives one handful of holy water from a monk. Like Phuntsho and Dorji, I take a sip of the water from my hand—and slap the remainder on my head.

We then descend to the Kuru River and turn right, with Tibet just an abandoned dream in our rearview mirror. We stop at the village of Autsho, which struck us as idyllic as we drove north this morning. We have tea—two cups each—and sweet candies, along with a bowl of spicy hot snacks. The bill is $2.

This mountain village with its tall pine trees, rushing river, wood homes, main street cattle, and archery competitors who shoot arrows over vehicles passing through, is beyond mesmerizing. Those of us on the cross-country road trip dream of a return. We will live in Autsho village, at least sporadically, for years. Perhaps we'll take turns occupying a house we think we'll buy.

After our second cups of tea, though, we return to Mongar. It's a city. A traveler can fall in love with it, too. The next morning, we mill among 300 Buddhist worshippers, who sit on a vast sea of pine needles covering the ground. Presiding over this gathering for world peace is the country's highest-ranking monk—the chief abbot of Bhutan. Phuntsho explains that the prayer being said while we observe is in the classical Tibetan language.

I am reminded of a time long gone. I haven't hitched rides since my 20s, when I waited in subzero temperatures for a 200-mile lift home from college in Minneapolis, when I spanned Southern California to the Texas School Book Depository on three rides, or when I hopped a freight train—one night sharing a box car with another bum.[37] But yesterday felt so much like I'd stuck out my thumb and was picked up by two guys on an all-day joy ride. We drove far up a river gorge and back—with a lark of a side trip to a mountaintop temple for a dash of holy water. I'd like to continue with Phuntsho and Dorji for months.

the abominable snowman and the queen

Here in the Himalaya Mountains of Bhutan, I carry a book that I open to just any page and start reading. Today's page takes me to "In the Tracks of the Migoi." With admiration and then foreboding, I absorb a bit of the tale.

"Bhutanese do not kill living beings, and some people avoid agricultural work because it kills countless insects and worms. But there are exceptions . . . In the highlands of Kurtoi, many men have been forced to hunt for the family's subsistence."

The tale continues: "As the forests dwindled, game moved higher in the mountains. Hunters were eventually away for days. They grew bewildered because the traps they set for deer were being disturbed,

---

[37] Riding the rails, hitching to Texas, a night jailed in Tijuana, entranced by a funeral bonfire in New Guinea's interior, and other old memories are peeled back as "Notes in Bottles" in *The Other Worlds: Offbeat Adventures of a Curious Traveler*, on pp. 243–54.

but there were never any animals in them. One day, near a trap, the hunters discovered footprints in the snow the size of a forearm of a large man. They were gripped with cold fear, and in a panic headed home, for the footprints had to belong to the mysterious *migoi*." Migoi, I must point out, is a Bhutanese name for yeti, or abominable snowman.

"Chaynga La, the youngest hunter, recklessly refused to go home, his mind filled with visions of himself as the hero who killed the migoi, and with visions that the village belle Lhazon, who'd always spurned him, would change her mind . . . He walked on without even glancing back at his departing friends."

Upon reading just three more sentences, fear makes me drop the book to the floor: "The hunter followed the huge footprints for three days. He then heard a growl and saw . . . [a] grotesque creature, agitated and waving its arms over its head . . . its blood-red mouth like a cave that was filled with jagged teeth . . ."

I plan to return to this story another day, and also read 21 others in Kunzang Choden's book, *Bhutanese Tales of the Yeti*.[38]

But first, let me start at the beginning, which takes place in the Tang Valley. The four-story house above the valley, and its predecessor destroyed by an earthquake, used to hold tons of barley, wheat, rice, and buckwheat on the second floor. For over six centuries, it has preserved documents of trade with Tibet and China, as well as tools, furnishings, and personal effects.

Visiting the massive wood house today evidences all this, and more. The fourth-floor library, for example, contains tens of thousands Buddhist documents, not only about the Bhutanese Tantric school of Buddhism, but about other major schools as well. The documents were printed one sheet at a time, centuries ago. It's quite easy climbing the steep ladder-like stairs from floor to floor, but it's better to go down facing the stairs, as if descending on a ladder.

---

[38] The excerpts are taken substantially verbatim, with permission, from the book by Kunzang Choden, *Bhutanese Tales of the Yeti* (Bangkok: White Lotus Co., Ltd, 2nd edition, 2007), 87–90.

Beginning in the 1300s, the Tang ("tong") valley was governed by one family. Today's senior member of the family is referred to as *adji*, or queen. At a picnic table outside the wondrous house, known as Ogyen Choling, guide Phuntsho, driver Dorji, and I enjoy a house-made lunch of fresh pumpkin soup and pears picked from a tree a few steps away. As we finish our meal, my road-trip companions surprise me with news that the Queen of the Valley is now walking through the yard. She's returning from Jakar town with fresh vegetables.

The queen, with wavy gray hair and carrying baskets, turns toward us and approaches. In beautiful English, she inquires where I am from. With a smile, she tells me her daughter attended Macalester College in Minnesota. The queen is part of the 20th generation to have lived on this property, I learn.

"I understand you've written a number of books," I say. I have heard that she is a writer and the first Bhutanese woman to have penned a novel in English.

"Yes, but I no longer have time," she explains. "I am now working on my new project. I'm dedicated to making the four floors of the house a permanent museum." (*As if they aren't already!* I say to myself.)

"The thousands of Buddhist manuscripts had been scattered all around the house," she tells us. "Our first priority was engaging a scholar to assemble and categorize them. Staff from the British Library of Endangered Archives then arrived and photographed every page over two months."

As the three of us cross-country road trippers leave the remote Ogyen Choling museum grounds, I buy two books authored by the queen, whose name is Kunzang Choden. One book relates 22 of Bhutan's tales about the yeti, including the tale I haven't finished reading yet.[39]

I'll pick that book up from my lodging floor momentarily. I must discover what happens to the brave but reckless hunter, Chaynga La,

---

[39] A photo of the queen of Tang Valley and the Minnesota traveler is inset in the map of Bhutan. The queen, Kunzang Choden, also appears on the cover of this book, right of center. Dorji, my fellow road tripper and driver, is on the book cover, far right.

to the girl of his dreams, Lhazon, and to the frighteningly abominable snowman. The queen's English will tell me. Does the hunter die, the girl now weep, and the migoi relate his encounter to an abominable snowwoman? Or does Chaynga La return to his village a hero, with a snowman's blood on his hands? Or . . . ?

I wonder what *your* guess is. We might pass on the lesson we're about to learn to a child in our families, as perhaps this tale and others were lessons for young Bhutanese who lived between 1490 and this century.

I now plunge ahead through the tale of the migoi, feeling it will be a simple winner-takes-all kind of ending. Let's see . . . Chaynga La swung his sword at the migoi that was hurling itself at him, and cut the migoi in two. Thrust onto his back by the impact, he then heard a wail so mournful that he shuddered and sat up. A second creature joined the fallen one, held the severed body passionately, and cast a sad glance at the hunter.

Upon Chaynga La's return home, the villagers did not believe a word he said, and Lhazom laughed and teased him. Two older hunters insisted that Chaynga La show them the proof. The three returned to the scene, where they found both creatures frozen. "The mate's face touched that of the slain animal," we read. "An expression of shock was frozen on the face of the victim, while genuine sorrow and defeat was written on the face of the mate."

The three hunters ran back to their village and rushed inside their homes, where the deity *Goi Lhamo* protected them. The Bhutanese believe that lurking evil spirits can harm people if they show fear. Goi Lhamo protects only those inside their home, where there is no cause for fear.

The tale now concludes: "Chaynga La was only one step away from the threshold of his house when he uttered the unmentionable expression of fear, *A zai!* He had been in a stressful, fearful situation for days, and now he showed the spirits how vulnerable he was by crying out that word. The young hunter's *sog*, or life force, was taken away only one step from the protective threshold of his house by the evil spirits that trailed him. He died within days of his adventure."[40]

• • •

Once I catch my breath, I turn to the introduction in Kunzang Choden's book, *Bhutanese Tales of the Yeti*. Ms. Choden, the queen of Tang Valley, tells us that the migoi, or yeti, is known by different names in different regions of the Himalayas: Glacier Man, Strong Man, Great Man, Snow Goblin, and Mountain Goblin. Its first contact with humans "cannot be dated . . . since the migoi has been around . . . much longer" than we have.[41]

Countless people of the high Himalayas have seen the yeti. While foreigner Eric Shipton took photos of footprints, all the foreign expeditions that sought to find a yeti have failed. The reasons given were that these expeditions were too large and opulent, had a poor understanding of the animal and its psychology, moved more than watched, and were unprepared for the hardships.[42]

The tales Ms. Choden presents are from a large body of legends in the Bhutanese oral folklore. She has heard many of these stories from people who heard them from their village elders or directly from eyewitnesses. And this is how the migoi lives on.

• • •

Kunzang Choden has her own story to tell. Most winters when she was young, her family used to travel over the mountains for three or four days to the warmer Kurtoi region. Since her family was privileged, they did not walk or carry heavy loads like other travelers but rode,

---

[40] Kunzang Choden, *Bhutanese Tales of the Yeti* (Bangkok: White Lotus Co., Ltd, 2nd edition, 2007), pp 87–93.

[41] Ibid., viii–ix.

[42] Ibid., x, citing Robert Hutchison, *In the Tracks of the Yeti* (London: Macdonald and Co., 1989).

first on mules and then on yaks, to get over the snow-covered Rodong La Pass.[43]

One day, while on her yak near the 13,140-feet-high pass, Ms. Choden was falling asleep with her cold, ungloved hands nestled under the long hair of the yak's neck for warmth. The day was gloomy, and a fierce wind blew, she explains. Then someone yelled out, "It's weather like this that brings out the migoi!"[44]

The thought of seeing a migoi jolted her awake. Her eyes scanned every bush, tree, boulder, and cave. Her group passed the spot where a man, Mimi Tashi, had once met a migoi. It was such a bad omen that he was sick for several months. But the royal family of the Tang Valley did not see any otherworldly creature on their journey.

"I had to be satisfied with stories of the migois," Ms. Choden relates, adding that she was captivated by the soft and delightful dialect spoken by the people of Kurtoi, and "never grew tired of listening to their accounts."[45]

Now, thanks to Kunzang Choden's books, yeti tales and other equally delightful legends will live on forever, I hope, not only in Bhutan but around the world.[46] I know I'll never grow tired of reading them.

karma, and a dance after death

We all know the Old West town of American popular history: a single dusty street set on a long trail, horses waiting for action, the saloon, mail service of sorts, tailors, and wheel repair shops. All have disappeared, never to return; you may as well be "Back East." But it so happens that my road-trip companions and I, after traveling for days from the

---

[43] The Kingdom of Bhutan map, at pp. 236-37, traces the road trippers' route, points out the 20-generation home (Ogyen Choling), and shows the trail over the Rodong La Pass that Kunzang Choden traveled on a mule and yak.

[44] *Bhutanese Tales of the Yeti*, 78.

[45] Ibid., 79.

[46] For example, Kunzang Choden's *Folk Tales of Bhutan* and *Dawa: The Story of a Stray Dog in Bhutan* (and *Bhutanese Tales of the Yeti*) are available on Amazon in e-book and/or paperback.

country's west all the way to its distant east, discover an intriguing town. And I suddenly find myself transported to a different era—in America!

At one time, the street running into town also went out over a narrow bridge held up by iron chains made centuries ago. Today, the bridge is gone. It takes us a slow two minutes to walk the entire length of the street, which dead ends at a café and pool hall. There are no side streets or back streets. Horses and mules patiently stand—hitched, but ready for action. The only hardware store within miles is here, as well as two tailors and a mechanic who fixes wheels. Folks from town and the environs sit outdoors on wood boxes, shooting the breeze.

We're not on a movie set, so I'm free to get involved! I poke my head into the post office, wondering how mail gets delivered. The agent yells, I learn, if the addressee lives just across the street. More likely, the recipients live out of town. If so, the agent calls the cell phone number noted on the envelope, then dispatches an assistant on a motorbike to the abode higher in the mountains. This feels like a science fiction story set in the Wyoming Territory of 1868, or something equally as exciting.

Since there's no stagecoach to ship mail out, the agent hands letters to the driver of a four-wheel-drive vehicle who's carrying passengers to Trashigang, a prominent town that's a rocky, curvy, muddy hour away. Tomorrow, three letters will be dispatched, the agent tells me, pointing to three envelopes on his desk.

I ask the postal man whether the establishment across the street might serve tea to me and my traveling companions. It's not well-known for serving tea, according to the postal agent. He nonetheless hollers to a young woman standing in the street who helps run the place, and she agrees to make tea.

We travelers while away time in front of that old joint. Upon entering, we see it is in fact a saloon! It's all weather-worn wood and liquor bottles lined up on shelves. Since it has no bar stools, we sit at

In front of the saloon that served tea, in the "Old West" karma village of Duksum. Guide Phuntsho (left), driver Dorji, the establishment's owner, and a girl in the family.

one of the two tables it does have. We savor our drink and snacks, and the fact that our Hyundai SUV is having its flat tire fixed at the nearby shop. We then take time to wander to the roaring river's banks, where the iron bridge once stood. We pick lemongrass to freshen our mouths, and the car, too.

Soon, the horses and mules depart, hauling cargo to their owners' farms and ranches in the "uppers"—higher up the mountain. We too must leave this Trashiyangtse district town of Duksum ("duke-some") before it gets dark.

We drive two miles south along the Kulong River to experience the beginning of the three-day Gomphu Kora festival at an ancient Buddhist temple and monastery. Next to the temple sits a black rock the size of a house. This is where the second Buddha, meditating in a very small cave in the rock, stood up suddenly upon seeing a demon, leaving an imprint of his head in the cave roof—so unmistakable and permanent that we cave explorers can vouch for it today. The demon, it is said, escaped through a tunnel and was next seen by the river.

This happened in 747 AD, and for the last 1,270 years, no one has explored that tunnel, or the "how" and "why" it ends in the river, Phuntsho tells me. And into that tunnel we dare not tread. Instead, just before sunset, we make a beeline for Trashigang, for there is no lodging near the rural festival, here in the remote eastern edge of the country.

The next morning, Phuntsho and Dorji make it clear that we must observe a dance ritual back in the festival temple. In our eagerness, we leave Trashigang city very early and arrive with an hour to kill. Something tells us we should go back to Duksum, a place I cannot get out of my head and was already lamenting I would never see again. We thus journey beyond the temple along the river to the three-horse town and its one dead-end street.

"By Karma, we returned," Phuntsho says as we sip our morning tea in the saloon.

"How has Karma worked?" I inquire.

"Tom, you love Duksum," he explains. "You had a subliminal wish to come back. The wish was like a prayer. Because the prayer was accompanied by your good intentions, Karma let your prayer be answered. By Karma, we returned."

"Yes," I tell Phuntsho. "By Karma, we traveled back to the American Old West; or at least as close to it as I'll ever get."

• • •

An eternity later, it seems, we find ourselves back at the Gomphu Kora festival. We sit on the wood floor of the small Buddhist temple that abuts the black rock and cave of the second Buddha. About 30 monks from the nearby monastery comfortably sit cross-legged in a U shape, with the head lama on an elevated chair at the open end of the U.

A dozen of the monks play Tibetan drums called *nag*, which originated in antiquity. Two play *dung-chen*, horns seven feet long that emit a very low tone. Two others play a flute-like instrument known as *jailing*. Two more hold in one hand a small bell—or *deap*—and in the other, a castanet-sounding instrument called *tangti*. (Names and spellings vary.)

A monk sitting next to the lama intones a Buddhist prayer in a very low voice, amplified just a little and matched in tone by the seven-foot-long trumpet-like horns. Monks not playing music read along in soft voices from prayer books in their crossed-leg laps. These books are written in classical Tibetan, I am told, not Bhutanese.

Three monks, until now unseen, glide into the temple through the ancient door. The three, wearing beautiful multicolored, flowing robes, dance as if they are flying through the heavens.

"Concentrate your mind on their dance," Phuntsho urges me, "so that it's familiar to you after death—when you are in the intermediate stage, before rebirth into one of the six worlds. You may recognize this dance while you're in that stage, though it will be performed by illuminations, not physical beings. You may then follow these illuminations where they lead and move more quickly through that painful stage after death, when your soul can be disturbed by bad forces."

I'm eager to learn a bit more. And I do. If I have earned it by doing good deeds while alive, I will be reborn as a god, a demigod, or a human being—not as an animal, a hungry ghost, or in hell.

How lucky I am to have seen the monks perform their once-a-year ceremony, for I may now recognize the dance after I die. If I do, I will know to follow the illuminations.

children play in buddhist bhutan

"Look at the children playing in that tree house," I comment offhand-edly as Phuntsho and I shuffle down a gravel road in Bumthang Valley toward the Chamkhar River. Phuntsho looks and laughs.

"They are playing—" Before he can complete his sentence, I finish it silently to myself: "playing house," for I know what kids look like when they're playing house.

"Playing monk," Phuntsho exclaims. We stop and watch.

"Playing monk?" I ask in a doubting voice.

"Two of them are 'monks.' They've dressed for the part by wearing their school uniforms," Phuntsho observes. "The other boys and girls are members of the 'host family.' They're playing out an ancient Buddhist ritual that in reality takes place over two days.

"On the first day," Phuntsho explains, "monks visit the host family to prepare offerings to the gods from items the family has assembled, like flour and butter. Most importantly, they make a 'ritual cake.' The next day, the monks, headed by the temple's head lama, visit the family's house in greater number and recite religious texts.

"A specific need, such as curing an illness, may motivate the ritual," Phuntsho continues. "Each home also has an annual ritual—all family members gather for that one. The purpose is to protect the family. It's done by making an offering to a deity that may live in the mountains, a tree, a lake, or a river."

As we watch, the children begin leaving the tree house. They are about to carry the offerings they've just prepared in their tree house to a place where a spirit typically resides, such as a tree.

"They won't make an offering where a spirit actually lives—that would be disrespectful—but at a comparable place," Phuntsho assures me.

"The children were very serious about their mission until they saw us," he points out a few minutes later. "They suddenly became self-conscious. When we asked them to pose for a photo, one said something that cracked them all up. At that point, their mission of making an offering ended. We disrupted their play, and the serious drama was over!"[47]

---

[47] The blog page of the website provides a link to a YouTube video of the Kingdom of Bhutan—and the children. It is Episode 5 of Tom Mattson's Virtual World Tour. Check www.TomsGlobe.com.

Treehouse children in Bumthang Valley, while enacting a solemn Buddhist practice, crack up as a visitor snaps a photo. The two "monks" (holding ritual "cakes") and the "host family" were about to head to a place a spirit typically resides.

"Playing monk," Phuntsho explains, "is a way for children to act out and understand a centuries-old tradition that is alive and well in many parts of Bhutan." But we were fortunate to witness the kids in Tamzhing village playing monk: nowadays, this play is not common in urban areas where, like in so many other countries, old traditions are getting lost.

• • •

The children in the tree house had created two offerings, Phuntsho explains to me later. One was a small plant in a basket. The other represented a ritual flour cake decorated with butter artistically designed to look like flower petals that monks have made for centuries. The children used *mud* to create their cake! Not flour. And perhaps because it's much faster—or just wishing to do the absurd—the children picked real flowers to represent the butter flowers.

Minutes and just meters before coming across the children in the tree house, Phuntsho and I had meandered through the temple of the Tamzhing Lhakhang monastery, built in 1501. As we walked a circular corridor around the inner temple, we counted 108 candles. They were burning—and made of butter. We also admired the details of many ritual cakes, all set as offerings.

Only Phuntsho and I and a few of the monastery's 95 monks were inside the temple with its ritual cakes and 108 burning candles, antiquated banners and fabrics hanging from above, Buddha statues, wooden masks from the 1500s still used in ceremonies, and fading 500-year-old wall paintings. Those paintings have never been retouched, says Phuntsho, and may never be.

Outside Tamzhing Lhakhang temple, we watched—from a distance —part of a funeral ceremony for the mother of a main lama. Many local faithful chanted mantras on the temple's veranda, then shared a meal.

I sensed I was at one of the most incredible places on earth. As we departed, a supernatural tug on my soul was calling me back inside the temple, but we sauntered away toward the Chamkar River. We happened upon the tree house, and promptly entered Bhutan's world of rural children.

HOMEBOUND

HOMEBOUND

History in the Making
NOVEMBER 16, 2008

Only once in my lifetime might I get a chance to knock on the doors of complete strangers in the 98-percent-white iron mining towns where I grew up, asking people to vote for a black man for president, and then make a good faith attempt to pal around with a "domestic terrorist" in revolutionary Chicago.

"Hi, I'm Tom Mattson, and I'm working for Tom Rukavina, Jim Oberstar, Barack Obama, and Al Franken. How ya doing today?" Pretty darn good I find out—at least in the four mining towns I cover. We get a chance to vote an entrenched party out and bring in an exciting and smart guy (not to mention make history while we're at it).

The exceptions stand out. Alaska's Sarah Palin, on the Republican ballot for vice president with John McCain, "is just like us, and I'm voting for her," says an 80-year-old woman with a Finnish accent working in her garden. "I'll never vote for a Democrat again. I lost my mining company pension, and it's the Democrats' fault," says a stern man cleaning his Harley. As I walk away, I tell him I've got two Harley Sportsters. He smiles a bit.

"Abortion is putting a needle into a baby's brain and drawing out the blood," says a man working outside on what looks like a home-made high chair for a child. He's very articulate and doesn't want me to walk away, but I say I'll let him get back to his work. As I depart, he explains he's building a deer stand. I imagine he'll be taking aim at a big buck in a week.

Two men in their 20s walk out of a house onto the street. I ask if they'll be voting. "No," says one, and after hesitating, adds, "I'm a felon." I look at the other one. He says, "I'm a felon too."

An Ojibwe boy invites me into his home to talk to his white great-grandmother. She's 92. After a while, the boy informs me that she's sometimes confused and doesn't understand what I'm saying. I let the older brother know how he can register to vote. At another house, a man with a cane hobbles to his door. "I'm 90 years old and blind and deaf, and I can't read anything to know how to vote," he tells me. I learn he was an elementary school principal for decades.

A young Ojibwe mother explains that she is voting for Obama because of the color of his skin and because she wants change. Her nine-year-old daughter wants pamphlets I have about Obama. She is eager to learn. "Can you give me something about McCain?" she asks. I can't.

I mark down on the campaign's computer-generated forms information like "Strong Obama supporter," "Lean Obama," "Undecided," "Lean McCain," or "Strong McCain." I jot notes like "been a registered Republican all his life but for Obama, and will try to bring his wife along."

I walk up and down the streets of Biwabik, my hometown. I no longer hear foreign languages in these mining towns, like I did when growing up. Serbians, Croatians, Italians, Finns, Welsh, Cornish, Jews, Slovaks, Greeks, Polish, Montenegrins, Slovenians, Austrians, Germans, Norwegians, and Swedes immigrated just before and after 1900 to mine the country's richest deposits of iron ore. It was said after the turn of that century—and in more than one language—that just 3 percent of miners spoke English.

Now the steep mine dumps from abandoned Biwabik Mine block the setting sun on First Avenue. One winter afternoon, when I was nine or 10, my friend and I were sledding down the dumps piled up from no-value overburden that had lain above rich iron ore. The only Native American person in town appeared at the bottom. She yelled up, asking if her son was there. "No!" we answered, but my friend then hollered racial names at the woman. I joined in. I've never figured out why. The woman's husband told our parents, and we boys were obligated to knock on that family's door and apologize to the woman. Now I'm knocking on all the doors on that street for an African American man running for president.

A few days later, it's Halloween, just before dark. My friend Eric Johnson from Mountain Iron and I divide up streets in the town of Aurora. We then meet to drive to the next neighborhood.

"People are coming to the doors with big bowls of candy," he says. "They think we are trick or treating." I get the same reaction, and I'm thinking of greeting the next one with, "Trick or treat! The treat is if you vote for Obama. The trick on all of us is if you vote for McCain." Instead, I stick to our talking points. No drama!

A girl about 18 comes to a door. It must be her mother yelling, from far inside, that I shouldn't bother leaving literature because they are all voting for the Democrats. An unseen man yells back, "He's just blowing smoke up your ass!" which is met with laughter in the house and causes the girl to blush.

An elderly Finnish-American man says he will pull the lever for Obama, who "is smart and will appoint good people." He then tells me that, when he worked on the railroad, he pulled the track switch for Harry Truman as his Duluth, Winnipeg, and Pacific train arrived in Duluth. "The security was tight. I guess I passed muster," he concludes.

During the 1960 presidential campaign, John F. Kennedy visited Hibbing, Bob Dylan's hometown. In front of a packed auditorium, he declared that the Minnesota Iron Range was the most heavily Democratic region of the United States he'd campaigned in. "I used to think they were pretty good in South Boston, but we are going to send them out here for indoctrination," JFK told my mother Elmy, Aunt Lil, and thousands of others. Last month, Hillary Clinton probably matched Kennedy as far as raucous crowds go. In a Hibbing hockey arena, she spoke for Obama to thousands of hockey moms, hockey sisters, washed-up hockey players, and to me and my next-door neighbor, Judy Little.

Back in Biwabik, kids on hands and knees are writing big letters in chalk on Fifth Avenue. The letters spell McCAIN.

"Do you know how to spell Obama?" I ask. They're silent. I take a step closer, holding an Obama flyer in my hand, telling them, "This shows how to spell his name."

"No," a girl says, dismissing me, "we are all voting for McCain."

It's the night before the election. It's getting cold, so houses in Biwabik are closed up tight. With time running short, I just open one of my last house's storm doors and hang a list of candidates on the knob of the main door. Odors drift through the nearly airtight doors and tickle my nostrils. A woman inside this house must be getting a permanent. Next door, a family is cooking spaghetti. People living in the house down the street must smoke all day long.

Election night! Some 72 percent of my hometown has voted for Barack Obama, almost exactly the same percentage as those who had voted for Kerry, Gore, Clinton, Kennedy, and all the Democrats of the past.

• • •

A week later, I'm driving to Chicago. I stop to visit farm friends Craig and Vicky Trytten in Southern Minnesota. Until recently, they farmed near Wasilla, Alaska, where they were on a first-name basis with John McCain's running mate, Sarah Palin. I've asked a few Northern Minnesota friends to share with me questions they have about Sarah, who was relatively unknown until McCain picked her.

Some of the questions I feel duty bound to ask are not deeply philosophical. "Is that daughter of hers and that redneck boyfriend really getting married?" "What is Palin's church denomination?" "Did her son really get his girlfriend pregnant?" "Find out what her real hair color is, because it looked red one time when she was harping about domestic terrorists"—as washed up as they may be.

With the discussion about Sarah out of the way, my farm friends and I patronize several businessmen and women in farm homes scattered on country roads near the town of Mabel. We buy cheese, butter, homemade blueberry jam, salsa, relish, and knives. These are not two-pickup-truck farmyards. They are, instead, horse-drawn-buggy farms.

We pass three rifle-toting boys climbing out of their buggy to hunt deer. A teacher's horse and buggy are stationed in front of a one-room school. No electrical current runs anywhere near the farms, since all the power poles have been pulled out.

"Who did these people vote for?" I ask Craig.

"The Amish do not vote," he answers.

• • •

I arrive in Chicago one week after the election. I phone my neighbor Judy Little back in Minnesota. She describes the endgame of a campaign faceoff. Before the election, I didn't want to poke my finger in the eyes of the family across the road by displaying an OBAMA-BIDEN sign in my yard, since I was sure they voted Republican for religious reasons. But once they stuck a McCAIN-PALIN sign in their yard, I hammered one for Obama and Biden in mine and another one in Judy's for good measure.

Now I was in the lead, 2–1. But the friendly opposition hit back with a second McCain-Palin sign at the extremist edge of their property, near their discerning neighbor's home. He got down to brass tacks and built his own sign, which stared the McCain-Palin sign in the face. His creation urged passersby to "Vote for a REAL Republican—Elect Ron Paul."

By the first light of dawn the day after the election, the McCain-Palin signs had disappeared, retired from public view by their owner. A couple days later, the real Republican went his own way. The Obama-Biden signs continued to let passersby know who had supported the winners. A few nights ago, however, these signs disappeared, Judy told me by phone, and we are now wondering who the guilty party is. But of one thing I am certain: the sign contest started out 0–0 and ended up 0–0.

• • •

On Chicago's South Side, employees at a State Farm office tell me how to get to the Obamas' street. They call him "President-Elect Obama." They also tell me the Valois Restaurant is close by. I'd seen pictures of the Valois in Minnesota's *Mesabi Daily News* the day after the election. Everyone visiting that establishment could enjoy a free meal to celebrate a neighbor who loved to eat his breakfasts there, the paper reported.

"What do you want?" I'm asked at the cafeteria-style Valois.

"What is Barack Obama's favorite breakfast?" I inquire.

"Eggs, hash browns, sausage, toast, and coffee," comes the rat-a-tat-tat answer.

"That's for me!" I bark back.

Regular customers make up most of the crowd packed into the large restaurant. They know this place is now part of history. And they are living it!

After my presidential breakfast, I park my Pontiac Grand Am two blocks from the Obama home—no traffic is allowed anywhere near the house. One may walk past the home, but on the opposite side of the street only. A Brazilian TV reporter hopes I'm from the neighborhood, so he can interview an Obama neighbor. I dash his hopes, but a woman walking two dogs does not.

"I suppose you know we don't want you to stand around too long," a friendly Chicago cop soon tells me. She's one of 40 officers assigned to the neighborhood when the Obamas are in town. I assure her I'm on my way. Besides, I don't want to be late for my historic event, which starts at 6 p.m. on the north edge of downtown.

• • •

I arrive at the Northwestern University legal clinic event before 6 p.m. The clinic is celebrating 10 years of successful work, having helped many wrongfully convicted men and women in Illinois get released from death row or long prison sentences.

"I spent 15 years on death row," an innocent man resting in a chair at a reception tells me. He's moved from the South Side to a suburb. He prefers to spend most of his time at home. Another man, who spent six years on death row, now lives back on the family farm, cultivating organic vegetables. He'd been wrongfully convicted of murdering his parents on the farm. I've talked to him in years past and ask if he might make it to Minnesota someday. He says he will not: suffering from post-traumatic stress syndrome, he, too, stays home most of the time. I buy his book, helping to support the legal clinic.

Before the program starts, Rob Warden, the director of the university's clinic, introduces a man in the aisle to his family sitting in the row behind me in the packed auditorium. "You know Bill Ayers," he tells them. They do. I turn around and say to a son, "Amazing." Why? Because Sarah Palin had claimed Candidate Obama was "pal'n around with terrorists," meaning educator Bill Ayers who, in the 1960s and early 70s, was a famous radical who reportedly did participate in some bombings.

I notice that Bill Ayers has now taken a seat across the aisle from me. He is with his wife, Professor Bernadine Dohrn. I'm thinking, "I have a question for Bill Ayers that perhaps I can ask after the program: '*Did* you do it? Or *didn't* you? You know: pal around with Barack Obama in recent years, like Sarah Palin has alleged in campaign rallies.'" Admittedly, that would be like asking him point blank, "Are you the alleged domestic terrorist who pal'd around with the man who'll be inaugurated as our next president?"

After the program, people linger. I pal around with some of the men who had once been convicted and sentenced to death for heinous crimes, and have now been exonerated, thanks to the work of the clinic, legal volunteers, investigators, and journalists.

Bill Ayers and I practically run into each other. We smile like we're long-lost buddies. I mention to him that I represented a death row inmate in Texas for 11 years and volunteered on the legal clinic project that led the Illinois governor to commute the death sentences of the 156 people who were on death row in this state.

Now is my chance to ask Mr. Ayers if he did it or not! Alas, my interview is short-circuited. Before I manage to get the first interrogating syllable out of my mouth, someone else who has previously pal'd around with him interrupts our discussion.

But I do have an opinion. I observed that Ayers, who wore a sport coat, jeans, and tennis shoes, was the first and loudest to laugh at lighter comments during the program, and was the only one to whistle at eminently whistleable comments. He's an extrovert—friendly with a big smile. People like him. So I'm quite sure that, if Barack Obama had any opportunity at all, he did some pal'n around with fellow Chicagoan William Ayers.

That's November 2008 for you.

The Heroic Odyssey of the Loons of Lost Lake
SEPTEMBER 2012

20 million bc to 2011 ad

Long before Henry David Thoreau described the wild, wolf-like howl of the loons in Walden Pond in the 1840s, indigenous cultures told stories about the creation of this ancient bird and its relationship to humans. Yesterday, I met an Ojibwe woman working at the Bois Forte Heritage Center at 1,000-mile shoreline Lake Vermilion. She told me a native story that reveals the origin of the loon's voice, white necklace, and red eyes. The mythological story of love is passed from generation to generation orally, but not in writing. I agreed not to convey it in written form. In respect to the custom, I may pass it to others in the oral tradition only.

If the story about the Ojibwe involvement in the creation of the loon's remarkable characteristics is not, in the end, based on historical fact, the loon's unearthly calling was likely a sound in the wilderness millions of years before the first humans walked the earth. The loon's direct parentage developed over 20 million years ago. Some say it's the most primitive living bird.

the joyous months

Sometime later, in early spring 2012, two common loons left the Gulf of Mexico for a destination 1,200 miles away: Lost Lake. The two had likely reared chicks in this lake for several years in a row.

This couple had not wintered together on the Gulf, but now, in twos and threes and tens, loons by the thousand headed north at 100 miles per hour, when pushed by a tailwind. Over 12,000 left the Gulf for Minnesota, fewer for Wisconsin, Michigan, and other states.

Tens of thousands of common loons also left the Atlantic and Pacific coasts, most flying to Canada and Alaska (other species of loons nest primarily there, too).

The Lost Lake male, like other males, arrived at his destination up to a week before the female, landing on the frigid waters just hours or days after the ice melted. It's hard to say how loons know when the ice goes out on one of Minnesota's 13,000 lakes, but they may send scouts north from Southern Minnesota or Wisconsin on high-speed reconnoitering missions. They can make the round trip faster than a sleek Corvette.

For the beautiful summer ahead, the Lost Lake couple had one goal foremost in their minds: to raise healthy chicks. They knew they'd have to build a nest, protect it from predators, and avoid disastrous, inexplicable events. *But would this be the year that would terrify them?*

The adult pair built a nest on the Lost Lake shoreline in May, among bushes and water lilies. To the astute eye, loons aren't exacting nest builders. They use whatever is close at hand—lake bottom mud for the base, and then twigs, moss, and leaves.

Constructing the nest took about six hours over several days. They weren't trying to build the home of their dreams. They were, however, pleased with what they had made. They felt sure this nest would serve their purpose magnificently. They anticipated another great summer unfolding, especially below the lake's surface, where abundant prey in clear water was just a minute away from being swallowed whole.

The mother-to-be most likely laid two eggs (rather than one or three) in early June. The parents incubated the eggs, taking turns that probably averaged two hours. The tending parent turned the eggs over every hour or so, but in a frenzy or slough, the lapse time could be 12 minutes or six hours. The parents tended the eggs 99 percent of the time, the better to ward off predators like eagles, crows, ravens, gulls, and skunks. If a stethoscope were applied to the eggs, it would've detected the chicks' chirps, waiting for the day to break out, probably one day apart, just like they'd been laid. *If the eggs are not stolen or eaten or destroyed by a sudden and shocking event, that is!*

behold the spectacular future

After about 27 days of incubation, the chicks would hatch. Soon, they'd flop into the water. They'd innately know how to swim, but diving for food and flying skyward would be a whole 'nother matter. As infants, they'd often ride around on their parents' backs. They'd soon peer downward from the surface as their parents chased and caught minnows and bigger fish, or selected mollusks, insects, and aquatic greens.

The adults may spend hours a day underwater, but they don't see in night waters well enough to fish. With brains that tolerate carbon dioxide, they'll frequently dive for 30 to 90 seconds—some even manage three minutes. They'll often dive 30 feet, and on deep lakes, can reach prey over 100 feet deep.

The chicks would have the freshest of diets, never being fed a dead minnow or anything that had been sequestered or regurgitated. With their high protein meals, they'd grow rapidly. They'd learn a little later how to chase down fish on their own.

When the family found a good fishing spot with just one species on the menu, they'd have no need for variety. The chicks might marvel at their parents' swallowing 100 four-inch minnows a day. They'd also notice the elasticity of their parents' esophagi with the intake of a six- or even 12-inch fish.

The chicks would begin learning vocabulary, too. They'd hear their parents and an occasional interloping or socializing neighbor scream out four basic calls. Loons may not have the 250 calls of crows, but each basic call can be modified, and different calls can be linked to create a one-of-a-kind message. A call is sometimes heard for miles. An outside loon with designs of encroachment may just fly over and not bother to land, thus avoiding wasting calories when taking off again.

The parents will teach the chicks how to run across the lake surface into the wind to take off. Once airborne, the novices will have to flap their wings four times a second because of their heavy weight, a highly informative book teaches us.[48] The loons' mass is partly due to quite solid, non-hollow bones that let them sink from the surface of the lake without a flap, kick, or splash noticeable to prey. Even after the chicks have learned the art and science of takeoff, they might lack the best landing technique and experience a total wipeout. The conflicting emotions that go through a parent's mind when witnessing a wipeout would have to be covered in a separate paper!

The chicks accept the fact that their bodies are made first and foremost for diving in pursuit of prey, not for flying. They'll never even think about taking off from land, for that is impossible. If perchance they mistake a rain-slicked highway for a lake in their lifetimes and land on it, they'll survive only with expert human relocation assistance, after which they may go on to enjoy a 20- or 30-year life span.

Come autumn, these young chicks will not fly south with their parents. Instead, they'll let their bodies grow bigger and leave weeks

---

[48] Stan Tekiela, *Fascinating Loons—Amazing Images and Behaviors* (Cambridge, MN: Adventure Publications, 2006), 83–84.

later, before the lake freezes. They'll join a coterie of 2012-born loons from other lakes. Lacking experience, instinct will guide them to the Gulf. They'll fly high and fast, but probably lower and slower than their parents' 5,000 to 9,000 feet and 60 to 80 mph (plus any tailwind).

The young ones (like their parents) will winter in the US Gulf of Mexico, although some go all the way to the Florida Atlantic coast. The 2012 chicks won't return to Minnesota next spring—they'll live in salt waters until 2015. With luck, they'll avoid the Gulf's speedboats, commercial fishing nets, and oil slicks. They'll start to nest in Minnesota at age five or six, and until then, may never have touched land since birth.

As of June 19, 2012, this is what awaits the incubating chicks on Lost Lake. Unless, God forbid, the eggs are stolen by a ravenous raven, scrunched and scrambled by a revolting raccoon, or destroyed by an untoward event!

the untoward event

The heavens opened up at 4:30 p.m. on Tuesday, June 19. Five inches of rain fell on the lake, even more in surrounding areas. Further south, Duluth and nearby towns experienced the flood of the century.

A stream that usually trickles out of Lost Lake and into the St. Louis River a few hundred feet away gushed like seldom seen. The river's upper watershed was already saturated by a foot of rain that fell in the previous 30 days. It now overflowed its banks and flooded the forests.

At first, the river had nowhere to go but up. But two days later, on Thursday, it found a new destination. The river stopped Lost Lake's outlet stream dead in its tracks. It then reversed the stream's flow with a vengeance. Every single second on Thursday afternoon, 1,880 gallons of river water poured into the crystal-clear lake—112,800 gallons a minute—every drop laden with sediment from the river's forest watershed. The lake surface rose two and one-third inches per hour.

By luck, I had duct taped a measuring stick to a tree that was two feet above lake level. It was a super yard stick—48 inches long. By 7 a.m.

on Saturday, the lake covered the lower 45 inches. Lost Lake had risen by almost six feet in two days.

Pity the people whose docks are far underwater and those who are sandbagging their homes. *Pity them, or pity the loons of Lost Lake?*

the months of melancholia

Two weeks later, as I float in a kayak in the middle of the subsiding lake, the pair of adult loons near me are lackadaisical, perhaps even despondent. "Why?" I wonder. I sit and ponder. No loon chick is anywhere to be seen, watching and learning how to fish, how to make the unearthly, wild sounds of its parents, and how to go airborne in a body built for underwater dives. Why?

The lake—rising over two inches an hour that Thursday—quite certainly nudged, lifted, twisted, and tore the nest the adults had been tending for weeks. The eggs spilled out of the nest and into the lake.

"The eggs were too heavy to float," the Ojibwe woman in the museum told me. "They sank!"

"The loons are in shock," I tell myself as I watch the adult couple from my kayak. "They were primed to teach their offspring how to dive into Lost Lake, fly above it, and preen themselves for countless hours. Now they only have each other."

To my human eye and the brain wired to it, they appear almost morose. They seldom bother flying. Their unearthly calls are fewer and farther between. It's more difficult to chase down prey, too, since the sediment carried in every drop of floodwater turned the lake turbidly opaque.

swimming with loons

More often than during summers with chicks, the pair of loons suddenly surface near me on my swims and during evening voyages in my kayak with a salad and *The New York Times*. If the loons need comforting, I'm willing to do it!

"The flood was a terrible event," I tell them. "It was an act of nature. We feel bad about what happened to you. Please don't leave the lake early. Stay a long time. We now have global warming through no fault of yours, and the autumn will be long and pleasant. Pay no heed to a prediction that Lost Lake is in for more floods in the future."

I catch myself and steal a glance toward shore to make sure no one is listening in on us. Whew, no one is.

The next time, I speak to them in Spanish, in case they've picked some up where they winter. After that, I whistle to them at every chance meeting. It's always the same call. It says, "Hey. It's me again." Do they laugh at my one-phrase whistling vocabulary?

The nearer they are, the redder their eyes, but below the water, they're gray or dark, it's said. They have double eyelids. You can frustrate yourself contemplating the visual powers and physiology of their eyes. One avenue to enlightenment, naturally enough, is to make an appointment with your eye doctor. Ask the eye technician if he's studied loon eyes. "Not me, but ask the doctor. I imagine their eyesight underwater is incredible," the technician comments. Next, I walk into the ophthalmologist's office.

"No, I haven't examined loon eyes, just cat eyes," she tells me. "And we operated on pig eyes as students. They are tough." I learn no more at the doctor's office.

• • •

"Did you have a big weekend?" asks the bank teller, as she usually does on Mondays. "No, I was just swimming with the loons," I mention. She booms incredulously for everyone to hear, "Swimming with the loons?" Now a mine captain, YMCA lifeguard, and even my loan officer might evaluate me through a different prism. I walk out happy I didn't confide in her that I've been talking to the loons, too. And in a foreign language. I'll hold some secrets dear.

Back on the lake, I sound-record the male in a rare talkative mood. Would it be scornful or overlording if I play back his call for him? Not wanting to step off the deep end, I consult my friend Roy Coombe, age 88.

"Would playing my recording for the loons be mean of me?" I ask Roy.

"No, not mean at all; you're just trying to have a conversation with them," he assures me.

That evening, I play the call to the loon and his partner. They turn their heads to and fro, wondering, "What gives and where?" The male then breaks out in calls so loud he drowns out my recording. Now that's recorded too. An expert may transcribe it someday.

"Roy, do you think the loons have feelings of grief about losing their eggs?" I ask my venerable consultant a day later.

"Yes," he answers, "and ducks feel grief too. And deer. You can hear a deer cry when its fawn gets shot. It's a sad world we live in."

I swim farther out in the lake than most anyone in years. The loons suddenly appear. They've come near me, I believe, because they think that's where the fish are. "That animal knows how to fish," the loons believe. "We've seen them in boats pulling up nice ones." Looking at me, I'm quite sure they think, "That animal is admirable, beautiful, and smart. He can fish from a boat or do it like us, buck naked." (In the turbid waters, they've failed to notice my swim trunks.)

I give the loons a whistle and swim back to shore. If they wonder whether I go swimming to fish, what would they think if they actually saw me surface with a fish fighting for its life clenched in my mouth?

The next day, I've motorcycled north toward the Canadian border, to Cook, Minnesota. I'm in the Dollar Store, trolling the aisles. As luck would have it, the store sells toy porpoises, walruses and sharks. I ponder over which fish will most impress the loons of Lost Lake once I hold it in my mouth. I buy the six-inch long rubber shark that cries when you squeeze it.

I'll swim with the loons, carrying the shark in my swim trunks pocket. I'll submerge, come up with the wiggly shark in my mouth and watch the loons' reaction. I'll discover what they think and tell you. But would it be mean, scornful, or overlording to the loons to swim near them with a shark in my mouth?

I'm still thinking. I need guidance before the loons of Lost Lake lift off and head south.

the miracle chick of lost lake

What should appear in the middle of the lake in late August but a loon the size of a 2012 chick! This small gray bird, not yet having developed the black and white pattern of adults, floats by its lonesome self. Its head jerks left and right, thinking there must be something more to this great lake than a man in his kayak. Soon, something more appears —the two adults. One swims on the far side of my kayak. It calls out, either not seeing the chick or, perhaps, eager to observe the chick's reaction when it hears but does not see the adult. I take my eye off the chick for a few seconds to watch the adult's cat-and-mouse game. Just then, the other adult surfaces and makes a splashy ruckus right at the spot where the chick is. The chick disappears and takes forever to resurface.

Darkness falls. Those three kindred spirits drift into the black-ening night. Or are they kindred? I never see the young loon again. It seems unlikely to me that this chick is the offspring of the loons of Lost Lake. So, who are its parents? How did it get to the lake? Was one adult's splashy ruckus an attempt to force the young loon to dive and search for food? To scare it off the lake? The answers are forever untellable, unless you have a good friend who happens to be a loon expert. If so, clue me in. In the next breath, give me guidance on whether I should surface near the loons of Lost Lake with that shark in my mouth.

I will, in return, relate to you the Ojibwe story about the origin of the loon's call, its white on black pattern, and its red eyes. Remember, though, the story is only to be told, never to be written down.

Such is this corner of the universe.[49]

I will, in return, relate to you the Ojibwe story about the origin of

I will, in return, relate to you the Ojibwe story about the origin of the loon's call, its white on black pattern, and its red eyes. Remember, though, the story is only to be told, never to be written down.

Such is this corner of the universe.[49]

A Summer's Search and Rescue Mission

JULY 29, 2017

Swimming peacefully in a northern Minnesota lake, the last thing I could imagine is that in just seconds, I'd be involved in a one-person search and rescue mission. As I breast stroked back toward my dock without a care in the world, I noticed a figure panicking in the lake. As I swam closer, I realized it was helpless.

"I couldn't let it die," I explained to neighbors that evening. I did the crawl in record speed to the dock, turned my kayak upright on the shore, and slid it into the water. Grabbing the paddle and an empty Chobani Greek yogurt container, I stepped in a crouch from the dock into the kayak. After paddling 100 feet, I rediscovered it. Still flapping its wings and helpless, the bumblebee was almost dead in the water! Placing the Chobani container on the lake, the bee floated right in.

I soon spilled the bee onto the dock. It will surely fly away, I felt, but it just flailed flightlessly. After nudging it back into the Chobani, I walked up the hill to the southwestern corner of my house. I laid the bee on the ground, next to a mysterious flowering plant that generations of bees have hovered about. They partake of the sacred nectar, unwittingly collecting pollen on tiny hairs all over their bodies, even their eyes. Climbing a blade of grass, the bee reached a clover leaf.

---

[49] "The Loons of Lost Lake: And Their Heroic Odyssey of 2012" was published in *Hometown Focus* (Virginia, MN), October 19, 2012. The paper's scrutinizing editor requested that the writer furnish evidence for his claims, such as that 112,800 gallons of floodwater flowed into Lost Lake every minute on the cloud-burst Thursday, and 216 million gallons poured in by Saturday. The writer's detailed calculations passed muster. Read his answer—which *Hometown Focus* published—on the blog page at TomsGlobe.com (or request that it be reposted).

Atop it clung, but fly it still did not. At least it will die in a familiar place, I thought, resting atop a leaf of clover, the highest one around, next to a bed of flowers known to its sidekicks, ancestors, and perhaps its queen. Later, I returned to the flowers and clovers to wish the bee a somber farewell, though by now it would certainly have fallen dead to the ground.

"Dead on the ground, it wasn't," I told my enrapt neighbors. "It had flown away!"

• • •

By and by, the next day I visit my Biwabik childhood friend, Ed Turk.

"Eddie," I pose, "if a bee finds itself in a pail of water, or on a lake, is it able to take flight?"

"No," Ed answers.

"Do you know that from observations when we were kids?"

"I never observed that," Ed replies, "but what I did was capture bees in a jar with holes punched in the cover, feed them, and let them escape before they died. You did that too, Tom."

"Why do you say bees cannot take flight from water?"

"A bee weighs only one-thousandth of a pound," Ed explains without a moment's hesitation. "It's incredibly heavy when it's soaked with water. If you were in a lake with all your winter clothes on—your heavy parka, your wool pants, your big boots—you wouldn't be able to swim, Tom; face it!"

A day later, after another sojourn on the lake, I visit my knowledgeable friend again.

"Eddie, say a young bald eagle, perched at the top of a tree above the lakeshore, dives into the water to grab a fish but fails miserably, rising up with empty talons. If the eagle sees that I'm in a kayak watching, is it embarrassed?"

"No!" Ed exclaims.

But that is a different story—this one is about the bee and not the bird.

Autumn's Hours Outdoors
NOVEMBER 13, 2017

During a walk in a bit of woods, I approach a tall spruce that, 10 years ago, was small enough to be encircled with Christmas lights. I'm startled near out of my boots, though, by a partridge flapping from under the spruce and straight toward my house. It smacks a window!

My hunch is that the partridge has the sense knocked out of it but will survive. But am I right? I watch the partridge for two minutes, the first time I've ever been able to observe one that long. For the first minute, it appears stunned. It then jerkily looks left and right, as if determining where it is. It soon tiptoes off, in no mood to risk flying again so soon.

I wonder why partridges have recently appeared in my yard for the first time ever. I recall one day last month, when I had my chainsaw running at peak efficiency. During a break, I chatted inside on the phone with my cousin Alice, who celebrated her 103rd birthday this year.

"Alice," I said, "I'm about to cut down a wild crab apple tree that's crowding out white and red pines. Even though the fruits are ripe and red, they're just pea-sized, and sour! I see that migrating robins and other birds like them, though."

"Tom, I wouldn't cut that tree down if I were you," Alice advised me.

Once Alice and I ended our half-hour call and I was outside again with my whirring chain saw, *I did not* cut the tree down. In the weeks afterward, robins, partridges, and other birds pecked more of the fruits off the tree's springy branches.

"Alice," I'll say when I visit her in a few days, "If I'd cut the apple tree down, I would have deprived myself of the enjoyment of seeing so many birds this fall, to say nothing of the sustenance the tree offered to many a creature. Thank you. Life and lives are better because of your words of wisdom."

Might another chapter yet be written in this saga?

Winter and Its Nomads
DECEMBER 2017

Days turn, like pages on a calendar. The ice on the lake thickens. The remaining fruits on the wild crab apple tree shrivel in the cold. The robins have long left, and the partridges no longer return. The tree will be left to itself until the stirrings of spring, I'm certain.

On December 12, usually a nondescript date, I look toward the frozen lake, to be snow covered until April. The apple tree stands, as always, between my sight and the lake. Today, though, the tree has new life!

A bird of December seeks to pluck one of the few remaining frozen fruits from a bouncy branch. This bird is mostly red, with black and white wings and a body filled in with small patches of soft gray. It is surprisingly round. Never have I seen a bird like this. Another such bird alights on the tree too. And a third, but this one is mostly gold, and not red like the others.

Although they are only 35 feet away, I put binoculars to eyes to study these creatures and their companions flitting about from a small flock. My powers of observation and intuition tell me that they are exploring a new territory. I scribble down a description of the birds and make a rough drawing, the first time I've ever done such a thing. I resolve to locate my Minnesota bird book and identify this bird, also the first time I've done such a thing.

• • •

In the 5 o'clock darkness on the very same day, there is a knock on the door, uncommon at this hermitage. A UPS driver hands me a frozen package. After an hour of warming, I study the wrapping. I find it is from Cousin Alice and Janet, her daughter.

Cutting open the box, I discover a flip calendar for the approaching year, 2018. The Cornell University Lab of Ornithology created my

Christmas gift, with its colorful photos of North American birds, one for each of the 365 days we'll soon be enjoying. An app will teach me how these 365 birds chirps, offering a feast not only for my eyes, but for my ears as well.

Now is my opportunity! Like a four-year-old who has ripped open a Christmas gift and beholds a longed-for toy that must be grabbed, pulled, and tossed, I begin to flip the pages of the calendar, anxiously looking for any hint of the mysterious bird I watched this morning in the tree now known as Alice's Apple Tree.

Flip goes January 1st and 2nd and 3rd, and successively to the 31st. None of the images are like the bird of this morning. Nor are any in February or March. Having gone through 90 dissimilar birds, my fingers now tell me it will be easier to turn the pages from the back of the weighty tablet calendar. Thus goes the 31st of December, the 30th, and so on.

Quickly, you can understand, I come to Christmas Day. Appearing resplendent on December 25 is the bird that I'd resolved to learn

The Christmas gift calendar that arrived after dark with a knock on the door.

The white-winged crossbill, resplendent on Christmas Day.

about sometime soon in my life. It is mostly red including its head, with black and white wings and patches of gray. It's as round as a bird can be. It is, we may join in calling it, the white-winged crossbill.

The calendar's range map explains that the white-winged crossbill is prevalent through most of Canada and inhabits bits of Northern Minnesota and other northern states. They feast on spruce seeds year-round and seeds of many summertime plants. The gold-colored crossbill is the female. The reds are males.

The birds are nomadic, I learn. They appeared at Lost Lake from the north, perhaps for the first time ever, a few hours before the Christmas gift arrived from the south in a frozen package with a knock on my door after dark.

God bless Alice's Apple Tree, a tree that I would have buzzed down last fall without a second thought—had I not been dissuaded in the nick of time. Every fall, it will keep birds well fed. And every spring, its myriad of white blossoms will make it the most beautiful thing in the plant kingdom.

Alice's Apple Tree in luxurious bloom in May 2018, and in every May, perhaps in perpetuity.

Springtime at Alice's Apple Tree
MAY 26, 2018

I have just erased the thousand words of this story of springtime, and in their place, show a picture I took 60 seconds ago. It is the apple tree Alice Lundblad saved for the world.

A note to readers: Sadly, Alice passed away in January, having lived for over a century caring about, engaging, and even regaling so many, and recently offering advice that nurtured robins and partridges and white-winged crossbills. And a human's mind, too.

If someday I may communicate with the birds that flock to the apple tree, I'll tell them about Alice.

SLOW
GOODBYES

SLOW GOODBYES

As a young boy on the Mesabi Iron Range, I didn't envision venturing afar. I hadn't heard of most of the 90 countries then existing on our planet, like Ecuador, Burma, Bhutan, and Cambodia. And I certainly hadn't met anyone from those countries.

But on the streets of Biwabik and nearby towns, immigrants or their children spoke Slovenian, Italian, Serbian, and other languages. And Finnish was de rigueur for the two generations older than mine at my grandmother's house, near a mine on the edge of the great northern wilderness.

Between 1890 and 1920, tens of thousands of immigrants from 40 nations arrived in these 20 frontier towns, built in a jiffy next to 100 mines that melded together, forming larger mines. To varying degrees, these immigrants learned to comprehend and speak a new language. Unknowingly, they created a new English dialect—one that folks in Minneapolis later pinpointed from my speech. This dialect is slowly fading into a more standard American speech, but even today, people from New York to California wonder where I'm from.

Did my childhood experiences at home plant the seeds for my later explorations of other continents and my desire to rub shoulders with people in their own cultures? All I know is that curiosity is still bubbling in my blood, and my thirst to learn remains unquenched.

My effort in publishing these stories is worthwhile, I believe, because it is important that others "live" these experiences too, albeit through a bit of imagination. I hope these stories never become outdated. I do not think they will. In an ever-changing world, they may, in fact, appear even more original two generations from now.

Just so you know, I'm wrapping gift packages for my cousin Marvin's two grandchildren, Alyson and Nick Maki, 10-year-old twins. Each label says, "Do not open until your birthday in January 2060."

I anticipate that in 2060, Alyson and Nick will cut open the faded packaging paper. They'll each discover two books that they'll have already read: *The Other Worlds* and *Meeting Strangers, Making Friends*. An enclosed note will request that they pass the books to readers who, like you today, may enjoy discovering the experiences I've had. The future readers' comments on "stories from the past" just might create a small wildfire on their social (or post-social) media.

My challenge to you: what do you envision a future reader (circa 2060) will say about these earlier world travel adventures? I dare say my challenge is a first of a kind in the four thousand years since a story was first written.[50] You may answer via the website's Contact page. I'll tuck your comments into the packages that Alyson and Nick open in that distant year. Your prognostics—perhaps including two or three choice adjectives—might appear on 2060's social (or post-social) media!

• • •

We never know what a new day will bring. I hope to once again visit people you've gotten to know in these stories and to keep meeting strangers in several corners of the world. I'm eager to let you know.[51]

Since this is a slow goodbye, perhaps you and I will meet by chance in one of the 195 countries the world has today. I'd like to give you a hug. And we'll tell each other stories.

---

[50] The oldest story ever written is thought to be "The Epic of Gilgamesh." It was written on clay tablets in Sumer over four thousand years ago. See *The Other Worlds: Offbeat Adventures of a Curious Traveler*, p. 174.

[51] Check my website and sign up for my newsletter. And please let your adventuresome acquaintances know about TomsGlobe, too. They may appreciate your suggestion.

Tom Mattson

Tom Mattson grew up in Biwabik, Minnesota. After receiving his Juris Doctor from the University of Minnesota, he spent years—punctuated by sabbaticals for travel—advocating on cases ranging from family law, fires, explosions, and price-fixing, to the death penalty and nuclear bomb cleanup and compensation. Tom has enjoyed a parallel career —an ad hoc one that has its seeds in childhood Chevy and Greyhound explorations. He's ridden atop railroad boxcars in California, took the controls of a Peruvian locomotive, crawled through a Bolivian silver mine, and criss-crossed the kingdom of Bhutan. In other adventures, he's joined an indigenous family at its feast of the year in a 920-year-old New Mexico pueblo and admits he was once hauled off in a Mexican police car for a Saturday night in the infamous Tijuana jail.

Tom now divides his time between his Minnesota abode near Biwabik on a lake named Lost, his tin-roofed shack in the Guatemala mountains of the Maya people, and motorcycling the American and Canadian West —and revisiting friends in some of the 75 countries he's experienced. For more information about Tom, please check out tomsglobe.com.

Connect with Tom online at:

TomsGlobe.com

TomsGlobe

TomsGlobe

MORE BY
TOM MATTSON

"None of it was meant to be: the stories and anecdotes that appear in this book, my travels to far-flung other worlds, being face-to-face with hundreds of strangers. Yet here we are, and there I've been, and somehow, strangers became friends." *(From the Introduction)*

Meet Tom Mattson's friends including Maribel, on a park bench in Havana; Braulio, a silver miner in Bolivia; Chema, a fisherman on unfathomably deep Lake Atitlan in Guatemala; and Hisako, a Japanese activist for most of her 101 years—and many more around the world. Discover the stories of their lives, their experiences, and their histories, so different from your own.

Be charmed by the Minnesota storyteller who draws you into *The Other Worlds* with ease and who delights in sharing the sights, sounds, smells, and serendipities of his adventures with active and armchair travelers everywhere.